TRUTH & PERSUASION

IN THE DIGITAL REVOLUTION

R. W. CHAPMAN II

Copyright © 2024 by AEVI Books
All rights reserved.

1441 W. Long Lake Rd.
Ste 310
Troy, MI 48098

First Edition
ISBN: 9798304737777

Disclaimer:
This publication is designed to provide accurate and authoritative information concerning the subject matter covered. It is sold with the understanding that the publisher does not render legal, accounting, or other professional services. If legal advice or other expert assistance is required, the services of a competent professional should be sought.
Printed in the United States of America
Cover design by Lauren Jefferson
10 9 8 7 6 5 4 3 2 1

To the Memory of Dr. Mark Allen Rigstad

(1965-2024)

Your profound political philosophy and ethics teachings ignited my passion for these disciplines. The wisdom you imparted to me lit my path to the United States Marine Corps as a Federal Trial Lawyer and an author. Your early instruction on logic, the Greek philosophers, the philosophy of law, and the philosophy of war and peace occupied my mind in pivotal moments with far-reaching consequences on the battlefield and in life. I would not be here today without your passion and dedication to filling young minds with centuries of knowledge.

The unwavering commitment to critical thought and moral integrity you bestowed upon me is a gift I am undeserving of and eternally grateful for. I wish I could continue seeking the light of your knowledge, but I hope some of you are on these pages. You were with us for too short of a time, and with that, you left the impact of a thousand lifetimes.

Til Valhalla. Professor Rigstad.

R. W. Chapman II

TABLE OF CONTENTS

Liminal Spaces   ix

Part One: Navigating Hyperreality and Postmodernism   1
Understanding the Dangers of a Fragmented Reality

Hang the DJ: The illusion of choice in a simulated world   2
How Hyperreality and Digital Choices Shape Our Perceptions

Between the Hammer and the Anvil: Lessons from Post-War French Thinkers   8
How French Philosophers Predicted Today's Cultural and Social Crises

The Information Age and the Rise of Postmodernism   16
How Hyperreality and Endless Information Reshape Our Understanding of Truth

Feeling Machines that Think: Capitalism's Commodification of Humanity   29
How Capitalism Exploits Our Emotions and Sells Them Back to Us

Following Orders: Authority, Morality, and the Danger of Compliance   42
How We Surrender Our Morals to Authority in the Age of Obedience

Death of the Follower: Algorithms and the Loss of Individuality   61
Why Algorithms Drive Us Toward Conformity and How We Can Resist

Target Knows Your Daughter is Pregnant: The Dark Reality of Surveillance Capitalism   67
Understanding the Impact of Data Collection and Privacy Invasion

Birth of the Liminal Guru: The Rise of Unoriginal Thinkers   73
How the Atrophy of Critical Thinking Has Led to a Culture of Conformity or Worse

The Illusion of Knowledge: Surface-Level Thinking and Modern Ignorance   79
How Superficial Understanding Fuels the Rise of Dangerous Ideologies

Majority Report: How Data and Algorithms Influence
Democracy   85
How 5,000 Data Points Can Sway a Nation

Part Two: Emerging from the Cave   91
A Journey to Clarity in an Era of Distortion

Don't Yank the Chain: Reviving Ancient Rhetoric in
Modern Times   92
What We Can Learn from Greek and Roman Philosophers about Influence

The Time Tested Tools of Philosophers: Rhetoric's
Role in Shaping History   101
How Ancient Rhetorical Techniques Shaped Iconic Moments in History

Mobocracy: Lessons from Cicero and Modern Mob
Mentality   121
How the Ancient Roman Statesman and Recent Events Warn of the Dangers of Groupthink

The Demon Haunted World: Lessons from Carl Sagan
on Reason and Passion   127
Using Critical Thinking to Combat Deception and Find Purpose

The Nesting Dolls of Language: Deconstructing
"Truth" Beyond Semantics   135
Examining How Language Shapes Reality and Meaning

Part 3   142
Alchemy, Integration and L'Art de la Persuasion Postmoderne

Confronting the Shadow   143
Our inner truth is our path towards purpose

Megapint: Shadow-work and the Honest Depiction
of Self   151
The refreshing glare of radical acceptance and individulization

The Art of the Question: How Stories Shape Our
Perceptions   159
Larry King teaches us about the power of the story and the unassuming question

The Trial of the Century   166
O.J. teaches us that unifying is more powerful than dividing

Hinduburger: Appropriate Cultural Appropriation   185
How the nation's largest restaurant confronted religion and cultural norms

Think Different: Steve Jobs and the Creation of the
Commercial Subculture   194
Creating your own culture and integrating your consumer

Let's See Paul Allen's Card   201
What American Psycho tells us about our future selves

L'Art de la Persuasion Postmoderne: Mastering
Persuasion in a Postmodern World   210
The Ten Essential Rules for Persuasion in an Age of Ambiguity

The New Dawn of Authenticity   247
Ushering in a new age of originality and creativity

Bibliography   253

LIMINAL SPACES

THE MICROCOSM OF REDDIT AND THE PERVERSION OF TRUTH AND POWER

"One does not discover new lands without consenting to lose sight of the shore for a very long time."

André Gide

In the vast expanse that is the internet, there is a place called Reddit.

Reddit is a collection of forums, a digital conglomerate of things called threads discussing literally anything — everything from the news and identity politics to "cats with jobs" and obscure hobbies. Reddit is where you go to watch a live Q&A with a celebrity who might actually respond to your comment. Reddit is where you go to search whether a late-stage career change has been possible for others in your demographic. Reddit is where you go to waste precious minutes of life in any waiting room, a curated feed of followed topics presenting itself to you right when you need the ultimate distraction.

When you go to Reddit, you may be searching for something ultra specific or you might be in the mood to voyeur a place called "relationship advice," where disgruntled family members or spouses lay out the entirety of their problematic interpersonal dynamics in ten-thousand characters or less. And, if you're lucky, you'll get an update on such dynamics through a place called "Best of Redditor Updates." If you're looking for something spicier, you'd be better suited to "Am I the Asshole," a forum committed to telling "OPs" or, original posters of the thread, whether they were an asshole in a specific instance.

Reddit is a place to complain about your children, to brag about your promotion, to comment on someone's lack of self-awareness, and to debate politics; where you rate a complete stranger's resume or physical attractiveness, where you determine someone's celebrity doppelgänger or watch a cat dive off the edge of a fridge in a gif looped for eternity.

It's the internet as it lives and breathes.

This is all, of course, anonymous — as of the time of this writing, Reddit users usually forgo profile pictures and instead opt to keep the default alien mascot silhouette given to them by the website upon signing up. Their usernames, if not deliberately chosen, are random assignments of verbs, adjectives, and nouns such as "proper_washing_machine" or "racing_baguette758." You don't even need a Reddit account to peruse — users can simply visit the website and seek what they will eventually find.

Reddit, then, is a perfect revolving door of the things we think about on impulse in our daily lives, the things we judge at a glance, the people we don't want to talk to but are dying to know more about, the relief that we're not in a certain predicament or the jealousy that we're not in another. Reddit is a mirror of our intrusive thoughts, a carousel of distraction, and a conveyor belt of content for dopamine-starved brains.

It's not surprising, then, to know that on Reddit there is a place devoted to liminal spaces.

The forum r/LiminalSpace — the r/ being the formal way of writing out the name of a particular forum on Reddit — defines liminality and its spaces as "transitional areas with no humans, no life, and a vague sense of nostalgia." Definitions also include that "In abstract terms [liminality] is usually things like the act of waiting, the state of being between uses, transitional stages in life, transitional times of day, etc - things that could be compared to a state of limbo."

The user who posted these definitions is considered a Liminal Space "elder" or, in more practical terms, an accomplished moderator. This person has reached a level of trust within the community devoted to Liminal Space such that they are responsible for defining the very meaning of liminality for any new users in a guide designed to help users post about liminality according to stringent guidelines.

Posting successfully, according to the rules set out by community moderators, is where Reddit incentivizes good and truthful behavior through the use of a social score called Karma. If a post is good and follows the designated truth of a community, it will receive "upvotes" or positive points from people in and even outside the community, thereby verifying its truthfulness — its adherence to truth. If a post is bad, it will receive "downvotes," or a negative score to correlate with its fall from, or subversion of, the prescribed truth.

Hinduism defines Karma as the sum of a person's actions in this and previous states of existence. On Reddit, Karma can arguably be defined as how witty you are at following the moderator's rules, and it can be reset by the process of reincarnation—voluntarily deleting a Reddit account and beginning a new one. As a result of this, most Redditors have several Reddit masks they use to navigate various corners of Reddit. Karma goes up, and Karma goes down. Thumbs go up, thumbs go down.

This machinated existence plays out thousands, if not hundreds of thousands, of times a day on the website that is Reddit, but something interesting happens to its forums which lack the steady hand of a ruling moderator — a fate which philosopher Hobbes warns of as "poor, brutish, and short." This happened to the incel (**in**voluntarily **cel**ibate) Reddit community— a group that formed a hateful echo chamber so loud that members didn't think twice about doxxing women or wishing for acts of violence against them. It was eventually quarantined (cut off from the general public) and then banned from the website.

When a group like r/incel swells and its members are not properly controlled by the herd, it becomes a community of rot. In order to prevent community rot, something must be done to keep order. A restriction of the communal definitions and rules for posting is just that kind of thing. Imagine, instead of allowing any old expression of "liminal space," a group could control their view of liminal space for all. Such a movement would favor the insiders—who presumably all have clout—and exclude outsiders who must adjust to the rules.

It goes like this: someone with authority changes the rules of the game in an obscure way that is generally only understood by the ruling class, i.e. the moderators and highest-performing Karma earners. The modification is used to gatekeep the purity of the members and immediately isolate and reject those who fail to conform. Post a photo of a "liminal space" without respecting the abstraction of a transitional waiting period sprinkled with a sense of nostalgia? Sorry, downvote to obscurity—berate user—backslap over victory to improve morale—attempted coup quashed.

The shallow and pedantic junior intellects of Reddit have no issue with the endemic hypocrisy of this: Endless communities creates an environment where inclusion in a group is voluntary through a social contract yet a mass exodus could happen at any moment when the moderation of the group fails. Reddit and evolution both have the goal of improving the strength of the species, and those groups that have maneuvered this careful balance have struck a bargain with their members that helps both sides feel respected.

Then, after the moderators are fat and happy off of their success and not watching their backs, a young star on the way up is born and learns the system in a way that Machiavelli would be proud of. Rubbing elbows with "big Karma," he gives the appearance of conformity. Then, at just the right time and after sufficient support is achieved, a post too controversial to ignore could spark a powerful debate on a socially important issue within the community. A fracture splits users and spurns warnings of an attempted coup. Others join, the IRA of Reddit, if you will, setting off little Reddit bombs here and there to destabilize the leadership and the forum until one day an overthrow is possible. One might subvert the definition of "liminal" in a way that demolishes the moderator elder's original intent, and the corresponding social boost may give that controversial poster enough social proof, votes, to open a competing "liminal spaces" Reddit so that they can become a moderator.

In this microcosm, the "truth" is dictated by the moderator or their rightful heir, another moderator. Lacking a democratic process in favor of "eye of the beholder" logic and order, users seem to prefer limited incremental rule changes to frequent regime changes. Power flows from the ruler until a new ruler is established and a new contract is struck.

The irony is that our friends in the subservient class are in a "liminal space," lacking an anchor, direction, or guide. Unable to rise to the ruling class or the favored class, they are transients sowing and plowing endlessly with little traction, operating on a logic that serves the liminal.

Under the r/LiminalSpace moderator's definition, the images on r/liminalspace are panic-inducing to experience: They provoke the same feelings experienced by those lost in an incorrect feedback loop. The photos of spaces are often dark, frozen in time, lacking an exit and infinity that will continue on with you in transit. Viewing a liminal space is tough to experience because we can't imagine ourselves existing in such a reality. Our minds search for the subject, and lacking one, we assume it's intentionally avoiding us—which we perceive as a threat. We have no anchor, and we are on the precipice of transition.

In the age of Reddit, with the hoarding of fake internet points—or likes, or saves, or engagement—digital power struggles, fake news, and AI-generated content, it's easy to see where logic has taken on an element of liminality.

We are now in a state of panic. We are in a state of in-between truths, all dictated by moderators of different flavors: political leaders, forum leaders, journalists who slant a certain way, AI-generated video producers, and deepfakes. Even the way a friend asks for input on a controversial opinion can induce fear of repercussions where social standing is everything, online and elsewhere.

It's impossible to remain logical where there's liminality because liminality requires that we assume tenancy of two places at once — we are to stay while we are expected to leave; we are to accept when all we want to do is reject. We are to wait, possibly forever, while a decision on our version of the truth is delivered.

On Reddit and in life, liminality is clear: In an endless hallway of endless threads to walk through, we can choose our reality and, thus, choose our own truth while we wait for someone to approve of it. And in this day and age, we can now abandon our chosen truth for something more attractive to our various overlords, our moderators.

And this is *illogical*.

Logic is a thing of structure and reason, whereas liminality is defined by the lingering ghost of reason. When you combine the two, you have a world which lives and dies on waiting in the trenches to capture what *could* be logical, only to change that logic when nebulous, more powerful forces act upon the truth.

Why this book?

How can I effectively communicate my message in an era where the shelf life of information is getting shorter?

And then the other questions: How did we get here, and where are we going? Then, what can we do about it?

As you will later learn from Al Gore, fear without action is inadvisable.

Humans are different, the German philosopher Kant explains. Instead of being satisfied with adapting to our environment and following the Darwinian conveyor belt to dragonhood, we are unsatisfied.

For centuries, we have not just evolved but flourished. And then we didn't — we let others do that for us: Amazon, Apple, Google, Pfizer; harnessing human technology to move adaptation further to a point we humans cannot comprehend.

Our main purpose is no more and we are adrift. We went from cattle rancher to cattle. We graze, lay, graze some more and fatten ourselves up so that we may feed the machine.

Sad, right? It doesn't have to be this way. A revolution is coming and it is coming from within. An individual awakening.

The key is embracing your true self and only your true self. One by one, as we learn that feeding the machine is a poor, brutish and short existence, we will wake up. We will reject the simulated world laid out before us. We will seek pleasure, pain, sadness, happiness and adversity. When we speak to this human need, we will reach those looking for a more authentic experience.

In order to wake, you will need to understand postmodernism, the simulacrum, hyperreality and behavioral economics. With this foundation, we can explore the impact of authenticity and messages that satisfy the human condition.

It doesn't matter whether Maslow, Jung, or Kahneman are your guides. The key to persuasion is finding the right entry point to connect and create genuine relationships. The space between these covers holds the secret to finding that entry point and satisfying the need.

Truth & Persuasion is the result of countless hours exploring the complexities of persuasion, psychology, behavioral economics, and logic to find an answer to my pressing question: Where do we go from here?

This book is shaped by lessons drawn from public speaking engagements, courtroom trials, high-stakes negotiations, and late-night debates in the philosophy department. It's also shaped by lessons learned on the battlefield in Kajaki, Afghanistan, where justice and logic must hold higher esteem than passion. It was honed in situations where outcomes could mean the difference between justice and ruin, life and death.

The experiences shared in this book come from interactions with diverse groups—from jurors with differing backgrounds to international discussions across cultures and borders. Whether I was training Afghan police and prosecutors to uphold human rights, sharing meals with Taliban leaders, or questioning a chief medical examiner with 3,000 autopsies under his belt, every moment offered profound insight into the universal nature of communication and persuasion that I now share within these pages.

Amidst the penultimate classics in this field lies an unfortunate layer of works on persuasion and influence. Seven rules for this, twelve steps for that, game-changing formulas for yadda yadda. They're about as effective as gas station erectile dysfunction pills, and the dysfunction stems from the fact that they were never intended to be used, only purchased. These charlatan works use the heuristics and mind traps contained in their pages to persuade you that the key to success lies between their covers.

Oh, how meta.

Let me be very clear from the outset—and I'm breaking a rule here — I'm supposed to tell you this book will perform absolute magic on you. Sorry to say that, after reading this book, you will not be more successful. Your life won't measurably change. You'll be the same as you were, with one subtle difference.

Properly digest this book, and for the first time, you'll see the game as it's being played all around you. Slowly, it will appear as your eyes adjust until reality, like a blue light on a hotel sheet, eventually emerges. You'll be Neo, post-pill, glancing at the Matrix. You're no longer an easy mark but a participant in the game, elevating above the charlatans, tricksters, and false prophets—many of whom have made millions.

Apply the skills, and you'll have a sixth sense and a new coat of armor. You'll recognize persuasion immediately and engage your what Daniel Kahneman calls your System 2 thinking, your wise mind. You'll avoid mind traps. You'll be able to develop a message, product, presentation, or even a persona that cultivates trust. I hope you'll have some fun while doing it and perhaps gather some interesting anecdotes to share with your friends, partner, or kids.

Marine Corps operations briefings always start with orientation: You are here. Seems obvious, but it's crucial. What if we didn't all agree on where we are? Believe me, it's possible in our modern world. So first, we'll orient ourselves.

In the beginning of this book, we'll pinpoint precisely where we are and where we're going in this hyperreal digital age. The dopamine wars of the post-2004 internet age made "the follower" a currency, but that's short-lived as we enter the age of the "death of the follower."

Descending into a new layer of our glass onion, we're entering a postmodern, algorithm-dominated reality dishing up vastly different worldviews to people. Information is adjusted, packaged, and regurgitated so many times before filtering to the masses that vastly different interpretations are a certainty.

We're not a nation divided anymore—that would be nice. No, we're a nation fractured, a gallon Ziploc bag of puzzle pieces from seven different puzzles. Our curated feeds, inboxes, and commercials define our realities, and there are more versions of reality than grains of sand on the world's beaches. Yet we try to piece our picture together, create ourselves, and identify ourselves, grasping externally for anything remotely resembling truth that fits our image.

Kahneman's System 1 thinking tells us that information overload causes reflexive opinions, favoring the snap judgments of identity politics over the careful study of the ancient Greeks. It's natural; survival isn't an option—it's a mandate. Imagine reading the label on every food item at Walmart, starving before we allow a decision. No, we're Katniss in the woods, shooting the first image of a deer — we're starving. But dopamine is our food.

We lunge at labels, symbols, emotions, and our good friend dopamine. Flicking through people like packaged snacks on Tinder, scrolling through Instagram to confirm our self-importance, silently and rapidly judging their lives—we bounce the false construct of their reality against how we feel about ours. We never win.

The house takes 50% of every hand. Mark Zuckerberg takes the other 50%.

The world is at war with delayed gratification, which doesn't stand a chance. Overly optimized corporations know this, and they're ten light-years ahead.

Our data is tracked, brokered, synthesized, and now Target knows when your daughter is pregnant before you do.

... And before she does.

Target uses its vast data to target ads, track consumers, and provide the illusion of choice throughout the store, while our dollars vote our corporate jailers into monopolistic control of just a few brands. Nestlé owns over 2,000 brands in your local Target and growing—including Nespresso, Nescafé, Nestea, and Coffee-Mate, but also Gerber, Purina, and both of your favorite sparkling water brands, San Pellegrino and Perrier. Seriously, where is the Federal Trade Commission on the sparkling water monopoly? Was this merger even approved?

Thanks, Obama.

In later chapters, we will wind back the clock and look to the ancients for wisdom and insight to form our building blocks of logic and rhetoric. We must begin from this base, given that these insights intertwine into nearly all messaging. We'll learn how Socrates was slain by the Republic he sought to protect because he was obstinate and upset the delicate balance of power. He was rewarded with a trip to see the gods. He died—thoughtfully—but he still died.

Plato, his student, watched the death sentence take its toll, learned a bit about survival, and advocated for some guiding principles and restraint—perhaps he could have slipped Jesus a note. Aristotle refined these principles, ushering in a golden age of rhetoric until Cicero taught us why we can't have nice things.

Cicero, inheriting trust in his tradecraft as a rhetorician, became drunk on the power bestowed upon him to persuade, leading to the summary execution of his opponents without a trial. Cicero learned that when hysteria runs its course, sober minds always prevail, and the tables are turned. Senator Joseph McCarthy—a modern Cicero—learned this lesson in 1954 after being convicted by the Senate and dying in 1957 at a young age. His Cuban Missile Crisis, Red Scare, and communism antics capitalized on in-group bias. Cicero, too. Both names would become synonymous with reckless and unsubstantiated allegations.

Finally, we establish a more substantial base to enhance our understanding by applying the emerging field of behavioral economics and Jungian psychology to the ancient art of logic and rhetoric.

In the final part, we'll cover the principles of hyperreality persuasion—a set of principles unique to our modern perils and opportunities. These principles will guide your future communication while your depth of understanding in the delicate art of persuasion allows seamless integration into your processes. The anecdotes, stories, and pitfalls shared in this book will be what you remember most. You'll recall the case study or story when you finish. You may find yourself randomly sharing them with others, as I have done; this simple act will jumpstart your storyteller's journey.

This work wouldn't be possible without the hundreds of authors, creators, reporters, and professionals who have contributed to this book by authoring groundbreaking research in behavioral psychology, heuristics, logic, philosophy, economics, and business. I endeavored to cite every source I referenced at the end of this book, and this list will be updated—it's a compelling reading list for the avid student of these topics.

PART ONE: NAVIGATING HYPERREALITY AND POSTMODERNISM

UNDERSTANDING THE DANGERS OF A FRAGMENTED REALITY

HANG THE DJ: THE ILLUSION OF CHOICE IN A SIMULATED WORLD

HOW HYPERREALITY AND DIGITAL CHOICES SHAPE OUR PERCEPTIONS

"Freedom is what we do with what is done to us."

Jean-Paul Sartre

Like many aspects of our hyperreal existence, dating apps offer a never-ending buffet of options, making users more indecisive, evasive, and nihilist. Sure, some have found love, but these apps have sparked subcultures that reject this awkward window to the soul.

Sick of the paradox of choice, people crave something different. Capitalism spawned a dating app that didn't just match you; it told you exactly how long the relationship would last and eventually would match the user with the perfect companion. It could be hours, or it could be years. You'd never know until you tapped that screen and a countdown clock appeared, ticking away like a time bomb strapped to your love life.

Frank and Amy were two brave souls who decided to surrender their fate to this digital oracle. Although they were strangers, they were bound by the system's unbreakable rules.

Their first meeting? Awkward doesn't begin to describe it. Imagine knowing you have only 24 hours with someone you've just met. They shared small talk over dinner, each glancing nervously at the ticking clock on their devices. When they parted ways, it was clear something was missing. The connection felt stunted and artificial—like they were actors in a play directed by an algorithm. That's the point. The app was in control, not them.

Frank's next relationship lasted a year. Yes, 365 days with someone he barely knew and didn't love. The days blurred into weeks, the weeks into months, and the relationship morphed into an endurance test rather than a romance. Yet, through it all, Frank clung to the hope that this process—this grand simulation—was steering him toward something real. The algorithm was learning and adapting. After all, the system promised perfection—a match designed just for him—a genuine experience in a synthetic world.

Amy's journey wasn't a fairy tale either. One short-term relationship after another left her more disillusioned. But she kept going. Why? Because the app knew best. It had to. You'll learn about the sunk cost fallacy later.

Then, as if scripted by some cosmic playwright with a twisted sense of humor, Amy and Frank met again. After countless failed matches, heartbreaks, and enough frustration to fuel a reality TV show, they realized their connection was different this time. It felt actual—more accurate than any relationship they'd experienced within the system's confines. Finally, the algorithm worked! But why with the same person? What had changed?

They decided to rebel, run away together, and escape the digital puppet enslaver pulling their strings. But as they tried to break free, the truth hit them: Their entire relationship, along with every other relationship they'd experienced, was a simulation.

They were a simulation.

If you're a fan of *Black Mirror*, you've probably connected the dots to the episode "Hang the DJ." This parable allows us to explore the concept of simulacra—the copy (Frank and Amy) realize they're a copy, and the audience realizes it's a copy—yet the experience remains profoundly honest.

Philosopher Jean Baudrillard's *Simulacra and Simulation* developed this theory. Baudrillard outlines a haunting progression in which reality becomes increasingly mediated by copies, representations, and simulations. Initially, the copy reflects reality—imagine a painting capturing a landscape. But over time, the copy distorts and eventually replaces reality, leaving us lost in a hall of mirrors with no exit sign.

He defines three orders of simulacra:

The First Order: The copy faithfully reflects the original. It's like a photograph—it captures reality as it is. In "Hang the DJ," this dating app is designed to mirror real-life relationships, simulating them to help users find their ideal match. It is a tool, a means to an end.

The Second Order: The copy starts to distort reality. It doesn't just reflect; it alters. Frank and Amy's relationships in the simulation aren't exact replicas of real-world relationships. There are imposed time limits, rules, and constraints—all courtesy of the algorithm.

The Third Order: The copy has no relation to reality whatsoever. It creates its reality—a hyperreality that we accept as truth. Here, the simulation becomes more accurate than the original, and the original is forgotten. Frank and Amy's entire world is a simulation designed to test their compatibility. The simulation isn't a means to an end; it is the end.

We no longer distinguish between the original and the copy in this hyperreal state. The simulation is all that matters. Frank and Amy—and we, the audience—become invested in this simulated reality, forgetting about the "real" world outside the app. Baudrillard would nod vigorously.

Now, let's zoom out and look at our own lives. Social media influencers craft hyperreal versions of themselves. Their Instagram feeds are a curated gallery of perfection—flawless skin, exotic locations, perpetual happiness. Over time, this digital persona can overshadow the natural person. Followers engage more with this hyperreal version, and the influencer becomes a simulation of themselves. The copy replaces the original.

In online games like *Roblox*, *Minecraft*, or *Fortnite*, virtual economies mimic real-world financial systems with amplified rewards and risks. Players invest real time and money to gain virtual wealth, blurring the line between digital and physical value. The simulation becomes more significant than reality.

However, perhaps one of the most striking examples of hyperreality is the tale of Chris Moneymaker, whose name is so fitting that you'd think it was scripted. And maybe it is.

In 2003, Chris Moneymaker, an unassuming accountant from Tennessee, entered an online poker tournament on PokerStars. For a mere $39—the price of a mediocre dinner—he won his way into the World Series of Poker (WSOP), where the buy-in was a hefty $10,000. This should've been where the story ends—a guy gets a lucky break, rubs shoulders with the pros, and goes home with a great story.

But the universe had other plans.

The WSOP main event that year had 839 entrants—not small potatoes, but nothing compared to what's coming. The prize pool was substantial; the winner would receive a cool $2.5 million jackpot.

Poker at this level was a game of seasoned professionals—stone-cold bluffers who could read a soul through sunglasses. Yet, as the tournament progressed, Moneymaker started knocking out players left and right, including the legendary Phil Ivey. He pulled off a win that defied all logic in a hand that could've ended his Cinderella story.

His final opponent was Sammy Farha, a poker veteran with a penchant for chewing on unlit cigarettes and intimidating newcomers. In the final hand, Moneymaker, holding a modest 5 of diamonds and a 4 of spades, bluffed Farha out of a winning hand. Yes, you read that right—he bluffed a bluffer. The accountant from Tennessee took home $2.5 million and unknowingly changed the poker world forever.

This wasn't just a win; it was a seismic event. The "Moneymaker Effect," as it came to be known, triggered a tsunami of interest in online poker. The following year, WSOP entries tripled. People who had never set foot in a casino were logging on, convinced they could be the next overnight millionaire.

Here's where hyperreality kicks in.

Poker, traditionally played in smoky backrooms or glittering casinos, is a game of human interaction—reading tells, bluffing face-to-face, and the tactile feel of cards and chips. But online poker is a different beast. It is faster, accessible, and free of the physical cues that define the traditional game. The simulation doesn't just replicate poker; it reinvents it.

Online players developed new strategies—hyper-aggressive playstyles, multi-tabling, and relying on statistics rather than gut feelings. When these players transitioned to live games, they brought this hyperreal approach with them, transforming the very nature of poker. The simulation had not only become more popular than the original; it had fundamentally changed it.

Baudrillard's hyperreality had manifested in a card game.

The purists lamented. The soul of poker was dying, they cried. But for the new generation, this was evolution. The lines between the virtual and the real had blurred. The simulation was the new reality.

AND ISN'T that a reflection of our broader society? We swipe on dating apps, curate social media feeds, and invest in virtual currencies. We participate in simulations that often feel more fulfilling than the messy unpredictability of real life.

So, what does this mean for us?

Copies don't just reflect reality—they replace it. We find comfort in the controlled environments of our simulations, be it an app that dictates our love life or an online platform that lets us reinvent ourselves. The unpredictability and authenticity of the natural world are traded for the certainty and perfection of the hyperreal.

But in chasing this perfection, we risk losing touch with what makes us inherently human—the flaws, the surprises, the genuine connections that can't be quantified or programmed.

Yet, like Amy and Frank, we choose the copy because it more precisely addresses our emotional needs than reality.

BETWEEN THE HAMMER AND THE ANVIL: LESSONS FROM POST-WAR FRENCH THINKERS

HOW FRENCH PHILOSOPHERS PREDICTED TODAY'S CULTURAL AND SOCIAL CRISES

"The invention of a gaze that can be calculated, in which power makes itself more visible and more verifiable, has become a basic tool of coercion and control."

Michel Foucault

France had an advantage during the German occupation in World War II. Despite experiencing a totalitarian regime and the puppet Vichi Government, with a healthy risk of Communist occupation at the hands of Stalin, France's thinkers had plenty of time to think and observe.

In a modest apartment overlooking the Seine, a young Jean-Paul Sartre gazed out at the city he loved, now marred by swastika flags and the stern faces of German soldiers. Born in 1905, Sartre had already begun to make a name for himself as a philosopher and writer. The war and occupation profoundly impacted his thinking, leading him to ponder the nature of freedom under the most oppressive circumstances. His experiences crystallized into his existentialist philosophy, asserting that existence precedes essence and that humans are condemned to be free.

"Never were we freer than under the German Occupation," Sartre later wrote with a touch of irony in his essay "The Republic of Silence."

He observed that the constraints imposed by the occupiers forced individuals to confront the reality of their freedom—their choices carried immense weight, and the moral implications were inescapable. Yet, Sartre also recognized the insidious ways authoritarian regimes could infiltrate the mind, shaping desires and suppressing authentic choices.

Simone de Beauvoir, Sartre's lifelong companion and a formidable philosopher in her own right, navigated the same treacherous landscape. Born in 1908, de Beauvoir witnessed the rapid transformation of French society under the Vichy government, a regime that collaborated with the Nazis and embraced conservative, patriarchal values. The oppression of women intensified, reinforcing de Beauvoir's conviction to explore gender as a social construct in her groundbreaking work, *The Second Sex*.

"One is not born, but rather becomes a woman," she declared, dissecting how society molds individuals into prescribed roles. The occupation amplified her concerns about how external forces—be they political, cultural, or economic—could strip individuals of their agency. De Beauvoir saw parallels between the subjugation of women and the broader manipulation of the populace under both fascist and capitalist systems.

As the war raged on, another thinker began to stir the embers of radical critique. Guy Debord, born in 1931, was just a teenager during the occupation, but the experience left an indelible mark on his psyche. He would channel his disillusionment into the Situationist International movement in the postwar years, culminating in his seminal work, *The Society of the Spectacle* (1967). Debord argued that advanced capitalism had turned life into a mere representation—a spectacle where images and commodified experiences replaced authentic social interactions.

"In societies where modern conditions of production prevail, all of life presents itself as an immense accumulation of spectacles," Debord wrote.

Prophetically, he perceived capitalism as no different than the totalitarian regimes of the war, which could manipulate reality, shaping perceptions and desires to serve its ends. The spectacle was a new form of control, subtle yet pervasive, eroding genuine human connections in favor of consumption and passive acceptance.

Observing the neon lights flickering to life along the Champs-Élysées, Jean Baudrillard contemplated the rise of simulations—a reality where symbols and signs had overtaken the tangible. Born in 1929 in Reims, Baudrillard grew up amid the ruins of war, witnessing firsthand the transformative power of media and propaganda. The devastation and subsequent American cultural influence on Europe prompted him to question the nature of reality itself.

In *Simulacra and Simulation* (1981), Baudrillard introduced the concept of hyperreality—a condition in which the distinction between reality and simulation blurs, and individuals can no longer discern the authentic from the artificial. He posited that in the postmodern world, reality had been replaced by a series of simulations, copies without originals:

"The simulacrum is never that which conceals the truth—it is the truth which conceals that there is none. The simulacrum is true."

Baudrillard argued that both capitalist and communist systems could create hyperrealities, environments where manufactured images and narratives become more influential than objective truth. The use of propaganda by the Nazis and the Soviet Union during World War II demonstrated how mass media could fabricate realities that overshadowed the genuine experiences of individuals.

He observed that in capitalist societies, the proliferation of advertisements, television, and digital media contributed to a culture where signs and symbols became more real than the objects they represented. The result was a society immersed in hyperreality, where individuals are bombarded with images that shape their desires, beliefs, and perceptions without realizing the manipulation at play.

Baudrillard was mainly concerned with how powerful entities—governments, corporations, and media conglomerates—could use information to control and direct public consciousness. By constructing hyperreal environments, these entities could guide consumer behavior, political opinions, and social norms to align with their interests.

For instance, he cited how the Gulf War was presented through the lens of media as a sanitized, virtual conflict—a spectacle devoid of the gruesome realities of war. This presentation manipulated public perception, fostering support for political agendas without fully understanding the consequences.

In the context of the occupation, Baudrillard's theories reflect how both the Vichy regime and the Nazis employed propaganda to construct alternate realities. The dissemination of false information, glorification of the government, and demonization of the enemy were tactics used to maintain control over the populace.

Baudrillard's notion of hyperreality extends to the modern digital age, where social media platforms create echo chambers reinforcing existing beliefs. Algorithms curate content to maximize engagement, often at the expense of exposing individuals to diverse perspectives. The resulting hyperreal environment distorts reality, making distinguishing between genuine information and manipulated narratives challenging.

Michel Foucault, born in 1926 in Poitiers, France, was a child during the occupation. The war's impact on the structures of power and society profoundly influenced his philosophical inquiries. Foucault's work centered on the relationship between power and knowledge and how they are used as forms of social control through societal institutions.

In *Discipline and Punish* (1975), Foucault introduced the concept of the panopticon, a prison design proposed by English philosopher Jeremy Bentham. The panopticon allows a single guard to observe all inmates without them knowing whether they are being watched. This uncertainty compels inmates to regulate their behavior, effectively internalizing the surveillance.

"Power should be visible and unverifiable," Foucault wrote, emphasizing how the panopticon symbolizes modern disciplinary societies that

extend beyond prisons into schools, hospitals, and workplaces. He argued that power operates through overt repression and subtle means that shape norms, behaviors, and even desires.

During the occupation, the pervasive surveillance by the Gestapo and the Vichy regime instilled a culture of fear and self-censorship. Neighbors could be informants; conversations could be overheard. This environment forced individuals to internalize the watchful eye of authority, mirroring the panoptic effect.

Foucault extended his analysis to how knowledge itself is a tool of power. Those who control information—governments, media, educational institutions—can define what is considered valid, normal, or acceptable. This control over discourse shapes societal norms and limits the possibilities of thought.

Foucault observed that power manifests in capitalist societies through institutions that appear neutral but perpetuate existing power structures. The media, for example, can frame narratives to support the interests of the powerful and marginalize dissenting voices.

Modern data collection practices reveal how powerful entities use information to control populations. Corporations gather vast amounts of personal data to predict and influence consumer behavior. Governments may employ surveillance technologies to monitor citizens' activities and communications under the guise of security.

Foucault's concept of biopower—the regulation of populations through an array of institutions and practices—highlights how modern states exert control over territory, bodies, and minds. By managing health, education, and welfare, states can shape individuals' biological and social lives.

While approaching from different angles, Baudrillard and Foucault both dissected how the powerful wield information and representation to manipulate reality and control societies. Baudrillard focused on the saturation of signs and the erasure of the real, while Foucault examined the mechanisms of power embedded in institutions and knowledge systems.

Their theories converge in the understanding that in modern societies, control is exercised less through overt force and more through the shaping of perceptions and the internalization of norms. The powerful do not need to constantly exert pressure if individuals regulate themselves according to the constructed realities and accepted truths disseminated through media, education, and cultural practices.

During the occupation, the Nazi regime and the Vichy government exemplified these dynamics. Propaganda was meticulously crafted to dehumanize enemies, glorify the regime, and justify oppressive policies. Information was controlled to suppress dissent and maintain the illusion of legitimacy.

The philosophers' insights extend to concerns about capitalism and communism. The market dictates values in capitalist societies, often prioritizing profit over truth. Information becomes a commodity, and media outlets may cater to the interests of advertisers or owners rather than the public good. In communist regimes, state control over information reinforces the ruling party's ideology, suppressing alternative viewpoints.

While the French postwar philosophers were principally concerned with using information to consolidate power in governments, the ability to rapidly disseminate information allowed power to emerge from the people themselves. The rapid spread of information can even be used to riot, protest, or oppress. We saw this during the Arab Spring, the Me Too Movement, and the Black Lives Matter protests.

In another area, we see the Panopticon, biopower, and hyperreality clash. With our identities displayed in the open for millions to see, the preying eyes of content police have considerable influence. Social surveillance is prevalent. Modern culture emphasizes awareness, accountability, and sensitivity to identity, equality, and social justice issues. While these aims can promote positive change, the digital and social environments they play out often create intense surveillance dynamics akin to a virtual Panopticon.

Here, individuals may feel continuously scrutinized by visible and invisible observers—friends, strangers, and algorithms alike—who assess their actions, words, and thoughts against evolving cultural norms.

Social media, in particular, acts as a digital Panopticon where people monitor and record behaviors within one's network and an abstracted collective. "Wokeness," as a framework, becomes a set of cultural standards to which people must conform, often publicly, to avoid criticism or social ostracization. People may begin to internalize these standards, self-monitoring their actions, opinions, and language to avoid public backlash. This self-surveillance can feel oppressive, as the boundaries of acceptable behavior are constantly shifting and subject to scrutiny. The result is a culture in which individuals may feel compelled to adopt outward expressions of "woke" attitudes, sometimes suppressing genuine beliefs or nuances to appear aligned with accepted norms.

Furthermore, algorithms and data analytics play a significant role in this surveillance. Online platforms amplify certain behaviors and reward expressions of wokeness. Posts that align with popular sentiments are promoted and widely shared, while dissenting or nuanced views may be met with backlash or downranking, subtly nudging users toward performative compliance. This digital feedback loop creates a form of peer pressure, where conformity to social norms becomes both a protective measure and a social expectation.

Authentic self-expression becomes challenging in this landscape, as people continuously weigh their words and actions against potential social consequences. The effect is a society in which people are "always on"—constantly aware of the possibility of surveillance by an audience that can judge, comment, and respond. As with Foucault's Panopticon, this awareness creates a self-regulating population, where individuals monitor their behavior to align with perceived societal expectations, resulting in an often intense conformity.

The cultural Panopticon of "wokeness" can be both a positive force—encouraging empathy, inclusivity, and awareness—and a restrictive one, where fear of misstep or condemnation limits honest dialogue. In navigating this space, individuals may feel that they must sacrifice genuine perspectives for the appearance of correctness, raising questions about the balance between social accountability and personal authenticity.

Like our occupied French counterparts, we exist between a hammer and an anvil. Our self-expression is either mired by the preying eyes of social surveillance by our peers or by the algorithms bending our views into homogeneity.

THE INFORMATION AGE AND THE RISE OF POSTMODERNISM

HOW HYPERREALITY AND ENDLESS INFORMATION RESHAPE OUR UNDERSTANDING OF TRUTH

"We are not thinking machines that feel; rather, we are feeling machines that think."

António Damásio

Most social movements start with a simple yet profoundly resonant act of protest. The Arab Spring was no different and began with the self-immolation of Mohamed Bouazizi, a street vendor in Tunisia. After enduring years of systemic corruption, harassment, and humiliation from local officials, Bouazizi set himself ablaze in a desperate act of defiance. At that moment, his image became a powerful symbol of resistance, an icon of rebellion that resonated beyond Tunisia's borders and ignited protests across the Arab world. But in the age of hyperreality, as Baudrillard might argue, Bouazizi's story was not just a local tragedy; it was instantly transformed into a hyperreal event— a symbol that transcended his individual experience to become a simulacrum of oppression, courage, and the thirst for dignity.

In the days following Bouazizi's death, images of his charred body and his story of defiance were copied, shared, and disseminated globally, fueling an image of revolution that would resonate from Cairo to Damascus. The symbolism of Bouazizi's act was stripped down, simplified, and amplified into a universal rallying cry: "Enough." Yet this story, while based in reality, took on a life of its own through media coverage, social sharing, and the relentless news cycle. It morphed from an isolated act into a hyperreal representation of collective suffering and resistance across the region. One man's act was transformed into the "original" spark that fueled countless uprisings, each new protest carrying the weight and power of that singular moment.

In its hyperreal form, Baudrillard would argue that this story was more potent and mobilizing than Bouazizi's struggle could have ever been in isolation. It became a constructed symbol that was now perceived as "truth." As the image of Bouazizi's sacrifice spread, it fueled a simulation of revolution that felt inevitable and unstoppable. This simulation created a contagious energy, an unshakable sense that sweeping political change was within reach. The power of Bouazizi's story was not in its complexity but in its reduction, its oversimplified transformation into an iconic act that millions could appropriate.

As protests erupted, each movement across the Arab world became a variation of this hyperreal theme of defiance. Bouazizi's sacrifice was reborn, copied, and re-performed in every square and mass gathering, blurring the lines between his isolated tragedy and the collective demands of millions. This hyperreal revolution, fueled by the image of Bouazizi, captured the attention of the world, but it also, as Baudrillard might suggest, set up an impossible expectation. The reality on the ground—diverse, complex, and resistant to change—could never fully align with the simplicity and power of the hyperreal image.

This truth is now so deeply ingrained in the minds of the entire Arab world that refuting their growing movement with the depreciation of Bouazizi's circumstances would be futile.

Their equally powerful symbols—George Floyd, Rodney King, and Harvey Weinstein — sparked Occupy Wall Street, the Me Too Movement, the Black Lives Matter Protest, and the Los Angeles Riots. The individual plight of the symbol is irrelevant to the movement's emotions, opinions, and even deeply held beliefs. The movement is driven by a much deeper undercurrent of societal mistreatment and often degradation.

Welcome to the age of hyperreality, the undercurrent of social themes pulls harder than surface messaging. Social media, curated identities, and the subtle manipulation of symbols have made truth a fluid, ephemeral, and often nebulous concept.

The world is different now and it must be approached in a much different way. A picture can move a generation or, unmoved by the algorithm it can drag bottom into obscurity. Communication is not automatically recieved and its not automatically percieved as the creator intended.

Previous classics on Truth and Persuasion, such as Dale Carnegie's How to Win Friends and Influence People, Robert Cialdini's Influence, Robert Greene's The 48 Laws of Power, and Nick Kolenda's Methods of Persuasion, were the cheat codes for social interaction. But these venerable tomes are arcane in postmodernity.

These works assume a stable reality: Clear communication, interpersonal dynamics, and rational appeals drive persuasion. You can win friends and influence people without outsmarting an algorithm or competing with a cat meme for attention. Sure, classic techniques like Carnegie's emphasis on building relationships or Cialdini's principles of influence—reciprocity, scarcity, authority, and the like—still hold some water. But in today's fragmented audience, they're about as sufficient as a paper umbrella in a hurricane. Let's break it down.

Take Cialdini's principle of reciprocity, where someone does you a favor to make you feel obligated to return the gesture. This often translates to companies offering "gifts" or perks to get you to buy their products. But let's be honest—when was the last time a free keychain convinced you to drop serious cash on something? These tactics come off as transactional, lacking authenticity. It's a ploy, not a sincere act of goodwill.

Then there's the classic price manipulation tactic—the anchor and reel. Slap a high price tag on something, then "generously" offer a discount to make it seem like a deal. But today's consumers are savvy. We have Google and price comparison apps; we're not falling for that anymore. These obvious tactics alienate people.

Carnegie also emphasized the power of praise and flattery to win over others. But where every Instagram comment is "OMG, you're stunning!" or with a simple flame emoji, excessive or insincere compliments are the background noise of our lives. They can be perceived as manipulative or, worse, utterly meaningless. When people sense they're being flattered for ulterior motives, it backfires, diminishing trust instead of building it.

Cialdini's scarcity tactic—convincing people something is more valuable because it's rare—is another overplayed hand. "Limited-time offers," "only two left in stock," "sale ends at midnight!" Have you ever been to Kohl's or had a Starbucks star about to expire? How about Amazon Prime Day, Cyber Monday, or the consumerist gladiator arena known as Black Friday? While these tactics can spark a sense of urgency, people have grown wary. It's often seen as routine manipulation rather than genuine scarcity. We're not buying it—literally and figuratively.

Mirroring subtly copies someone's body language or speech patterns to build rapport. In sales and negotiations, mirroring is as standard as bad coffee but can easily be overdone. When detected, it feels about as genuine as a politician's promise. This tactic is so prevalent that many people recognize it and may react negatively if they think they're being mimicked. It's the social equivalent of plagiarism.

Robert Greene's advice to withhold information to maintain mystery and power might have worked in Renaissance courts, but it often misfires in today's culture of transparency. Think of collaborative workplaces or social movements in environments that value open communication. Saying less can make you seem aloof or untrustworthy. Overuse this tactic, and you risk creating distance or suspicion. It's like showing up to a potluck and refusing to reveal what dish you brought—no one's touching that mystery casserole.

Here's the bottom line: when persuasion tactics become too predictable, they lose their charm. Modern audiences are hip to the game. With the rise of digital marketing, these strategies are not just known; they're expected. And when the magician reveals his tricks, the magic disappears.

Many of these tactics rely on creating emotional connections or trust. But when overused or transparently deployed, they lose their persuasive power and come off as manipulative. As our world becomes more interconnected and social values shift toward authenticity, transparency, and trustworthiness, these older strategies feel ancient and predictable.

Today's persuasive environment is more dynamic than ever, with attention shifts that make a goldfish seem focused and engagement spans shorter than Snapchat stories. These old-school tactics are akin to the skills needed to win the World Series of Poker before Chris Moneymaker turned the game upside down.

Speaking of which, let's revisit our friend Moneymaker—the accountant who, in 2003, took $39 and spun it into $2.5 million at the WSOP. He didn't play by the old rules; he brought an online, aggressive style to a traditional, conservative game. He was the glitch in the matrix, the wildcard that disrupted the system. His victory signaled that the game had changed, and if you weren't adapting, you were dying.

Similarly, the hyperreality we live in demands different skills. Persuasion now isn't just about interpersonal dynamics; it's about navigating a labyrinth where truth is relative, identities are curated, and facts bend like light in a black hole to fit the narrative of the moment.

So, how do we navigate this new landscape? We need tools designed for a hyperreal age. We need to become fluent in the language of memes, understand the psychology behind viral content, and grasp how algorithms shape our perceptions. Knowing the principles is insufficient; we must also understand how memes are being hacked, remixed, and redistributed in real-time.

These postmodern challenges require an evolved strategy of influence that accounts for the volatility of modern discourse, the power of digital symbols, and the necessity of crafting narratives that resonate across rapidly shifting contexts. It's about being genuine in a culture saturated with artifice, building trust when skepticism is the default setting, and connecting on a human level even as we engage through screens.

In other words, it's time to update our playbook. The old maps won't guide us through this new territory. We're charting a course in uncharted waters, and the compass is still spinning. But one thing's for sure: clinging to outdated tactics is a surefire way to get lost.

Ever notice how the grand stories that once held our world together unravel like an old sweater. Religion, national identity, ethnicity—they were the glue keeping everything in place. These grand narratives gave us a script, a purpose, a reason to get out of bed in the morning. But now? We're flipping through channels in a postmodern world without a remote.

In his book Sapiens, Yuval Noah Harari nails this. For most of human history, he explains how religions like Christianity, Islam, and Buddhism provided the frameworks for understanding everything—morality, existence, and the whole shebang. These stories told us who we were, why we were here, and what rules to follow. They were comforting, like a warm blanket on a cold night.

Then came scientific thinking and rationalism, which eliminated religious grand narratives in many parts of the world. The Enlightenment replaced divine commandments with humanism, spotlighting human experience, reason, and individual rights. We went from "God wills it" to "We can figure this out ourselves."

Fast-forward to modern times and capitalism is the new grand narrative. It promises that endless economic growth and shiny new tech toys will lead us to Happinessville. Harari isn't buying it, though. He points out that despite all our gadgets and wealth, we're not necessarily happier. It's like chasing a mirage in the desert—you think you're getting closer but get thirstier.

But here's where it gets juicy. While Harari hints at the cracks in these grand narratives, postmodernism comes with a sledgehammer. Jean-

François Lyotard, in *The Postmodern Condition*, defines postmodernism as "incredulity toward metanarratives." Translation? We're skeptical of any big story that claims to have all the answers.

Western culture was built on grand narratives for centuries, such as the Enlightenment's faith in progress through reason or Marxism's vision of a classless society. These stories were the North Star guiding humanity forward. But postmodernism flips the script. By the late 20th century, people started losing faith in these one-size-fits-all stories. Instead of a single path, we now see countless trails branching off in every direction, each as valid—or questionable—as the next.

Lyotard believed that grand narratives—whether rooted in religion, nationality, or race—were often manipulated by those in power. People grew skeptical, much like when folks split from the Catholic Church during the Protestant Reformation. The result? A fragmented understanding of truth. No single story or framework can claim universal validity anymore. We're adrift in a sea of micro-narratives, each person navigating their tiny boat.

This fragmentation of truth is a game-changer. Philosophers like Michel Foucault and Jacques Derrida argued that truth isn't some objective reality waiting to be discovered. Nope, it's constructed, contingent, and often a tool of power dynamics. Foucault dissected institutions like prisons and hospitals, showing how what we accept as "truth" is shaped by social structures and those who hold the keys. "Power is everywhere," he said, "because it comes from everywhere."

Think about it: who gets to decide what's true? The Catholic Church? The government? Your Facebook feed? Those in power control the narrative and, by extension, the truth. Instead of fighting to become the Pope or the President, people are splintering into smaller groups, each with their version of reality.

Jacques Derrida took his theory of deconstruction a step further. He argued that language itself is unstable and full of contradictions. Since all knowledge is mediated through language, pinpointing a universal truth is like trying to nail Jell-O to a wall. His famous line, "There is nothing outside the text," suggests that everything—including truth—is filtered through language and context.

So, what does this mean for persuasion in our hyperreal age? If truth is no longer stable or universal, persuasion becomes a whole new ball game. You can't just trot out objective facts and expect everyone to nod along. Instead, persuasion is about aligning with the subjective truths of individuals or communities. Emotional appeal, storytelling, and relatability take center stage, pushing logic and reason to the back seat.

Look at modern politics. Successful campaigns now craft narratives that tap into emotions and resonate with voters' identities. In the 2024 Presidential race the Democrats chose abortion as their main policy position. While some regard this as a mistake, it was chosen because of its tendancy to allign with white women - a group that Deomcrats needed to sway to put Kamala Harris in office. In the 2015 Republican Presidential Primary Debate, Donald Trump was asked about vaccines causing autism, he said:

"Just the other day, two years old, [sic] 2½ years old, a child, a beautiful child, went to have the vaccine and came back, and a week later got a tremendous fever, got very, very sick, now is autistic."

Dr. Ben Carson, a respected physician, had just stated that there was no scientific link. But which statement sticks in your mind? Trump's anecdote wasn't about objective truth but about creating an emotional connection. Facts took a backseat to feelings.

In this landscape, persuasion isn't about facts but crafting a narrative that resonates personally. It's about acknowledging that truth is constructed differently for everyone and meeting people where they are emotionally.

Foucault's insights remind us that power shapes truth. Those who control the narrative wield the real power. Carefully curated images, advertisements, and influencer personas create a hyperreal environment that's more persuasive than reality itself. Jean Baudrillard famously said, "The simulacrum is never what hides the truth—it is the truth that hides the fact that there is none."

Gilles Deleuze took this even further, focusing on the fluidity of reality. For him, the world isn't fixed; it's always becoming, always in flux. Truth isn't something to discover but something to continuously redefine. We're all surfing an ever-changing wave, and there's no solid ground to stand on.

All these philosophical heavyweights—Foucault, Derrida, Baudrillard, Deleuze—set the stage for our current digital chaos. In the internet and social media age, information is fragmented, and truth is customizable. Algorithms feed us content that reinforces our beliefs, creating echo chambers where our version of truth is constantly validated.

Remember the early days of the COVID-19 pandemic? Platforms like Facebook and Twitter scrambled to control the narrative, suppressing discussions about the Wuhan lab leak theory. The dominant story was that the virus had zoonotic origins, and any deviation was labeled misinformation. Fast forward, and even Dr. Anthony Fauci acknowledged that the lab leak theory warranted investigation. The narrative shifted, highlighting just how fluid truth has become.

Nicholas Wade, a former *New York Times* science writer, published an analysis raising questions about the virus's origins, but his work was initially sidelined. Dr. Li-Meng Yan, a Chinese virologist, claimed the virus was manufactured, but her voice was silenced mainly on social media. Platforms wielded their power to shape the narrative, deciding which truths were acceptable.

In this postmodern maze, traditional authority structures are crumbling. Credibility isn't about expertise anymore; it's about relatability. Influencers hold sway not because they're experts but because they connect emotionally with their audience. Authority has become subjective, and emotional connection often trumps formal credentials.

So, who controls truth now? Content moderators, algorithms, and governments are the new gatekeepers, bending the river of information to fit certain narratives. Propaganda isn't just about spreading false stories; it's about selecting which truths to highlight and which to suppress.

Carl Sagan warned us about this in *The Demon-Haunted World*. He championed the scientific method as a defense against the seductions of unproven beliefs. "Science is more than a body of knowledge; it is a way of thinking," he wrote. Logic and reason offer a framework for navigating reality, even when truth feels quicksand.

The legal system is a testament to this. Despite the fragmentation of truth, courtrooms rely on evidence and logical argumentation to seek justice. Logic remains a universal language, a common ground in a divided world.

But here's the rub: logic doesn't always gain traction in a landscape dominated by emotional appeal. Social media platforms, driven by algorithms that prioritize engagement, feed us content that aligns with our beliefs. This creates echo chambers where we're rarely challenged, making emotional persuasion more potent than ever.

Daniel Kahneman's research on cognitive biases shows that we're wired to favor information that confirms our beliefs. Multiple truths coexist in our current age, and these biases reinforce our narratives, making us more resistant to alternative perspectives.

So, where does that leave us? In the postmodern age, a story's authenticity is less critical than its emotional impact. Facts take a backseat to feelings, and persuasion becomes a battle of narratives rather than a presentation of evidence.

The challenge is finding a balance between emotional resonance and objective truth. While postmodernism embraces the fluidity of truth, we can't abandon reason and logic entirely. They remain crucial tools for critical thinking and meaningful dialogue.

Postmodernism can also backfire and undermine society. During the anti-vaccination movement, elebrities and influencers shared emotionally charged stories linking vaccines to autism despite overwhelming scientific evidence to the contrary. The emotional narratives were compelling but ultimately harmful, leading to a resurgence of preventable diseases. In this instance, the postmodern emphasis on personal truth and emotional appeal clashed with objective reality, resulting in negative consequences for public health.

In 2006, Al Gore swapped his vice-presidential suit for a climate crusader cape. *An Inconvenient Truth* hit the global stage like a meteor, aiming to awaken us with dire warnings about our planet's future. Gore didn't just tiptoe around the issue; he went full throttle with fear as his weapon. Gore showed images of melting icebergs, costal cities sinking and polar bears drowning. The message was a constant catillion of fear.

The film was an instant sensation. Gore snagged a Nobel Peace Prize, and suddenly, climate change was the hot topic at dinner tables that usually reserved that spot for sports and celebrity gossip. But here's the twist: that aggressive, fear-laden approach started to rub people the wrong way over time. Some felt Gore was playing fast and loose with the facts, and as the years rolled by without the promised apocalypse, skepticism began to bubble up.

The pushback hit a crescendo when a UK court weighed in. In the case of Dimmock v. Secretary of State for Education and Skills in 2007, the court ruled that while the film could be shown in schools, it needed some disclaimers. They pointed out nine instances where Gore might've stretched the truth a tad—overstating the immediacy or scale of specific threats. For example, his dramatic claims about a 7-meter sea-level rise didn't mention that such a scenario would likely unfold over centuries, not next Tuesday. As for those poor polar bears? Turns out the drowning incident he cited was an isolated event, not the norm.

While Gore's sensationalism grabbed headlines, it also attracted the wrong attention. People started seeing his message as more theatrical than factual. The exaggerations fuelled climate change skeptics' questions about the entire movement. It was like shouting "Fire!" in a crowded theater with only smoke from a burnt popcorn kernel.

Another sticking point was how Gore directly linked specific extreme weather events to climate change. Hurricane Katrina? Blame climate change. The drying up of Lake Chad? Yep, that's climate change, too. The scientific community wasn't entirely on board with these direct correlations. Climate change might increase the likelihood or intensity of certain events, but pinning individual disasters solely on it oversimplified complex systems.

People tend to lose their appetite when fear becomes the main dish rather than the seasoning. Psychologists call this the "doomsday effect." Overwhelm your audience with catastrophe, and they might check out or push back. Effective fear-based messaging needs a balance—a way to empower rather than paralyze. While groundbreaking in many ways, Gore's film left some viewers feeling more helpless than motivated.

When done right, fear-based messaging can pack a punch— then Presidential Candidate Lyndon B. Johnson ran the most influential presidential campaign ad in history in 1964 - the infamous *Daisy Ad*. Amid the Cold War jitters, this ad didn't mince words—or images. A little girl picking petals off a daisy morphs into a countdown to nuclear annihilation. Subtle? Not even close. Effective? Absolutely. It aired only once but left an indelible mark, tapping into primal fears of survival and pushing voters to choose Johnson over the perceived trigger-happy alternative.

Contrast that with Steve Jobs strolling onto a stage in his iconic black turtleneck and jeans. In 2001, he introduced the world to the iPod with a simple, aspirational pitch: "1,000 songs in your pocket." There were no scare tactics, no doom and gloom—just a vision of personal freedom and endless possibilities. Jobs wasn't selling a gadget; he was offering an identity, a lifestyle. He tapped into our desires for esteem and self-actualization, those higher rungs on Maslow's Hierarchy of Needs.

While Gore aimed to motivate through fear, Jobs was inspired by clean and rebellious disruption. The iPod became more than a music player; it symbolized modernity and individuality. People didn't just buy it for what it did but for what it said about them. Jobs understood that the consumer base is saturated with choices, and offering a path to becoming the best version of oneself was the ultimate persuasive tool.

Fear can be a powerful motivator, but it's a double-edged sword. Wield it recklessly, and you might just cut yourself. Gore's *An Inconvenient Truth* was a wake-up call. Still, its overreliance on fear without sufficient actionable solutions left many hitting the snooze button instead;

conversely, when authentic and empowering, aspirational messaging can move mountains—or, at the very least, many iPods.

Persuasion is about connecting with people where they are, offering them a stake in the outcome, and giving them the tools to act. Whether through the chill of potential disaster or the warm glow of possibility, the most effective messages resonate on a profoundly human level.

FEELING MACHINES THAT THINK: CAPITALISM'S COMMODIFICATION OF HUMANITY

HOW CAPITALISM EXPLOITS OUR EMOTIONS AND SELLS THEM BACK TO US

"The propagandist's purpose is to make one set of people forget that certain other sets of people are human."

Aldous Huxley

Daniel Kahneman, born in 1934 in Tel Aviv and raised amidst the turmoil of Nazi-occupied France, carried within him the indelible marks of uncertainty and survival. The specter of war cast long shadows over his childhood, instilling a profound curiosity about the nature of human thought and the irrationalities that govern it. "My earliest memories are the uncertainties of war," Kahneman would later reflect. "The contradictions of human behavior during those times kindled my fascination with the mind." His family's narrow escapes from the Gestapo left an imprint that would shape his life's work, driving him to explore the complexities of perception and judgment.

Amos Tversky, born in 1937 in Haifa, was a man of formidable intellect and unyielding rigor. His military service as a paratrooper in the Israeli Defense Forces honed his analytical acumen under the pressures of life-and-death decision-making. Tversky possessed an uncanny ability to distill complex phenomena into elegant mathematical expressions—a skill that proved invaluable in his collaboration with Kahneman. Together, they embarked on a journey to deconstruct the myth of human rationality, venturing into the labyrinthine depths of the mind where intuition often usurps logic.

Their partnership was a crucible of ideas, melding Kahneman's psychological insights with Tversky's mathematical precision. At the Hebrew University of Jerusalem, they began a series of experiments that would challenge the bedrock assumptions of economics. The prevailing theories rested on the notion of *Homo economicus*—the rational actor who makes decisions based solely on logical analysis and self-interest. Kahneman and Tversky's work illuminated the cognitive shortcuts or heuristics that people employ when uncertain, revealing that these mental processes often lead to systematic errors.

Their seminal paper, "Prospect Theory: An Analysis of Decision under Risk," published in 1979, introduced a new framework for understanding economic behavior. Prospect Theory posits that individuals value gains and losses differently, leading to decisions that deviate from strict rationality. The value function concept, which is concave for gains, convex for losses, and steeper for losses than gains, reflected a fundamental asymmetry in human psychology. This asymmetry is known as loss aversion—the idea that losses weigh more heavily on the psyche than equivalent gains.

Loss aversion manifests in myriad ways, subtly influencing choices that seem, on the surface, entirely logical. Imagine an investor clinging to a declining stock, refusing to sell in hopes of a rebound. The initial investment becomes a psychological anchor, and the prospect of realizing a loss is so painful that it clouds judgment. This behavior contributed to the 2008 financial crisis, where homeowners and investors held onto depreciating assets, exacerbating the market collapse. The fear of loss led to inaction—a paralysis that rippled through the economy.

Marketers, ever attuned to the levers of human behavior, exploit loss aversion by emphasizing potential losses to spur action. Insurance companies paint vivid disaster scenarios to sell policies, tapping our primal instincts. Retailers use phrases like "Don't miss out!" or "Limited time offer!" to trigger fear of missing opportunities. These tactics compel decisions that may not align with our rational interests, nudging us toward choices driven by emotion rather than reason.

Anchoring is another subtle yet powerful heuristic uncovered by Kahneman and Tversky. It describes how initial exposure to a number or concept influences subsequent judgments. In an elegant experiment, participants were asked to estimate the percentage of African nations in the United Nations after spinning a wheel rigged to stop at either 10 or 65. Those who landed on 65 provided significantly higher estimates than those who landed on 10, demonstrating how arbitrary anchors can sway our perceptions.

Consider the art of negotiation, where the first offer sets the stage. Real estate agents might show an overpriced property to anchor buyers' expectations, making subsequent listings more reasonable. Car dealerships display vehicles with high sticker prices, knowing that any negotiated reduction still operates within a range influenced by the initial number. Buyers navigate within boundaries subtly dictated by the seller, often settling on prices higher than they might have considered without the anchor.

The availability heuristic reflects our tendency to estimate the likelihood of events based on how easily examples come to mind. Vivid or recent experiences disproportionately influence our perceptions of frequency and risk. After high-profile airplane crashes, fear of flying surges despite statistical evidence that air travel remains one of the safest modes of transportation. The vivid imagery of a plane crash lingers in the collective consciousness, skewing risk assessment. Following the tragic events of September 11, 2001, many opted to drive long distances instead of flying, inadvertently increasing the number of road fatalities. The availability heuristic led to decisions that, while emotionally comforting, heightened actual risk.

Media outlets amplify this effect by focusing on sensational stories, making rare events seem familiar. Marketers harness it by ensuring their products remain top-of-mind through repetitive advertising. The incessant jingles and logos that adorn every possible surface embed themselves in our memories, influencing choices in subtle yet profound ways.

The representativeness heuristic involves assessing similarity and assuming that like goes with like, often leading to neglect of statistical realities. In finance, this manifests as the gambler's fallacy—the belief that a string of losses increases the probability of a subsequent win. Casinos exploit this by showcasing near-misses on slot machines, encouraging the belief that a win is imminent. Players continue gambling, enticed by patterns that exist only in perception.

In hiring practices, managers may favor candidates who fit a stereotype of success, such as graduates from prestigious universities, potentially overlooking more qualified individuals who don't fit the mold. This bias perpetuates homogeneity and can stifle diversity and innovation within organizations. The mirage of patterns leads to decisions that feel intuitively correct but are statistically unsound.

The framing effect reveals how information is presented—the context and wording—and how it can significantly influence decisions. Kahneman and Tversky illustrated this with a study in which participants chose between two treatments for a disease expected to kill 600 people. When options were framed in terms of lives saved, participants preferred certainty; when framed in terms of deaths, they favored riskier choices. The underlying outcomes were identical, but the framing altered perceptions.

Political discourse often uses framing to sway public opinion. For example, describing a tax as a "benefit to society" rather than a "burden on taxpayers" elicits vastly different reactions. In healthcare, a procedure with a "90% survival rate" is more reassuring than one with a "10% mortality rate," though the statistics are the same. Framing manipulates perception without altering the facts—a tool wielded adeptly in marketing and politics.

Confirmation bias is the tendency to seek out or interpret information to confirm existing beliefs, disregarding evidence to the contrary. In the digital age, algorithms curate content aligned with users' preferences, reinforcing existing views and creating echo chambers.

Confirmation bias is a cognitive trap that profoundly affects decision-making processes, particularly in environments where high-stakes judgments need to be made, such as criminal investigations. It refers to the tendency to search for, interpret, and recall information in a way that confirms one's preexisting beliefs, while disregarding evidence that contradicts those beliefs. The effects of confirmation bias can be devastating, as seen in the case of Richard Phillips, who spent nearly 46 years in prison for a crime he did not commit.

Phillips was convicted in 1972 for the murder of Gregory Harris, a crime that hinged almost entirely on the false testimony of Fred Mitchell, Harris' brother-in-law. This conviction, despite the lack of any physical evidence, is a classic case of confirmation bias in law enforcement. Once police and prosecutors formed a theory that Phillips was involved in the crime, they selectively interpreted the evidence to fit this narrative, ignoring significant inconsistencies in Mitchell's testimony and failing to properly investigate other suspects or leads.

The central piece of evidence against Phillips came from Fred Mitchell, who had initially been a suspect himself. Mitchell provided a narrative that fit the police's early assumptions about the crime, claiming that Phillips and another man, Richard Palombo, were responsible for Harris' death. Despite significant inconsistencies in Mitchell's testimony and his obvious incentive to deflect suspicion from himself, law enforcement fixated on his account.

Once Phillips and Palombo were implicated, investigators interpreted all further evidence through the lens of their guilt. This "tunnel vision" led police to overlook exculpatory evidence, such as the absence of physical links between Phillips and the crime scene. Investigators also ignored or downplayed the contradictions in Mitchell's evolving story. Even though his testimony had clear flaws, it supported their theory of the crime, and that was enough to build their case.

The trial itself reflected this bias. Prosecutors leaned heavily on Mitchell's testimony, treating it as the linchpin of the case despite its dubious reliability. Confirmation bias is often reinforced in court settings, where the pressure to secure a conviction can lead to an overreliance on narratives that confirm guilt, while undermining the importance of contradictory evidence.

Once law enforcement decided that Phillips was guilty, every piece of evidence was interpreted through this lens. Investigators failed to thoroughly consider alternative explanations or pursue other suspects. For example, Fred Mitchell, who had his own violent history and clear motives to shift blame, was never properly scrutinized. His testimony was accepted at face value, and once it implicated Phillips, investigators stopped looking for other leads. The failure to critically evaluate Mitchell's credibility or question why he would accuse Phillips speaks directly to the impact of confirmation bias in the case.

This bias became entrenched over the decades. Every time Phillips appealed his case or presented new evidence, the courts rejected his claims, unwilling to revisit the original narrative constructed around his guilt. It wasn't until 2010, when Palombo himself confessed that Phillips had no involvement, that the wheels of justice finally started to turn in Phillips' favor. Even then, it took years of legal work by the University of Michigan Innocence Clinic to fully exonerate him.

Often, Once an initial theory of guilt is established, investigators, prosecutors, and even judges may become fixated on that theory, interpreting all evidence in a way that confirms it while ignoring or minimizing anything that contradicts it. This can lead to devastating consequences for innocent individuals, as seen in Phillips' case.

One of the most dangerous aspects of confirmation bias is that it often goes unrecognized by those who are caught in it. Investigators genuinely believe they are acting in the interest of justice, unaware that their own cognitive biases are distorting their view of the facts. In Phillips' case, the bias was so strong that it persisted for nearly five decades, through countless appeals and legal challenges, before finally being overturned.

The Phillips case teaches us several critical lessons about how confirmation bias operates in the criminal justice system:

Initial Theories Shape Perception: Once law enforcement has formed an initial theory about a suspect's guilt, that theory can distort how all subsequent evidence is interpreted. In Phillips' case, the initial decision to focus on him as a suspect led to years of wrongful imprisonment.

Ignoring Exculpatory Evidence: Confirmation bias often causes investigators to overlook or dismiss evidence that contradicts their theory. In Phillips' case, the lack of physical evidence and the inconsistencies in Mitchell's testimony were ignored because they didn't fit the narrative that had been constructed around Phillips' guilt.

The Need for Objective Review: One of the most important safeguards against confirmation bias is the objective review of evidence. Independent reviews by organizations like the Innocence Clinic or other external bodies can help ensure that investigations remain impartial. In Phillips' case, it was only after an external investigation that the truth finally came to light.

Prolonged Miscarriages of Justice: Once a conviction has been obtained, confirmation bias can continue to affect the case through the appeals process. Courts are often reluctant to reconsider evidence or re-examine the initial investigation, perpetuating the bias. Phillips' decades-long battle for justice demonstrates how deeply entrenched this bias can become.

Overconfidence bias leads individuals to overestimate their abilities or the accuracy of their knowledge. Long-Term Capital Management's (LTCM) fall in the 1990s exemplifies this peril. Led by Nobel laureates and esteemed economists, LTCM developed complex models predicting market behavior with high certainty. Their overconfidence led to massive leveraged positions, and when unforeseen events occurred—such as the Asian financial crisis and the Russian default—their models failed catastrophically. The resulting losses necessitated a bailout to prevent broader economic fallout. Overconfidence at high levels can have cascading effects on the global economy, a stark reminder of the Icarus-like risks of hubris.

The sunk cost fallacy is the inclination to continue an endeavor once resources have been invested, even when future costs outweigh the benefits. Despite mounting costs and diminishing profitability prospects of the Concorde jet, the British and French governments continued funding the project due to the substantial investments already made. The term "Concorde fallacy" became synonymous with the sunk cost fallacy.

While inherent to human cognition, these heuristics render us vulnerable to manipulation—particularly in the hands of those who understand their mechanisms. The insights uncovered by Kahneman and Tversky opened avenues for not only understanding human behavior but also influencing it. When merged with the rampant expansion of post-World War II capitalism, these cognitive shortcuts became tools to subtly guide consumer choices, often blurring the lines between persuasion and exploitation.

Companies craft interfaces that guide decisions through default settings, pre-checked boxes, and strategically placed buttons. Online subscriptions often employ dark patterns—design elements that trick users into agreeing to terms or making purchases unintentionally. The "Accept" button for cookies is prominently displayed, while the option to decline is hidden in less accessible menus.

Financial pitfalls abound as credit card companies and lenders exploit present bias and hyperbolic discounting, offering immediate gratification with deferred consequences. Leading up to the 2008 financial crisis, lenders offered subprime mortgages with low initial interest rates, downplaying long-term costs. Influenced by present bias, borrowers focused on the immediate possibility of homeownership while underestimating future financial burdens. The widespread default on these loans triggered a global economic downturn.

Recognizing the shadows that heuristics cast upon our decisions is the first step toward reclaiming agency. Governments and organizations play pivotal roles in safeguarding against exploitation. Regulations like the General Data Protection Regulation (GDPR) in the European Union enforce data privacy and transparency. Ethical guidelines for user interface design discourage dark patterns and promote informed consent. Companies adopting principles of conscious capitalism prioritize stakeholder well-being alongside profitability, fostering trust and long-term success.

The tapestry of behavioral economics does not end with Kahneman and Tversky; it extends into the works of scholars and authors who have explored how these cognitive biases are harnessed—sometimes insidiously—within modern society. Richard H. Thaler is a pioneer in behavioral economics who delved into practical applications in everyday life. In his book *Nudge: Improving Decisions About Health, Wealth, and Happiness*, co-authored with Cass R. Sunstein, Thaler examines how subtle policy shifts can guide people toward better choices without eliminating freedom of choice. They introduce the concept of libertarian paternalism, where choice architecture is designed to improve individual welfare while preserving autonomy.

Thaler and Sunstein argue that policymakers can "nudge" individuals toward decisions that enhance their well-being by understanding heuristics and biases. For example, automatically enrolling employees in retirement savings plans leverages the status quo bias to promote financial security. They advocate for interventions that correct market failures caused by cognitive limitations, positioning behavioral economics as a tool for societal benefit rather than exploitation.

Shoshana Zuboff's critical perspective in The Age of Surveillance Capitalism contrasts this principled approach. In it, Zuboff explores how corporations mine personal data to predict and shape behavior, creating new behavioral futures markets. She warns of a looming dystopia where exploiting behavioral tendencies undermines individual autonomy and democracy. "Surveillance capitalism unilaterally claims human experience as free raw material for translation into behavioral data," she writes, highlighting a paradigm in which manipulation supersedes mutual benefit.

Zuboff's work echoes George Akerlof and Robert Shiller's concerns in *Phishing for Phools: The Economics of Manipulation and Deception*. The authors argue that markets inherently provide opportunities for profit by exploiting human weaknesses. They illuminate how sellers can create artificial needs or exploit a lack of information, leading consumers into choices detrimental to their interests. "Competitive markets, by their very nature, spawn deception and trickery," they assert, challenging the notion of markets as inherently fair or efficient.

Drawing from historical contexts, Edward Bernays's seminal work *Propaganda* unveils how strategic communication can shape public opinion. Often referred to as the father of public relations, Bernays applied principles of psychology to influence mass behavior, recognizing the power of subconscious desires. His campaigns, such as promoting cigarette smoking among women as a symbol of liberation, demonstrate how exploiting heuristics can alter societal norms and consumer habits. Bernays writes, "Those who manipulate this unseen mechanism of society constitute an invisible government which is the true ruling power of our country."

On a different note, Dan Ariely's *Predictably Irrational* delves into the systematic and predictable ways humans deviate from rationality. Ariely conducts experiments revealing how emotions, social norms, and relativity influence decisions. While acknowledging vulnerabilities in human cognition, he explores how understanding these patterns can lead to better personal and policy decisions.

In *Thinking, Fast and Slow*, Daniel Kahneman extends his earlier work to a broader audience, dissecting the dual-system model of cognition. He elucidates how System 1 (fast, intuitive thinking) and System 2 (slow, deliberate thinking) interact, often leading to cognitive illusions. Kahneman expresses concern over the overconfidence bias, especially among experts, and its impact on decision-making in finance and politics. He advocates for humility and critical thinking as antidotes to overestimating our knowledge.

In marketing, Robert Cialdini's *Influence: The Psychology of Persuasion* dissects the principles that govern how we are persuaded: reciprocity, commitment and consistency, social proof, authority, liking, and scarcity. Cialdini's exploration reveals how these levers are pulled in advertising and sales, often without our conscious awareness. By understanding these mechanisms, individuals can defend against undue influence.

Moreover, in *Scarcity: Why Having Too Little Means So Much*, Sendhil Mullainathan and Eldar Shafir delve into how scarcity—of time, money, or resources—affects our cognitive bandwidth and decision-making.

They reveal that scarcity imposes cognitive loads that exacerbate biases and impair judgment. Their work underscores the importance of considering context and environment when evaluating decisions and advocating for systemic solutions to mitigate the effects of scarcity on populations.

In the wake of the Cambridge Analytica scandal, a disquieting question lingers: Have we, as a society, surrendered our agency to the invisible architectures of algorithms and data analytics? The convergence of behavioral economics, psychology, and technology has created a landscape where our choices are not solely our own but are subtly shaped by forces beyond our conscious awareness.

Behavioral economics provides the framework through which these algorithms can effectively nudge us. By understanding our cognitive biases—such as loss aversion, present bias, and confirmation bias—algorithms can present choices in ways that are most likely to elicit desired responses. This dynamic raises the specter of a feedback loop, where our actions reinforce the algorithm's predictions, narrowing the scope of our perceived choices.

Are our futures predestined based on perceived choice? The notion of predestination suggests a fixed path from which deviation is impossible. While algorithms can influence and constrain the options we see, they do not eliminate free will. However, they can create environments where confident choices become more salient, and others fade into obscurity. The danger lies in the gradual erosion of awareness, where the subtle shaping of options leads us to believe that the curated selection before us is all that exists.

Education plays a pivotal role in fostering this awareness and preventing its erosion. Learning to question sources, identify biases, and understand the mechanics of algorithms equips individuals with the tools to make informed choices. Another essential element is transparency. Tech companies and developers are responsible for making the workings of their algorithms more accessible and understandable. This doesn't necessarily mean revealing proprietary code but providing meaningful explanations of how data is used, and decisions are made. Initiatives like algorithmic audits and ethics boards can help ensure that systems are designed and deployed with consideration for their societal impact.

Regulation may also be necessary to safeguard against the most egregious abuses. Policies that protect data privacy prevent discriminatory practices, and promote accountability can create a framework within which technology serves the public interest. The European Union's General Data Protection Regulation (GDPR) is an example of legislation that gives individuals control over their data.

Moreover, fostering a culture that values human-centered design can shift the focus from exploiting cognitive biases to enhancing well-being. Ethical design principles encourage the development of technologies that align with users' interests rather than manipulating them for profit or power. This approach resonates with the "choice architecture" concept proposed by Thaler and Sunstein, where environments are structured to promote beneficial choices without restricting freedom.

Collective action and societal dialogue are also vital.

Engaging in conversations about the role of technology in our lives, advocating for ethical standards, and supporting organizations that prioritize transparency and user welfare can drive change. As consumers, we wield power through our choices and voices, influencing market dynamics and corporate behaviors.

On an individual level, cultivating mindfulness and introspection can help us become more attuned to the influences acting upon us. We can regain control by pausing to reflect on our motivations and the factors shaping our decisions. Techniques such as digital detoxes, setting boundaries for technology use, and seeking out diverse perspectives can counterbalance the effects of algorithmic curation.

Ultimately, moving forward requires a recalibration of humanity's relationship with technology. Algorithms are powerful tools that reflect the values and intentions of their creators. They are not sentient overlords but constructs that can be guided, modified, or restrained according to our collective will.

Philosopher Hannah Arendt once wrote about the "banality of evil," the idea that great harm can result not from evil intent but from thoughtlessness. She argued that we can avert the slide into a deterministic future of critical engagement. We can avert the slide into a deterministic future by bringing deliberate thought to our interactions with technology.

Revisiting cognitive science's insights can help us contemplate the balance between determinism and free will. While our brains rely on heuristics and biases to process information efficiently, we also possess the capacity for metacognition—the ability to think about our thinking. This self-awareness is a uniquely human trait that enables us to question, adapt, and transcend our habitual patterns.

The narrative that humans are slaves to algorithms is not a foregone conclusion. In the grand tapestry of human history, technology has always been a double-edged sword, capable of uplifting and undermining. The printing press disseminated knowledge but also propaganda; the Industrial Revolution improved living standards while disrupting societies. The digital age is no different, presenting us with choices about how we shape and are shaped by our creations.

FOLLOWING ORDERS: AUTHORITY, MORALITY, AND THE DANGER OF COMPLIANCE

HOW WE SURRENDER OUR MORALS TO AUTHORITY IN THE AGE OF OBEDIENCE

"The disappearance of a sense of responsibility is the most far-reaching consequence of submission to authority."

Stanley Milgram

In 1961, psychologist Stanley Milgram conducted one of the most famous and controversial experiments in social psychology. The study was designed to explore how ordinary individuals could commit acts of cruelty simply by following orders from an authority figure. This question arose in the aftermath of the Holocaust, where many Nazi officials claimed they were "just following orders." Milgram's experiment sought to test the limits of obedience, revealing unsettling truths about human behavior and the power of authority in influencing decisions.

Milgram's experiment involved participants who were told they were taking part in a study on learning and memory. The participants were instructed to administer electric shocks to a "learner" (actually an actor) whenever the learner gave incorrect answers to a series of questions. The learner was placed in another room, and the participant could hear their supposed responses to the shocks. As the shocks increased in intensity, the learner began to scream in pain, plead for the shocks to stop, and eventually fell silent, as if unconscious or worse.

Despite hearing these distressing reactions, the majority of participants—about 65%—continued administering shocks up to the maximum voltage of 450 volts simply because an authority figure (the experimenter) told them to continue. The authority figure wore a lab coat and maintained a calm, professional demeanor, which added to their credibility and influence. The participants, despite their visible distress and hesitation, deferred to this authority, following orders they knew were causing immense harm to another person.

Milgram's findings offer deep insights into the nature of persuasion and authority, and these insights have profound implications for understanding how people respond to power and control.

At its core, the experiment demonstrates how authority figures wield significant influence over people's actions, often in ways that bypass an individual's moral compass. When individuals perceive someone as an authority, whether due to their position, expertise, or appearance (such as a lab coat), they are more likely to comply with that person's directives—even if those directives conflict with their own ethical standards. This finding has vast implications for how society understands leadership, obedience, and the potential for abuse of power.

One of the key elements Milgram's experiment reveals is that persuasion through authority is incredibly effective when the person being persuaded feels they are not personally responsible for their actions. The participants in the experiment were often distressed and uncomfortable, yet they continued to administer shocks because they believed the responsibility for harm fell on the authority figure, not themselves. The sense of moral responsibility was displaced. This highlights how people can be persuaded to act against their own values if they believe they are simply following orders from a higher authority.

In terms of persuasion, Milgram's experiment shows how authority can override personal agency. It demonstrates the power of social influence, where people are compelled to act based on external directives rather than their own judgment. This principle has been applied in numerous contexts, including the military, corporate settings, and even everyday situations where individuals comply with authority figures (such as doctors, police officers, or political leaders) without questioning the orders they receive.

The lessons from Milgram's experiment extend far beyond the confines of a psychology lab. In today's world, the same dynamics of authority and obedience play out in various forms, especially through digital media. On platforms like YouTube, Instagram, or Twitter, influencers, celebrities, and figures of perceived expertise wield immense persuasive power. Their authority may not be formal, like the authority of a scientist or government official, but the vast number of followers and visible social proof confer upon them a similar influence.

The social media age has created a new type of authority—authority by popularity. When people see that a certain YouTuber or influencer has millions of subscribers, they may automatically defer to their opinions, viewing them as credible or "correct" purely because of their visibility and following. This creates an environment where individuals are persuaded to align with the views or behavior of influencers, often without critically examining the content or questioning whether the advice is sound.

In this way, Milgram's findings about the dangers of unthinking obedience to authority are just as relevant today, albeit in a different form. Instead of a lab-coated scientist, today's authority figures might be social media influencers with millions of followers who can persuade individuals to buy products, adopt lifestyles, or even espouse political beliefs—all based on the perception of authority created by follower count or online persona.

Furthermore, the ability of influencers to persuade large audiences without rigorous oversight or accountability raises ethical concerns, similar to those Milgram explored. Just as the participants in Milgram's experiment deferred moral responsibility to the authority figure, today's social media users may defer to the opinions of influencers, assuming that their popularity equates to reliability or expertise. This is particularly concerning when influencers promote questionable products, pseudoscientific ideas, or divisive political ideologies.

Beyond social media, Milgram's experiment reminds us to be cautious of authority in more traditional settings as well. Doctors, judges, police officers, and politicians hold formal power, and while their authority is essential for maintaining order and expertise in society, it also carries the risk of abuse. Milgram's work underscores the importance of maintaining critical thinking and personal responsibility when dealing with authority figures. It is a reminder that authority should be questioned, especially when the actions or orders being given contradict basic moral principles.

he findings of Stanley Milgram's obedience experiment have deeply influenced how industries like healthcare and aviation re-examine their internal power structures, particularly in high-stakes environments where authority can override individual judgment. Both sectors have learned that unchecked obedience to authority figures can lead to fatal errors, and they've implemented changes to mitigate the risks associated with hierarchical decision-making.

One prominent application of Milgram's insights has been in the medical field, especially in hospitals where doctors traditionally hold significant authority over nurses and other healthcare staff. The risk of harm arises when subordinates fail to challenge decisions from superiors, even when they know something is wrong. One famous example of this dynamic in action was the Hofling Hospital Experiment (1966), where 21 out of 22 nurses followed a doctor's telephone order to administer a dangerous dose of medication without question. The nurses obeyed because of the hierarchical structure and their assumption that the doctor held ultimate authority.

In response, healthcare systems began emphasizing open communication and flat hierarchy models to encourage staff to challenge decisions if something seems amiss. This approach has led to the development of Crew Resource Management (CRM) training in hospitals, which encourages a culture of safety by promoting assertiveness and communication among all team members, regardless of rank. Nurses and technicians are trained to voice concerns without fearing retribution, similar to the way aviation professionals are taught to cross-check decisions in real-time.

The airline industry, historically prone to accidents caused by miscommunications between crew members, also applied lessons from Milgram's work. Several high-profile crashes, such as the Tenerife airport disaster in 1977, were attributed to pilots' reluctance to challenge the authority of the captain, even when they had doubts about the captain's decisions. In response, the aviation industry adopted CRM programs in the 1980s, focusing on teamwork, communication, and decision-making under stress.

CRM dismantles the traditional hierarchical command structure that existed in cockpits by giving co-pilots and cabin crew the power to speak up and challenge decisions. This helps avoid the type of blind obedience that Milgram's experiments revealed and ensures that power is distributed more evenly across the team.

In both industries, these changes reflect the recognition that blind obedience to authority can be dangerous, and that individuals at all levels must feel empowered to challenge decisions when safety is at risk. Milgram's experiments demonstrated that individuals are often willing to commit harmful acts under the direction of an authority figure, especially when they feel that the responsibility for the outcome lies with the superior, not themselves. By creating a culture of shared responsibility, hospitals and airlines have reduced the potential for tragic outcomes caused by over-reliance on authority.

These shifts show how lessons from psychological research can reshape power structures in environments where lives are at stake, ensuring that authority does not become a liability but a tool for collaboration and safety.

False Confessions

There are notable parallels between the Milgram experiment and the Reid method of interrogation, particularly in how both use authority and psychological pressure to elicit compliance—whether that's administering electric shocks or extracting confessions. Both methods exploit individuals' tendencies to obey perceived authority figures, even when such obedience can lead to unethical or harmful outcomes.

The Reid Technique, developed in the 1950s, has been widely used by law enforcement to obtain confessions from suspects. It begins with an "interview" phase, during which police attempt to determine if a suspect is lying, often using heuristics and behavioral cues. If officers believe the suspect is guilty, the interrogation escalates, using psychological pressure, minimizing the seriousness of the crime, or offering implied promises of leniency. Over time, this technique has been heavily criticized for leading to false confessions, particularly when used on vulnerable individuals such as juveniles or those with low cognitive functioning.

The Milgram experiment, on the other hand, demonstrated that people are prone to following authoritative commands, even when it conflicts with their moral compass. Much like Milgram's participants obeying an experimenter's instructions to administer painful shocks, individuals subjected to the Reid method can feel coerced into providing confessions, even if they are innocent. The same psychological mechanisms are at play—compliance due to the presence of authority, the stress of the situation, and the belief that they have no real choice.

Both approaches share the tactic of reducing personal responsibility. In Milgram's study, participants were told they were "just following orders" from the authority figure in charge. Similarly, during Reid interrogations, suspects can feel as though the only way to alleviate the intense pressure of the interrogation is to confess, even if the confession is false. They may believe that confessing is a way to escape a stressful situation, especially when authorities imply that their cooperation will result in leniency.

There have been numerous cases of false confessions tied to the Reid Technique. In wrongful conviction cases, such as the infamous Central Park Five, suspects confessed under intense pressure despite being innocent. These confessions were obtained after hours of interrogation using Reid-style methods, where suspects felt overwhelmed by the psychological manipulation and authority figures' persistence. The interrogation method's focus on presuming guilt rather than seeking the truth has been a key contributor to such false confessions.

Moreover, studies and critiques have drawn parallels between how both the Milgram experiment and the Reid method exploit the heuristics of authority and compliance to push people into actions they would not otherwise take. Saul Kassin, a leading expert on false confessions, has discussed how the coercive nature of the Reid method mirrors the dynamics of obedience to authority observed in Milgram's study. This recognition has prompted calls for reforms in interrogation practices, including the recording of all interrogations and the adoption of alternative techniques that minimize the risk of false confessions.

The Third Wave Movement

The Third Wave experiment, conducted by Ron Jones in 1967, took place over the span of just five days, but in that short time, it vividly demonstrated how quickly ordinary individuals can be swayed into authoritarian behavior. Jones, a history teacher at Cubberley High School in Palo Alto, California, set out to teach his students about the rise of Nazi Germany and how the German population could allow the atrocities of the Holocaust to happen. However, Jones quickly realized that simply telling his students about history wasn't enough—they needed to experience how easily a group could slide into fascistic behavior. The result was an experiment that spiraled out of control, paralleling Stanley Milgram's findings on obedience to authority.

Jones started the experiment with the idea of creating a structured, disciplined group. He introduced the slogan "Strength Through Discipline" on the first day and required his students to sit upright in their desks and greet him uniformly. Jones himself shifted from his usual laid-back demeanor to that of a strict authoritarian, and to his surprise, the students complied immediately. Encouraged by the initial success, he escalated the experiment on the second day by adding the principle of "Strength Through Community," reinforcing a sense of unity and belonging. The students quickly embraced this, going so far as to create a salute, much like the Nazi salute, that they were required to use whenever they greeted each other inside and outside of class.

By the third day, the movement—now called "The Third Wave"—was gaining momentum. Jones added "Strength Through Action," tasking his students with concrete assignments, such as creating banners and recruiting new members. The group swelled in size as students from outside the class became intrigued and joined the movement. With this growing size came more structure, including membership cards, secret police-like monitors, and an emphasis on loyalty to the group. It was during this phase that students began reporting on each other for minor rule infractions, further embedding the authoritarian culture that Jones had inadvertently fostered.

On the fourth day, the environment had become so intense that students began turning on each other, betraying long-time friends and informing on classmates. The social structure of the class had transformed entirely, with students appointing themselves as guards and enforcing the movement's rules. As paranoia spread, Jones realized the experiment had gone too far, especially after hearing rumors that some students planned to beat up classmates who had expressed skepticism about The Third Wave. Jones knew he had to bring the experiment to an end before it became dangerous.

On the fifth day, Jones called a special rally where he promised to announce a presidential candidate for The Third Wave. The students eagerly gathered in an auditorium, but instead of introducing a leader, Jones revealed that the entire experiment had been a fabrication. He showed his students a film about Nazi Germany and explained that they had fallen into the same patterns of obedience, exclusion, and betrayal that allowed fascist regimes like the Third Reich to rise to power. The students were shocked to realize how quickly they had succumbed to authoritarianism, mirroring the behavior of ordinary Germans during the Nazi era.

The Third Wave experiment demonstrates a crucial lesson that aligns with the findings of Stanley Milgram's obedience experiment. Both studies reveal that people can be easily persuaded to act in ways that conflict with their morals when following the lead of an authority figure. In Milgram's case, participants continued to administer painful shocks to another person simply because an experimenter told them to. Similarly, in the Third Wave, students obeyed and participated in an authoritarian movement because of their respect for Jones as a teacher and the group identity he created.

What is particularly interesting about the Third Wave is that the authority figure—Jones—was not someone with formal power outside the classroom. He was a charismatic and likeable teacher, which made his students more willing to follow him without question. This brings us to a critical point about authority: it doesn't always need to come from formal power or overt dominance. In both Milgram's and Jones' experiments, the subjects were swayed by a figure they trusted, illustrating that likeability and charisma can be just as powerful in persuading people to act against their better judgment as formal authority.

In the digital age, this dynamic plays out on social media, where influencers and charismatic figures can lead their followers to adopt behaviors, opinions, or products simply because they are perceived as trustworthy or likable. Much like the students in the Third Wave experiment, social media users might find themselves conforming to group norms or following trends without fully questioning the implications of their actions.

Both experiments—Milgram's and Jones'—highlight the importance of understanding how authority, whether based on power, charisma, or trust, can influence behavior. The lesson is clear: individuals must remain vigilant and critically evaluate the instructions or movements they follow, lest they fall into the trap of blind obedience.

False Consensus

In 1977, psychologists Lee Ross, David Greene, and Pamela House identified a fascinating cognitive bias known as the False Consensus Effect. This theory explains how people tend to overestimate the degree to which others share their beliefs, attitudes, and behaviors. Essentially, we assume that our worldview is not just personal but universal. When we make decisions or express opinions, we often expect others to feel the same way, even when that isn't the case.

In their original study, participants were asked to make decisions—such as whether they would wear a sandwich board advertising a product—and then estimate how many others would make the same choice. Regardless of their decision, participants believed that a significant portion of others would make the same choice they did. The False Consensus Effect highlights our deep-rooted need to validate our own beliefs by assuming that others think the same way.

The reason for this bias lies in how we form our social circles and absorb information. We are naturally inclined to spend time with people who share our views, and we pay attention to sources that affirm our existing beliefs. This creates a feedback loop where we're surrounded by like-minded individuals, reinforcing our assumptions that our beliefs are the norm. This feedback loop was present long before the digital age, but social media has supercharged it in ways we're only beginning to fully understand.

In the age of social media, the False Consensus Effect has evolved and been magnified. Platforms like Instagram, Facebook, and Twitter have turned social proof into a quantifiable metric. Likes, followers, views, and shares serve as new forms of validation. When people see a post or a YouTuber with thousands of likes, they're inclined to think, "This many people can't be wrong." Social proof provides the illusion of consensus, which can deepen the False Consensus Effect. If a tweet with a particular political opinion gets tens of thousands of retweets, a person who already holds that opinion might think that their viewpoint is widely accepted, even if, in reality, it represents a minority perspective.

What's even more fascinating—and problematic—is that social media algorithms are designed to show users more of what they already like. If you engage with content that reflects your views, the platform will continue feeding you similar content. This leads to the creation of echo chambers: digital spaces where only familiar, affirming voices are heard, and opposing perspectives are excluded. The more you hear your own beliefs echoed back to you, the more you believe that those beliefs are not only common but correct. The False Consensus Effect thrives in these environments, making it harder for people to recognize when their opinions are not as widely held as they think.

One of the clearest examples of this is the polarization of political discourse. On social media, people are continually exposed to posts, videos, and articles that align with their political beliefs. The algorithms prioritize content with high engagement, which is often the most sensational or emotionally charged. This means users are more likely to see extreme viewpoints from their own side, reinforcing the idea that their perspective is both rational and shared by the majority. In reality, many of these views are held by a vocal minority, but the illusion of consensus makes them seem more popular than they are.

This false consensus also manifests in consumer culture, where likes and followers have become a modern currency. In industries like publishing and modeling, follower count is often equated with credibility or talent. Publishers are increasingly looking at an author's social media following before offering book deals, assuming that a large online presence guarantees an audience for the book. Similarly, modeling agencies are now factoring in social media engagement when choosing models, equating high follower counts with marketability. The assumption is that if someone has thousands or millions of followers, they must be influential or talented. However, this creates a distortion where popularity is mistakenly linked with expertise or authenticity. An individual may have gained followers through viral trends or superficial content, but their follower count gives them an aura of authority.

In reality, the number of likes, views, or followers is not always an accurate reflection of quality or expertise. In fact, social media's emphasis on numbers can encourage herd behavior, where people follow trends because they see that others are doing the same. Social proof becomes a mechanism for amplifying the False Consensus Effect. People who follow an influencer or agree with a popular post are not necessarily engaging critically with the content—they're simply responding to the visible endorsement of others. This can lead to a false sense of expertise, where individuals with large followings are viewed as authorities on topics they know little about.

At its worst, the False Consensus Effect can create polarization and entrenchment. As people increasingly believe their views are widely held and "correct," they become less open to opposing perspectives. Social media accelerates this process, as people engage more with content that reaffirms their beliefs and ignore content that challenges them. Over time, this can lead to the creation of deeply entrenched echo chambers, where opposing views are dismissed or attacked, and dialogue breaks down.

This digital amplification of the False Consensus Effect has serious implications. It encourages people to double down on their views, often without considering alternative perspectives. When everyone in your social feed agrees with you, it's easy to assume that your opinion is universal. However, this illusion can lead to misinformed decisions, whether in politics, consumer choices, or other areas of life.

The key takeaway is that social media has created an environment where the False Consensus Effect thrives. By leveraging social proof—through likes, shares, and views—social platforms make it easy for individuals to feel validated in their beliefs, regardless of how popular or accurate those beliefs are in reality. As a result, people may feel emboldened to dismiss dissenting opinions, assuming their worldview is not only correct but widely shared.

Breaking free from the False Consensus Effect requires critical thinking and exposure to diverse perspectives. It's important to recognize that social media can distort our sense of what's common or true. Seeking out content from outside our own echo chambers and questioning the consensus we see online can help prevent the false belief that our perspective is universally shared.

In the end, the False Consensus Effect reminds us that our assumptions about the world are often shaped by the limited circles we move in—both online and offline. As we navigate the social media landscape, it's crucial to remember that just because a belief is widely liked or retweeted doesn't make it true. Popularity and consensus are not always reliable indicators of correctness, and recognizing that can help us make better decisions in a world that increasingly equates visibility with validity.

The Problem of Social Proof

In 1984, psychologist Robert Cialdini introduced the concept of social proof in his book *Influence: The Psychology of Persuasion*, and it has since become one of the most widely studied principles in behavioral psychology. Social proof is the idea that people look to others' actions to determine their own behavior. When we see others engaging in certain activities, adopting beliefs, or endorsing products, we are more likely to follow suit, assuming that if others are doing it, it must be the correct or desirable thing to do. It's a powerful driver of behavior, especially in situations where individuals are uncertain about what to do or what decision to make.

Cialdini's work is rooted in the broader field of social psychology, which has long explored how human behavior is influenced by others. The principle of social proof is essentially about herd behavior—the tendency of individuals to mimic the actions of a larger group. The origins of the theory can be traced back to early studies on conformity, such as Solomon Asch's conformity experiments in the 1950s. Asch's experiments demonstrated how people would conform to group opinions even when they clearly contradicted their own perceptions.

Social proof is particularly influential in ambiguous situations. When people are unsure of what to do, they turn to others for cues. For example, in an unfamiliar environment, individuals are more likely to follow the crowd's behavior. If a restaurant is packed with customers, new patrons assume it's a good place to eat. If a product has hundreds of positive reviews, it's more likely to be purchased by someone who's unsure of its quality.

There are several mechanisms that make social proof so effective:

1 Uncertainty: When people aren't sure how to behave, they look to others for guidance. The assumption is that the group knows something they don't, and therefore it's safer to follow the crowd.

2 Similarity: People are more likely to follow the behavior of others who are similar to them. This is why peer reviews or recommendations from friends are often more influential than endorsements from strangers.

3 Number of People: The larger the group of people engaging in a behavior, the stronger the social proof. This explains why viral trends or mass movements can gain momentum so quickly—the more people who join in, the more others feel compelled to follow.

4 Expert Endorsement: People look to experts or those perceived as knowledgeable for cues on how to act or what to believe. For example, celebrity endorsements can act as a form of social proof, where the celebrity's perceived expertise or status influences the behavior of others.

One of Cialdini's classic examples of social proof is the bystander effect—a phenomenon in which people are less likely to help a victim in need if there are other people present. The logic is that if no one else is helping, then the situation must not be that serious. Each individual in the crowd takes their cue from the lack of action from others, leading to collective inaction.

In the digital age, social proof has evolved significantly, particularly with the rise of social media. Today, likes, followers, views, and shares serve as modern metrics of social proof. When people see a post or account with a high number of likes or followers, they assume it must be valuable or worth paying attention to, which in turn drives even more engagement. This phenomenon has had profound effects across industries.

A key shift in the digital age is the false equivalency between following and expertise. In today's world, a large social media following is often viewed as a marker of authority, regardless of whether the individual has real expertise. This has had significant implications in various sectors:

1 Book Publishing: Many publishers now look to an author's social media following before committing to a book deal. The idea is simple: if an author has a large, engaged following, they can leverage that audience to drive book sales. This has led to a situation where influence and marketability sometimes trump talent or the quality of the writing.

2 Modeling Agencies: Similarly, modeling agencies increasingly evaluate potential models based on their social media engagement. The reasoning is that a model with a large following can offer more exposure for the brands they represent. Agencies assume that a higher follower count will translate into a wider reach for the campaigns they work on, often prioritizing models with significant digital influence over those with more traditional credentials.

3 Hiring Decisions: In a range of industries, from fashion to tech, a strong social media presence can tilt hiring decisions. Companies see social proof in action when an individual has amassed a large following —they assume this person's ideas or aesthetics are influential and relevant, even when the quality of their expertise isn't necessarily clear.

The problem with equating followers with expertise is that follower count doesn't necessarily reflect true knowledge or competence. In many cases, followers can be bought, or they can accumulate due to superficial content that prioritizes entertainment over substance. Yet, because so many people rely on social proof, they equate popularity with credibility, a cognitive shortcut that doesn't always lead to the most informed decisions.

The danger of social proof is that it can lead to herd mentality—the tendency to follow others even when they are wrong or when their behavior is not based on informed decisions. This is particularly evident in viral trends or social media fads, where people often engage with content simply because it's popular, not because they truly find it valuable. This can also manifest in financial markets through phenomena like stock market bubbles, where investors pile into a stock or asset because everyone else is, creating a cycle of increasing prices that eventually collapses.

Another concern is that social media algorithms often exacerbate social proof by prioritizing content that already has high engagement. This creates a feedback loop where the most popular content becomes even more popular, while content that might be of higher quality but has fewer initial views gets buried. The result is that people are exposed to what's trending, not necessarily what's valuable or meaningful.

While there are dangers, social proof remains a powerful tool in marketing and social influence. Brands and influencers leverage it by showcasing customer testimonials, high follower counts, and "as seen on" badges to instill confidence in potential buyers. The idea is simple: if others trust or engage with this product, you should too.

Savvy marketers use social proof to create momentum. For example, when launching a new product, companies might use limited-time offers to create urgency, which in turn drives early adopters to purchase. Once enough people have bought the product, it gains momentum, and others follow suit, trusting that if others are buying, it must be good.

In essence, social proof remains a double-edged sword in the digital age. It can be an effective way to build trust and drive behavior, but it also has the potential to lead to poor decision-making when followers, likes, or views are mistakenly equated with expertise or quality.

Cognitive Dissonance

In 1957, psychologist Leon Festinger stumbled upon a fascinating human quirk—one that would change how we understand our decision-making processes. It all began with a doomsday cult. Festinger and his colleagues infiltrated a group that was convinced the world was about to end. The members believed that aliens would come down, save the faithful, and leave the rest of humanity to face destruction. They were so certain of this event that they quit jobs, sold their possessions, and severed ties with skeptical family members.

But here's where things get interesting. The apocalypse didn't come. The aliens, predictably, didn't show up. Now, logic would suggest that when faced with such a catastrophic failure of belief, the cult members would abandon their faith, return to their former lives, and possibly feel a bit embarrassed.

Instead, they doubled down. The cult leader quickly spun a new narrative: their faith had saved the world. Far from feeling defeated, the cult members were more committed than ever.

Festinger realized he was observing a powerful psychological phenomenon. How could people cling more fiercely to beliefs that had just been debunked? The answer, he discovered, was something called cognitive dissonance.

At its core, cognitive dissonance is about the tension we feel when we hold two conflicting thoughts or beliefs—or when our actions don't line up with our beliefs. This tension is uncomfortable, and humans don't like to feel uncomfortable. So, we do what we can to reduce the dissonance, often by changing one of the conflicting elements.

The real beauty of Festinger's theory is that it doesn't matter whether the belief makes sense. What matters is the internal discomfort that arises when it's challenged.

The cult members had invested so much into their belief in the apocalypse that when reality failed to align with their expectations, the mental friction was unbearable. Giving up their faith would have meant admitting that they had thrown away their lives for nothing, and that kind of admission is brutal. It was easier, mentally speaking, to invent a new reason for why the world didn't end and keep the faith alive.

But Festinger's insight wasn't limited to extreme cases like doomsday cults. He soon realized that cognitive dissonance was a universal experience, playing out in everyday decisions and behaviors in subtle but significant ways.

In 1959, Festinger teamed up with James Carlsmith to put cognitive dissonance to the test. They devised an experiment that's become a classic in psychology: participants were asked to perform a mind-numbingly boring task—turning pegs on a board for an hour. After completing the task, participants were asked to tell the next person in line (who was, in fact, a confederate) that the task was enjoyable.

Here's the twist: some participants were paid $1 for lying, while others were paid $20. Afterward, when asked to rate how enjoyable they found the task, the participants who were paid $1 rated the task as far more enjoyable than those who were paid $20.

Why? Cognitive dissonance. The participants who were paid $20 had an easy way to justify their lie: the hefty payout. But for the $1 participants, the payment wasn't enough to justify lying, so they had to resolve the dissonance between their behavior (lying) and their belief (the task was boring). To reduce the mental discomfort, they convinced themselves that the task was actually kind of fun. The mind, after all, is very good at rationalizing behavior.

Festinger's theory also explains why people sometimes justify actions that required significant effort, even if the outcome isn't as great as expected. This was demonstrated in a 1959 experiment by psychologists Elliot Aronson and Judson Mills, which showed the effect of effort justification—a phenomenon where the harder we work for something, the more we value it.

In the experiment, women were invited to join a discussion group. Some had to go through an embarrassing initiation, while others did not. Afterward, all the women found the discussion to be rather dull. But the women who went through the more severe initiation rated the group as much more interesting than those who didn't. Why? Because they had to justify the effort they had put in. If they admitted to themselves that the discussion was boring after enduring a humiliating initiation, they would experience dissonance. Instead, they convinced themselves that the discussion was more engaging than it actually was.

Another classic cognitive dissonance experiment was conducted by Jack Brehm in 1956. In this study, participants were asked to choose between two equally attractive household items. After making their choice, they were asked to rate the items again. What Brehm found was that after making a decision, people tended to increase their preference for the chosen item and decrease their preference for the rejected one.

This is called "spreading the alternatives." It's a classic case of cognitive dissonance: when faced with two appealing options, choosing one can create discomfort because we're rejecting something equally desirable. To ease that discomfort, people convince themselves that the chosen option is significantly better than the rejected one.

Cognitive dissonance isn't just something that happens in the controlled environment of psychological experiments. It plays out in the real world in ways big and small.

Consider the example of a smoker. Smoking is widely known to be harmful, but many smokers continue the habit. The dissonance here is clear: on the one hand, the smoker knows that smoking is bad for their health, but on the other hand, they continue to smoke. How do they resolve this? Some might rationalize the behavior by saying, "Well, I know someone who smoked their whole life and lived to be 90." Others might downplay the risks or tell themselves they'll quit soon. The goal is to reduce the dissonance between their behavior and their beliefs.

You can see cognitive dissonance everywhere once you know what to look for. People justifying buying a new car they can't afford because "it was such a good deal." Politicians sticking to positions that have been debunked because admitting they were wrong would be too painful. Consumers remaining loyal to brands even after a scandal because switching brands would create dissonance with their prior choices.

Festinger's cognitive dissonance theory has endured for decades because it reveals something fundamental about the human condition: we are not rational creatures. We like to think we are, but our minds are constantly working behind the scenes to resolve dissonance and preserve a sense of internal consistency, even when that means bending reality just a bit.

We don't just seek the truth—we seek comfort, and cognitive dissonance explains how far we'll go to maintain it. By understanding this, we gain a clearer picture of why people act the way they do, and perhaps even a little more empathy for the mental gymnastics that we all perform from time to time.

Finally, the primacy and recency effects, discovered by Hermann Ebbinghaus, reveal that people are more likely to remember the first and last items in a sequence. This principle has important implications for the structure of cross-examination. By strategically placing the most critical questions at the beginning and end of the examination, cross-examiners can maximize the likelihood that these points will be remembered by the jury, helping to anchor the jury's perception of the case in the lawyer's favor.

DEATH OF THE FOLLOWER: ALGORITHMS AND THE LOSS OF INDIVIDUALITY

WHY ALGORITHMS DRIVE US TOWARD CONFORMITY AND HOW WE CAN RESIST

"The surest way to corrupt a youth is to instruct him to hold in higher esteem those who think alike than those who think differently."

Friedrich Nietzsche

In the summer of 2014 videos of people dumping ice-cold water over their heads began to go viral. Everyone—from your next-door neighbor to celebrities and politicians—seemed to participate in the Ice Bucket Challenge. A simple campaign to raise awareness for ALS (Amyotrophic Lateral Sclerosis) became a global phenomenon. It was a testament to the incredible power of digital platforms to mobilize collective action when fueled by genuine human emotion and connection.

The Ice Bucket Challenge wasn't engineered by algorithms or backed by sophisticated engagement strategies. It was pure, organic virality at its finest. People participated not because unseen forces manipulated them but because they genuinely connected to the cause. It was a movement grounded in empathy and community, demonstrating how persuasive messaging could ripple through the digital landscape and inspire millions.

But as the years rolled on, a shift occurred. The platforms that once empowered such authentic movements began to change. Algorithms—the invisible puppeteers of platforms like Facebook, Instagram, and YouTube—grew increasingly powerful. They started prioritizing content based on user behavior and engagement metrics. Social media transformed from a space of genuine connection into a game dictated by the unseen hand of machine learning systems.

Initially, social media offered an egalitarian experience. Your feed displayed posts chronologically from friends, family, and creators. If you followed someone, you'd see their content—straightforward. The engagement was driven by genuine interest, not by calculated manipulations. However, as these platforms expanded, they realized there was a more profitable path. Algorithms designed to maximize user engagement became the new gatekeepers of visibility.

Facebook was among the first to embrace this shift. What began as a tool to show users more relevant content became a mechanism to increase time spent on the platform. Metrics like likes, comments, shares, and even the time users hovered over a post became critical in determining what appeared in their feeds. The outcome was a highly curated experience, less driven by individual choice and more by what would keep users scrolling endlessly.

In some ways, this was a masterstroke. User engagement skyrocketed, and people spent more time online than ever before. But there was a darker side. As algorithms grew more sophisticated, they didn't just personalize content—they manipulated it. Posts eliciting solid emotional reactions—outrage, joy, or fear—were amplified. Users became passive consumers, subjected to the whims of systems designed to engage rather than inform.

This seismic shift was unsettling for content creators. They could no longer rely on their follower base for visibility. They found themselves at the mercy of algorithms, compelled to produce content that the platform deemed "engaging." This led to a homogenization of content, and creators felt pressured to adopt sensational tactics to survive in an increasingly competitive, algorithm-driven environment.

Take YouTube, for example. Once a haven for niche content and personal expression, it now favors clickbait titles, sensational thumbnails, and extreme content. The algorithm rewards videos that generate more interaction, pushing creators to escalate their tactics. Authenticity takes a backseat to sensationalism. Complex ideas are distilled into soundbites, and pursuing virality overshadows the quest for truth.

As algorithms dictated what users saw, the very fabric of the internet began to change. The digital utopia of creativity and self-expression started to resemble a system optimized solely for engagement. Creators on platforms like Instagram, TikTok, and YouTube are all vying for visibility, but the game's rules have changed. To be seen, they must cater to the algorithm—crafting content that generates immediate clicks, likes, and shares.

This has led to the rise of clickbait and sensationalism. Consider YouTube's emphasis on 10-minute videos to maximize ad revenue. Creators stretch their content to fit this "magic" length, even if it means diluting the substance. The pressure to meet algorithmic expectations fuels an arms race of shock value—dramatic headlines, over-the-top reactions—all designed to provoke emotional engagement. Quality and depth are often casualties in this race for attention.

In the quest to capture eyeballs, nuance becomes another victim. Complex topics that require thoughtful exploration are sidestepped in favor of content that delivers instant emotional payoff. This leads to cognitive overload, where users are bombarded with endless streams of shallow content. The algorithm favors simplicity and emotional resonance, prompting creators to dumb down their messages. It's akin to fast food for the mind—quick, tasty, but ultimately unsatisfying.

Algorithms shape what creators produce and dictate what viewers consume, creating a closed feedback loop. The more creators conform to algorithmic demands, the more the platform reinforces that content. Individuality gives way to conformity, and the digital landscape becomes a monotonous sea of replicated ideas. Creators mimic popular trends to stay afloat, and originality becomes a rare commodity.

At the heart of this transformation lies a powerful force: dopamine. This neurotransmitter, associated with pleasure and reward, is the secret ingredient social media platforms exploit to keep users hooked. Every like, comment, or share triggers a minor dopamine release, encouraging us to seek more of the same. Platforms employ variable reward systems—the same psychological tricks used in casinos—to make these rewards unpredictable and, therefore, more addictive.

Think about the infinite scroll feature or autoplay videos. These design elements are crafted to keep us engaged without realizing it. Each refresh is like pulling the lever of a slot machine—the possibility of a rewarding hit of content entices us. This unpredictability fosters a compulsive engagement cycle, trapping users in a loop that's hard to break.

While this cycle keeps us glued to screens, it doesn't necessarily make us happier. Excessive social media use has been linked to increased feelings of anxiety, depression, and loneliness. Constantly comparing ourselves to carefully curated portrayals of others' lives can leave us feeling inadequate. Moreover, the endless stream of information leads to cognitive overload, diminishing our ability to think critically or engage deeply with content.

As algorithms prioritize content that generates immediate, solid reactions, meaningful discourse causes a noticeable decline. Sensationalism has become the currency of the digital realm. Outrageous headlines, viral memes, and clickbait videos overshadow nuanced discussions and in-depth analyses. The algorithm rewards content that keeps users engaged longer, not content that educates or enriches.

Echo chambers further exacerbate this issue. Algorithms feed us content that aligns with our beliefs and preferences, reinforcing our biases. This creates a polarized environment where opposing viewpoints are rarely encountered, and critical thinking is stifled. For instance, divisive content amplifies political tension because it drives engagement, deepening societal rifts.

In this landscape, virality often trumps credibility. The pursuit of viral content leads to the spread of misinformation and fake news. Emotional manipulation becomes a tool to generate shares and clicks regardless of the truth. False information spreads faster than factual reporting because it often evokes more robust emotional responses.

This race to the bottom has homogenized online content. Creators, driven by the need to appease the algorithm, produce similar types of content, leading to a lack of diversity in ideas and expressions. On platforms like TikTok, trends dominate, and originality takes a backseat. Everyone is doing the same dance, lip-syncing the song, and following the script.

In response to this environment, many creators seek alternatives that allow them to reclaim their voices. Platforms like Patreon have emerged as havens for those desiring independence from algorithmic tyranny. Founded in 2013 by musician and filmmaker Jack Conte, Patreon offers a subscription-based model where fans—patrons—directly support creators financially.

Patreon enables creators to prioritize quality over quantity. They are no longer pressured to produce content that fits the algorithm's mold. Instead, they can create what they're passionate about, knowing their income isn't tied to ad revenue or fleeting engagement metrics. This model fosters genuine connections between creators and their audiences, built on shared interests and mutual support.

Jack Conte envisions platforms like Patreon as catalysts for a "Second Renaissance"—a revival of creativity unshackled from corporate algorithms. Educational content creators, artists, and niche enthusiasts have found success on Patreon by offering in-depth, thoughtful work that might not thrive on mainstream social media. They can engage with their audience on a deeper level, fostering communities that value substance over spectacle.

Patreon harkens back to the historical model of patronage but democratizes it. Instead of relying on wealthy benefactors, creators are supported by a collective of fans who each contribute a small amount. This decentralized support system empowers creators to pursue their vision without compromising integrity.

However, Patreon isn't without its challenges. Building and maintaining a patron base requires effort and marketing savvy. Creators often still need to use traditional social media to attract new patrons, which means they're not entirely free from the influence of algorithms. Moreover, not all creators can generate enough support to sustain themselves financially, especially when starting.

Despite these hurdles, platforms like Patreon represent a hopeful shift. They offer a path forward for creators and audiences alike to escape the pitfalls of algorithm-driven content. By prioritizing direct relationships and valuing authenticity, we can begin to reclaim the internet as a space for genuine connection, creativity, and meaningful discourse.

TARGET KNOWS YOUR DAUGHTER IS PREGNANT: THE DARK REALITY OF SURVEILLANCE CAPITALISM

UNDERSTANDING THE IMPACT OF DATA COLLECTION AND PRIVACY INVASION

"The invention of a gaze that can be calculated, in which power makes itself more visible and more verifiable, has become a basic tool of coercion and control."

Michel Foucault

There's nothing quite like a father's love—especially when it's mixed with confusion and a dash of anger. On a crisp autumn morning in Minneapolis a middle-aged man marches into a Target store, clutching a stack of coupons and advertisements. His face is a cocktail of bewilderment and frustration. "I need to speak to the manager," he demands. My daughter got this in the mail!" He waves the booklet with ads for maternity clothes, nursery furniture, and baby care products. "She's still in high school. Are you trying to encourage her to get pregnant?"

The manager, probably blindsided by this unexpected confrontation, profusely apologizes. A few days later, he calls to express further contrition. But this time, the father's tone has softened.

"I owe you an apology," he admits sheepishly. "Turns out there's been some activities in my house I wasn't fully aware of. My daughter's due in August."

This unsettling anecdote, first reported by *The New York Times* journalist Charles Duhigg in 2012, pulls back the curtain on a startling reality: Target knew about the man's daughter's pregnancy before he did. How? Our data knows more about us than our fathers do. And sometimes more than we do. Target engaged in a relentless and invisible collection and analysis of consumer data—a practice that's become the backbone of modern marketing and digital persuasion.

Data is now hailed as the new oil—a resource so valuable that entire industries revolve around its extraction, refinement, and distribution. Giants like Amazon, Target, and Google have mastered this domain, leveraging vast amounts of information to predict consumer behavior with almost eerie accuracy.

Target wanted to identify customers at pivotal life stages—like pregnancy—when shopping habits are most susceptible to change. Andrew Pole, a statistician, developed a "pregnancy prediction score" by analyzing purchasing patterns. Women buying unscented lotion, calcium and magnesium supplements, or large bags of cotton balls were likely in the early stages of pregnancy.

By assigning these scores, Target could tailor promotions and ads to expecting mothers, securing brand loyalty before competitors even knew there was a new customer to court. This was a commercial bullseye, but it raised serious ethical questions about privacy and the limits of corporate surveillance.

Then there's Amazon, the e-commerce titan that's built an empire on personalization. When you log in, you're greeted with recommendations —products you might like based on your previous searches, purchases, and even how long you lingered over an item. This isn't some friendly shopkeeper remembering your last visit; it's a sophisticated algorithm analyzing every digital breadcrumb you leave behind.

A 2020 report by McKinsey & Company noted that personalization can deliver five to eight times the return on investment and lift sales by

10% or more. Amazon's recommendation engine is estimated to drive 35% of the company's total sales. By understanding individual consumer preferences, Amazon enhances your shopping experience and subtly guides purchasing decisions. It's digital persuasion at its most effective.

Let's not forget Google, whose entire business model revolves around data. Every search query, email in Gmail, location history, and YouTube viewing habits contribute to your detailed profile. This information feeds into Google's advertising platform, allowing marketers to target ads precisely.

In 2019, Google's advertising revenue topped $134 billion. By leveraging data, Google enables advertisers to reach audiences based on demographics, interests, behaviors, and even life events. For example, if you search for "moving companies," you suddenly see ads for real estate agents, furniture stores, and home insurance. It's a seamless integration of data and persuasion.

So, how do these corporations gather such granular data?

• Cookies and Tracking Pixels: Tiny code embedded in websites tracks your online activity. Third-party cookies follow you from site to site, building a comprehensive picture of your browsing habits.

• User Accounts and Profiles: When you create accounts on platforms like Amazon or Google, you provide personal information such as name, email, and phone number, as well as sometimes more sensitive data like payment information and addresses.

• Mobile Apps and Devices: Apps often request permission to access contacts, photos, locations, and other data. This data is harvested to enhance personalization and target advertising.

• Public Records and Purchases: Companies link purchase data to individual customers through loyalty programs or credit card information. This data is analyzed to predict future behavior.

• Data Brokers: Corporations purchase additional information from data brokers—companies that collect and sell consumer data from various sources, including public records, online tracking, and offline purchases.

Understanding consumer behavior is the holy grail of effective marketing. By leveraging data, companies tap into psychological principles to influence decisions.

• Behavioral Targeting: Companies analyze past behavior to predict future actions. For example, if you frequently purchase organic products, you're more likely to respond to ads for eco-friendly goods.

• Emotional Triggers: Data reveals what content resonates emotionally, allowing marketers to craft messages that elicit desired responses.

• Social Proof: Showing you what others like you have purchased leverages the principle of conformity.

• Scarcity and Urgency: Personalized messages about limited-time offers or low stock levels can prompt immediate action.

A 2018 study published in the *Proceedings of the National Academy of Sciences* showed that psychological targeting—in which persuasive messages are matched to individuals' personality traits inferred from digital footprints—increases the effectiveness of advertisements. Extroverted individuals responded more positively to ads emphasizing sociability, while introverts preferred ads highlighting quiet and solitude.

Moreover, a 2018 Accenture report revealed that 91% of consumers are likelier to shop with brands that provide personalized offers and recommendations. Data-driven personalization is not just practical—it's expected.

But there's a dark side. The aggressive collection and use of personal data have sparked significant concerns over privacy and ethics.

Remember the Cambridge Analytica scandal in 2018? It revealed that the firm had harvested data from millions of Facebook users without their consent to influence political outcomes. This scandal was a wake-up call about the potential for massive data misuse.

Regulatory bodies are starting to push back. The European Union's General Data Protection Regulation (GDPR), enacted in 2018, imposes strict rules on data collection and grants users greater control over their personal information.

Yet, consumer trust is eroding. A 2019 Pew Research Center survey found that 79% of Americans are concerned about how companies use their data. This erosion of trust poses risks for corporations reliant on data-driven models.

As data analytics become more sophisticated, so do the methods of persuasion. Companies invest heavily in artificial intelligence and machine learning to enhance predictive capabilities. Chatbots and virtual assistants, powered by natural language processing, engage users in personalized dialogues, further blurring the lines between service and marketing.

Amazon's Alexa doesn't just respond to your commands; she suggests products and services based on past interactions. Google's algorithms can predict search queries before you finish typing, subtly guiding you toward specific content.

So, where does this leave us?

Consumer awareness is crucial. Understanding how data is collected and used empowers us to make informed choices about our digital footprint. Here's how to defend against the piercing gaze of our capitalist big-brother:

• Privacy Settings: Review and adjust the privacy settings on your devices and platforms regularly to limit unnecessary data sharing.

• Opting Out: You can opt out of targeted advertising through industry programs like the Digital Advertising Alliance's Consumer Choice Page.

• Use of Privacy Tools: Browser extensions and tools like ad blockers and VPNs can reduce tracking. Ethical data practices are becoming a legal obligation and a competitive advantage for businesses.

• Transparency: Communicating data practices build trust with consumers.

- Consent: Obtaining explicit consent for data collection respects user autonomy.

- Security: Investing in robust data security measures protects the company and its customers.

The dance between data collection and digital persuasion is delicate—balancing innovation with privacy and personalization with intrusion. Companies like Amazon, Target, and Google have revolutionized marketing by harnessing data to create experiences tailored to individual preferences. This has undoubtedly brought convenience and value.

However, as the boundaries of data utilization expand, so do the ethical and societal implications. The ability to predict and influence behavior raises questions about autonomy and consent, and the line between persuasion and manipulation becomes ever more precarious.

Perhaps the most effective persuasion in this era will not come from the most advanced algorithms or the deepest data pools but from respecting consumers' intelligence and agency. Transparency, ethical practices, and genuine value creation can foster trust and loyalty that no amount of data analytics can replicate. The problem is gaining traction where the noise will be much more attractive. Thankfully, Humans were built for that; it may just take a bit of, dare I say, evolution. Daniel Kahneman discusses this new evolution in his groundbreaking book Thinking Fast and Slow. He argues that humans have a built-in system for surviving modern marketing's persistent and persuasive attacks on our psyche.

BIRTH OF THE LIMINAL GURU: THE RISE OF UNORIGINAL THINKERS

HOW THE ATROPHY OF CRITICAL THINKING HAS LED TO A CULTURE OF CONFORMITY OR WORSE

"There is no greatness where there is no simplicity, goodness, and truth."

Leo Tolstoy

Some creators in our digital renaissance seem to surf the chaos of our modern world like it's a perfectly predictable wave. Tim Ferris, Joe Rogan and Andrew Huberman are just a few. These are the "grey gurus." They don't plant their flag on any particular hill; instead, they glide between multiple realities, riding the social currents of outrage, mania, and condemnation without ever getting wet. Often, they play the interviewer or mediator role, promoting others' views while keeping their cards close to the vest. They dabble in niches that aren't overtly divisive—venture capital, life extension, or alternative medicine.

Unlike the Walter Cronkites, who earned their paychecks by chasing Nielsen ratings, these gurus offer something else: a product, a lifestyle, and a philosophy wrapped up in just enough charisma to keep you hooked. They exist in that twilight zone where old norms haven't entirely faded, and new paradigms haven't fully taken hold—a space ripe for exploitation and innovation.

Tim Ferriss is perhaps the original gangster of this realm. The life hacker extraordinaire who penned *The 4-Hour Workweek*, a bestseller that made us all question why we were grinding away for 40-plus hours. But read between the lines; Ferriss rarely takes a firm stance. Instead, he invites you into a world of lifestyle tinkering, floating atop the river of information without diving deep enough to get caught in the currents.

A Princeton grad with a BA in East Asian Studies, Ferriss focused on entrepreneurship's political and cultural challenges in China. He leveraged this into a career in marketing nutraceuticals and became an early adopter of biohacking, eastern medicine, and even psychedelics. As podcasts began to bloom, Ferriss found himself in the perfect storm of pseudo-experts and seekers of zen, offering life hacks to a generation drowning in complexity.

The irony?

This self-improvement movement preached blocking out the noise but became a cacophony itself. The goal wasn't just self-improvement; it was the birth of a new podcast economy where products could be sold without the flashy, worn-out messages of traditional advertising. The liminal grey guru sells you a product and an alignment of values—a lifestyle. You start wearing the same clothes, adopting the same morning routines, and popping the same supplements. Is it all placebo? Maybe. However, placebo offers a lifeline of perceived stability.

To Ferriss's credit, he sparked a movement, fueling personal experimentation and venture capital that launched some great companies—and a plethora of failures. In 2012, Harvard Business School's Shikhar Ghosh pointed out that about 75% of venture-backed startups don't return cash to investors. Venture capitalists might bury their dead quietly, but the landscape is littered with the bones of startups that followed the gospel of hustle without the substance to sustain it.

Speaking of hustle, enter Gary Vaynerchuk, or Gary Vee, as the internet knows him. This guy is a whirlwind of energy. He is a serial entrepreneur who turned a wine business into a digital empire. He preaches hustle, self-awareness, and the gospel of grinding in the digital age. Gary Vee makes money by igniting the entrepreneurial fire in others, convincing them that untold wealth is just a few Instagram posts away.

But let's be honest—Vee's game is akin to selling shovels during a gold rush. It doesn't matter if there's gold in those hills; what matters is that people believe there is. His advice often lacks nuance, offering oversimplified repackaging of stale ideas with a fresh coat of digital paint. The liminal grey space he occupies is perfect for this. His strategies and "simple steps" are often so generalized that when they don't work, the onus falls on the follower, not the guru. You're not succeeding? You must not be hustling hard enough.

The first rule of hustle culture is to work harder.

The second rule of hustle culture is that you're still not working hard enough.

This concept of liminal grey space is critical to understanding the rise of these internet gurus. It's the foggy borderland where claims can't be easily verified or debunked, creating a sense of mystery and authority. It's the petri dish where the mold of disinformation grows, warm and damp, unchecked by the harsh light of scrutiny.

In this in-between zone, old ideas are being questioned, and new ones have yet to solidify. It's a playground for those comfortable with ambiguity, who can bridge different worlds without being pinned down. Many respected experts started here, oscillating in the liminal grey before taking a definitive stand.

Take Malcolm Gladwell, for instance. He's a left-leaning liminalist who straddles academic rigor and popular writing. He challenges conventional wisdom while appealing to mainstream audiences, revisiting history to cast it in a different light. Then there's Jordan Peterson, a right-leaning liminalist oscillating between psychology, philosophy, and politics. He discusses traditional values infused with modern psychological concepts, appealing to conservatives and liberals at different times.

Nassim Nicholas Taleb floats between academia and popular discourse, his ideas on risk and uncertainty challenging traditional and mainstream thought are business school classics. Yuval Noah Harari explores the grand narratives of human history while remaining intriguingly ambiguous about our future, appealing across political and cultural spectrums. And Elon Musk is a liminal shapeshifter, navigating between roles as a futurist, entrepreneur, and cultural icon. He's disrupted industries while maintaining elements of traditional capitalist structure, positioning himself in that grey space where innovation meets the status quo.

These liminal experts have provided significant value to society, mainly sidestepping the harsh judgments of postmodernism by avoiding absolute beliefs. But lurking in their shadows are some who exploit this space to peddle their wares, using powerful emotional tools under the guise of human advancement.

They're hard to pin down—and more challenging to hate—because they're slippery. They shift between ideas, adapt to cultural currents, and avoid strict allegiances. Their flexibility allows them to navigate conflicts without ever fully committing, giving them influence on all sides.

Consider someone like Gary Brecka. Seemingly, he flooded our social media feeds out of nowhere, his claims making us question if we were living life all wrong. A self-proclaimed "human biologist," he paces the stage with frenetic energy, blending emotional and scientific jargon into a poetic yet frightening tapestry. He claims to predict lifespans based on biomarkers, spilling the so-called secrets of big insurance companies. While his claims sound scientific, they often lack empirical validation. But in the liminal grey space, that doesn't matter. The allure of a personalized secret to longevity is too tempting.

Take his crusade against seed oils. Brecka and other biohacking advocates argue that oils high in omega-6 fatty acids—like soybean, canola, sunflower, and safflower—are inflammatory villains lurking in your pantry. They push for alternatives like olive, avocado, and coconut oil, claiming these are the keys to health. Modern science offers a more nuanced view, suggesting balance rather than outright elimination. But nuance doesn't sell; fear does.

At the core of the internet guru's allure is the psychological pull of fame and social proof. High follower counts and viral posts create an illusion of credibility. People are naturally drawn to these signals, mistaking popularity for expertise. It's the same reason Dan Bilzerian, with his Instagram full of yachts, women, and exotic cars, amassed millions of followers. Never mind the questions about how he accumulated his wealth or the authenticity of his persona; the spectacle was enough.

Followers don't just admire these gurus—they aspire to be them. Gary Vaynerchuk taps into this desire, telling people they can achieve extraordinary success with the right mindset and relentless hustle. It's a seductive message where traditional pathways to success feel increasingly inaccessible.

The algorithms of social media platforms like TikTok, Instagram, and YouTube pour gasoline on this fire. They reward engagement, pushing content that sparks solid emotional reactions—surprise, awe, fear—into more feeds. That's how Tai Lopez became a household name with his infamous "Here in My Garage" video, standing next to a Lamborghini while preaching about knowledge and success. Curiosity and envy are potent hooks.

Then there's Chef Pii, Veronica Shaw, who introduced the world to Pink Sauce—a mysterious, vibrant condiment that took TikTok by storm. The ingredients list was a head-scratcher, including items like dragon fruit and, yes, milk, all packaged without proper labeling or refrigeration. Despite (or because of) concerns about food safety, the sauce went viral. Negative attention only fueled the fire, turning skepticism into sales.

Social media algorithms create a feedback loop. The more engagement a post gets, the more visibility it gains, pushing these figures further into the spotlight, regardless of the substance—or lack thereof—behind their claims.

A common tactic among these gurus is exploiting emotional triggers, particularly the fear of missing out (FOMO). They present their products or services as exclusive opportunities available only to a select few for a limited time. It's psychological warfare, preying on the anxiety that you'll be left behind if you don't act now.

In this digital age, virality is the new currency of fame. Internet gurus like Tai Lopez, Chef Pii, and Gary Brecka build their brands on the velocity of their messages. Their dubious claims reach millions in the blink of an eye, amplified by algorithms and psychological manipulation.

People are drawn to those who promise solutions to their most pressing problems—wealth, health, personal fulfillment. Gurus like Tai Lopez or Dan Bilzerian tap into this by showcasing a lifestyle that's ostensibly within reach if you follow their lead.

They leverage social proof, creating a bandwagon effect where popularity begets more popularity. They manufacture scarcity and urgency, tapping into FOMO to drive impulsive decisions. They engage in emotional manipulation, telling stories that tug at fears and desires. And they present themselves as relatable, authentic figures, sharing personal struggles to build trust.

However, the same algorithms that elevate them can also hasten their downfall. As their influence grows, so does the scrutiny of their claims. The platforms that propelled them into the stratosphere can just as swiftly turn against them when their promises are exposed as hollow.

The combination of emotional manipulation and operating within the grey areas may create viral fame, but without substance or ethics, that fame is often short-lived. The rise contains the seeds of the fall.

Let's dive deeper into this downfall cycle, exploring how public backlash and legal scrutiny can bring these modern-day Icaruses crashing back to earth.

THE ILLUSION OF KNOWLEDGE: SURFACE-LEVEL THINKING AND MODERN IGNORANCE

HOW SUPERFICIAL UNDERSTANDING FUELS THE RISE OF DANGEROUS IDEOLOGIES

"The greatest enemy of knowledge is not ignorance; it is the illusion of knowledge."

Stephen Hawking

At the heart of a groundbreaking vision was a simple yet revolutionary idea: a machine capable of running hundreds of diagnostic tests from just a few drops of blood. No more needles, no more vials—just a tiny prick and a sleek device called the "Edison" that promised to empower patients, slash costs, and save lives. This was Elizabeth Holmes's emotional narrative, captivating the world with a promise that seemed too good to be true.

Elizabeth Holmes was everything Silicon Valley adores: charismatic, young, and ambitious. At 19, she dropped out of Stanford University and founded Theranos in 2003 with the audacious goal of disrupting the medical testing industry. The allure was irresistible: a simple finger prick replaced the dreaded needle, democratizing diagnostics for everyone.

Money flowed in like a tidal wave. High-profile investors poured over $700 million into Theranos. Media titan Rupert Murdoch, Oracle's

Larry Ellison, and former Secretary of Education Betsy DeVos all bought into the dream. The company's board was a who's who of power brokers: former U.S. Secretaries of State Henry Kissinger and George Shultz, General James Mattis, and other political heavyweights. They weren't just investors but validators, lending their reputations to bolster Theranos's credibility.

I remember speaking with a family friend who invested in Theranos early on. He was enamored by Holmes's vision and convinced that this young woman was about to revolutionize healthcare. "She reminded me of Steve Jobs," he said. I didn't want to miss out on the next big thing."

With her signature black turtleneck and baritone voice—a calculated homage to Steve Jobs—Holmes became a media darling. She graced the covers of *Forbes* and *Fortune* and was hailed as the world's youngest self-made female billionaire. Theranos soared to a valuation of $9 billion, and Holmes became an innovation icon.

But behind the façade, cracks were forming. By 2015, whispers of skepticism emerged from former employees who questioned whether the technology worked. The dam broke when John Carreyrou, an investigative reporter for *The Wall Street Journal*, published a bombshell exposé revealing that Theranos's technology was fundamentally flawed. In many cases, it wasn't being used at all.

Carreyrou's investigation was relentless. Tipped off by Tyler Shultz—the grandson of board member George Shultz—and Erika Cheung, both former employees, he uncovered a web of deception. They revealed that the company was faking test results and that its proprietary technology was neither accurate nor reliable.

One patient, who wished to remain anonymous, recounted a terrifying experience: "I received test results indicating I had a severe vitamin D deficiency and elevated cholesterol levels. I panicked, changed my diet, and started medication. Later, I found out the results were completely inaccurate."

The exposé ignited a firestorm. Regulatory bodies descended on Theranos. The Centers for Medicare & Medicaid Services conducted a surprise inspection of the company's lab, uncovering dangerous inaccuracies and unsafe practices. Faulty tests for potassium levels could have led to life-threatening misdiagnoses. By mid-2016, Theranos was barred from operating clinical laboratories, and Holmes was prohibited from owning or operating a lab for two years.

The U.S. Securities and Exchange Commission and the Department of Justice launched investigations into potential fraud. In 2018, the SEC charged Holmes and former president Ramesh "Sunny" Balwani with "massive fraud." They alleged a years-long scheme to deceive investors, doctors, and patients about the capabilities of their technology.

Statistics from the SEC revealed that investors lost over $700 million due to the deception. This is a stark reminder of how easily even savvy individuals can be misled by emotional appeals and the allure of groundbreaking innovation.

Holmes settled with the SEC without admitting wrongdoing but relinquished control of the company and paid a $500,000 fine. Balwani chose to fight. The DOJ then filed criminal charges, including wire fraud and conspiracy to commit fraud. Both faced the possibility of decades in prison.

The trials peeled back the layers of Theranos's deceit. The Edison machines—touted as revolutionary—were exposed as essentially nonfunctional. Internal concerns were ignored or silenced. Traditional machines from companies like Siemens were covertly used to run tests, while the Edison devices produced erratic and unreliable results.

Elizabeth Holmes was a maestro of emotional appeal. With her deep voice and unwavering gaze, she crafted an image of a visionary on a humanitarian mission. She wasn't just selling a product; she was selling hope. She spoke passionately about democratizing healthcare, about her fear of needles driving her to spare others the same discomfort.

"I grew up terrified of needles," she'd say. "I decided that nobody should have to go through what I went through."

She tapped into universal desires—accessibility, empowerment, and equality. She framed Theranos as a solution for underserved populations, promising affordable and accessible healthcare for all. "Every person should be able to order their tests, and we should be able to afford them," she declared.

Holmes also leveraged her status as a female entrepreneur in a male-dominated industry. She positioned herself as a trailblazer, a symbol of progress for women in tech. "We need more women to be part of changing the world," she told *Glamour* in 2015. "I hope to be an example for young girls that they can do anything."

Her emotional narratives won her accolades and bolstered her image as a savior. But behind the emotive storytelling was a stark reality: the technology didn't work, and the grand promises were built on a foundation of sand.

Psychologists refer to this phenomenon as the "halo effect," where the perception of one positive quality leads to the assumption of others. Holmes's charisma and confidence led investors and the public to overlook glaring inconsistencies. As psychologist and writer Dr. Maria Konnikova noted, "We are often persuaded by emotion rather than logic, making us susceptible to manipulation by those who can tell a compelling story."

Holmes didn't just fool investors; she conned some of the sharpest minds in America. General James Mattis, Betsy DeVos, and Henry Kissinger fell under her spell. Perhaps they believed that their fellow board members had done due diligence. Each layer of assumed credibility amplified her message, creating a hyperreal version of Holmes—a competent CEO with a viable product.

This is the collision of hyperreality and postmodernism in the tech world. The illusion became so pervasive that it was accepted as reality.

Around the same time Theranos was unraveling, another figure emerged in the digital landscape: Tai Lopez. In 2015, he burst onto the scene with his viral "Here in My Garage" YouTube ad. Standing beside a Lamborghini in a Hollywood Hills garage, he spoke about how he acquired wealth through knowledge, gesturing to bookshelves filled with titles that seemed suspiciously untouched.

"Here in my garage, I just bought this new Lamborghini. But you know what I like more than materialistic things? Knowledge."

The video amassed over 71 million views, catapulting Lopez into internet fame. He used symbols of wealth as social proof, implying that viewers could achieve similar success by following his teachings.

But savvy observers saw through the facade. The books appeared to be hastily assembled props. His claim of reading a book a day rang hollow. Those who've achieved real success recognized the telltale signs of a charlatan. Yet, Lopez wasn't targeting the discerning; he was aiming for those susceptible to his brand of allure.

Lopez operated in the same liminal grey space as other internet gurus. He thrived on unverifiable promises, marketing recycled self-help advice as exclusive wisdom. He exploited the fear of missing out, creating a sense of urgency with limited-time offers and exclusive access.

Criticism mounted as more former customers shared their experiences online. One Reddit user wrote, "I paid for his program, and it was nothing more than generic advice I could've found for free. It felt like a scam."

The exact viral mechanisms that elevated him began to expose him.

This pattern isn't unique to Lopez. Internet gurus like Gary Brecka and Chef Pii follow a similar trajectory. They rise rapidly, fueled by social media algorithms that reward engagement—positive or negative. They exploit psychological triggers like social proof, scarcity, and emotional manipulation to build a following.

Chef Pii, also known as Veronica Shaw, introduced the world to "Pink Sauce" on TikTok. The mysterious condiment went viral despite—or because of—concerns about its safety and labeling. The intrigue drove sales, but the lack of proper food safety led to backlash and regulatory scrutiny.

These gurus capitalize on the algorithms that amplify sensational content. Emotional triggers like fear, envy, and excitement drive engagement, creating a feedback loop that propels them into the spotlight. But their rise often contains the seeds of their downfall.

As they gain prominence, scrutiny intensifies. Claims are fact-checked, and credentials are questioned. The same platforms that elevate them can turn against them when their promises crumble under investigation.

This leads to the emergence of the "anti-guru." Figures like Coffeezilla step in as watchdogs, exposing the deceit behind the curated personas. In a postmodern world where truth is fragmented and hyperreality blurs perception, anti-gurus deconstruct the narratives these influencers spin.

They reveal that they rent mansions, lease cars, and buy followers. They dismantle the psychological tricks used to manipulate audiences, challenging the constructed identities and bringing audiences back to reality.

Some might argue that these gurus offer inspiration and that it's up to individuals to exercise critical thinking. While personal responsibility is vital, the influence of psychological manipulation and sophisticated marketing tactics can't be underestimated.

So, how do we protect ourselves from falling prey to these modern-day sirens? Awareness is the first step. Understanding the psychological mechanisms (like the halo effect, social proof, and fear of missing out) can help us recognize when we're being manipulated. Critical thinking and skepticism are our safeguards.

As information consumers in an age of hyperreality, we must resort to our old way of experiencing the world. We must question the narratives presented to us and not accept regurgitated information as social proof. Look beyond the glossy images and emotional appeals. Seek independent verification, consult experts, and consider multiple perspectives.

This transformation has already begun. Progressive internet advocate Jack Conte predicts that the algorithm will kill followers and has already created a way to save us.

MAJORITY REPORT: HOW DATA AND ALGORITHMS INFLUENCE DEMOCRACY

HOW 5,000 DATA POINTS CAN SWAY A NATION

"Until you make the unconscious conscious, it will direct your life, and you will call it fate."

C. G. Jung

In the months leading up to the 2016 presidential election in the United States, voters were inundated with tailored messages, each crafted to pluck the strings of their psyches. After the rise in social media, especially Facebook, online behaviors were now quantifiable. The likes, shares, and clicks accumulated over the years were siphoned into a vast reservoir of data. This digital footprint was the raw material for constructing intricate psychological profiles.

At the core of this operation was a fusion of behavioral economics and cutting-edge data analytics, wielded with a precision previously unimaginable. Cambridge Analytica claimed to possess up to 5,000 data points on over 230 million American voters. "We were able to form a model to predict the personality of every single adult in the United States of America," boasted Alexander Nix, the company's CEO, at a 2016 conference.

The methodology hinged on the OCEAN model—an acronym for Openness, Conscientiousness, Extraversion, Agreeableness, and Neuroticism—a framework from personality psychology. Cambridge Analytica aimed to classify individuals along these dimensions by analyzing Facebook activity and other online behaviors. This psychographic profiling was then used to micro-target voters with subconscious messages to influence their decisions.

The OCEAN model, also known as the Big Five personality traits, is based on decades of psychological research. It distills the essence of personality into dimensions that can be measured, analyzed, and manipulated as Cambridge Analytica intended. The company's strategists saw in OCEAN not just a model but a map—a way to navigate the uncharted waters of individual minds and, by extension, the collective consciousness of a nation.

At the helm of this initiative was Michal Kosinski, a young Polish psychologist whose work at the University of Cambridge explored the intersection of digital footprints and personality assessment. In 2012, Kosinski published a groundbreaking study demonstrating that a person's Facebook "likes" could predict intimate details about their personality and life with startling accuracy. A mere ten likes could appraise someone better than their work colleagues; seventy likes surpassed what friends knew; and with 300 likes, the algorithm could see a person better than their own spouse.

"We are looking at a world where machines can understand us better than we understand ourselves," Kosinski remarked at a symposium. His research caught the attention of political operatives and marketers alike, all eager to harness this predictive power. Cambridge Analytica saw an opportunity to weaponize the OCEAN model on an unprecedented scale.

The plan was as audacious as it was clandestine. The company constructed detailed psychographic profiles by harvesting data from millions of Facebook users—often without explicit consent. Each individual was assigned scores across the five OCEAN traits, creating a multidimensional personality portrait. This data was then used to micro-target voters with customized messages to resonate profoundly and personally.

For those high in Openness, the campaign emphasized themes of innovation and change. Advertisements highlighted progressive policies, appealed to creativity, and envisioned a bold new future. Sarah, an artist from Portland with a penchant for avant-garde music and abstract painting, found her feed filled with messages about pioneering environmental initiatives and groundbreaking social reforms. The content spoke to her spirit of exploration, subtly nudging her toward a candidate who promised transformation.

In contrast, individuals scoring high in Conscientiousness received messages stressing duty, responsibility, and stability. Michael, a small business owner in Ohio who prided himself on his work ethic and meticulous attention to detail, saw ads focusing on economic growth, law and order, and traditional values. The messaging appealed to his sense of discipline and reliability, framing the political choice as one between chaos and control.

Invitations to rallies, social events, and community gatherings were targeted at those with elevated levels of extraversion. The campaign knew that extraverts like Jasmine, a college student in Florida who thrived on social interaction, were more likely to be mobilized through collective experiences. Her feeds buzzed with energetic calls to action, group endorsements, and images of enthusiastic crowds.

Individuals high in **Agreeableness** were approached with messages centered on unity, compassion, and social harmony. For Raj, a social worker in Michigan who is deeply invested in his community, the ads emphasize collaborative solutions, bipartisan efforts, and stories of people coming together to overcome adversity—the content aimed to align his voting behavior with his intrinsic desire for cooperation and empathy.

Perhaps most controversially, those with high Neuroticism were bombarded with fear-based messaging. Lisa, a mother in Pennsylvania who often worried about her family's safety, found her social media filled with warnings about threats to national security, economic collapse, and moral decay. The campaign tapped into her anxieties, presenting a candidate as the bulwark against imminent dangers.

The precision of these tactics was both impressive and unsettling. The campaign bypassed rational deliberation by aligning political messaging with the deepest facets of individual personalities, speaking instead to instinctual drives and emotional responses. Voters were not merely being informed; they were being orchestrated.

Brittany Kaiser, reflecting on the process, acknowledged the ethical quagmire. "We were using the OCEAN model to peer into people's minds," she admitted. "It was like having a psychological X-ray of an entire population." The power to influence had crossed into the realm of manipulation, raising questions about free will and the sanctity of personal thought.

Public reaction to these revelations was a mixture of shock, indignation, and introspection. How much of our behavior is our own when others can predict and shape it accurately? The scandal ignited debates about privacy, consent, and the moral responsibilities of those wielding such technologies.

In academic circles, discussions intensified around the implications of psychographic profiling. Dr. Jennifer Stevens, a psychologist specializing in personality assessment, voiced concerns at a conference. "The OCEAN model was never intended to be used as a tool for mass manipulation," she asserted. "Its misuse threatens to undermine the very foundations of personal autonomy."

Christopher Wylie, a former Cambridge Analytica employee turned whistleblower, later revealed the depths of these strategies. "We exploited Facebook to harvest millions of people's profiles," he confessed to *The Guardian*. "And built models to exploit what we knew about them and target their inner demons." The operation blurred the lines between influence and manipulation, raising profound ethical and legal questions.

Yet, amidst the controversy, some saw potential for approving applications. If understanding personality could help tailor educational programs, improve mental health interventions, or enhance user experiences without infringing on autonomy, perhaps the model could be redeemed. Richard Thaler and Cass Sunstein's concept of libertarian paternalism offered a framework for such ethical use, advocating for nudges that guide without coercing.

As the election unfolded, social media feeds became battlegrounds. Voters were bombarded with "dark ads"—sponsored posts visible only to targeted users, leaving little room for public scrutiny or counter-narratives. The traditional safeguards of discourse eroded in this fragmented landscape. "It's no longer about persuading people with facts," Nix declared. "It's about playing into the psychology of the voter."

When the extent of Cambridge's involvement in the election was revealed in 2018, pure outrage ensued. Mark Zuckerberg, Facebook's CEO, testified before Congress, acknowledging the breach of trust. "We didn't take a broad enough view of our responsibility," he admitted. That was a big mistake."

Grappling with her role in these events, Brittany Kaiser became a whistleblower herself. In her testimony before the UK Parliament, she reflected on the implications. "The methodologies we used may have been very effective," she conceded. "But they also may have been unethical and disrespectful of individual privacy."

The heuristics and biases that Kahneman and Tversky painstakingly mapped are the fault lines along which influence can be exerted. The framing effect, social proof, and authority bias all become levers in the machinery of persuasion.

The digital footprints we leave behind are not just remnants of our online wanderings; they are the breadcrumbs that can lead others straight into the recesses of our minds.

The story of Cambridge Analytica begins not in the halls of academia or the offices of tech giants but within the intricate pathways of the human mind—a place where logic and emotion entwine, where the echoes of ancient survival mechanisms resonate amidst the hum of modern life. We must turn our gaze here to navigate the present challenges and chart a course toward a future that honors the power and vulnerability inherent in our humanity.

PART TWO: EMERGING FROM THE CAVE

A JOURNEY TO CLARITY IN AN ERA OF DISTORTION

DON'T YANK THE CHAIN: REVIVING ANCIENT RHETORIC IN MODERN TIMES

WHAT WE CAN LEARN FROM GREEK AND ROMAN PHILOSOPHERS ABOUT INFLUENCE

"The greatest blessing granted to mankind comes by way of madness, which is a divine gift."

Socrates

The *Socratic Method* sends fear into the hearts of prospective law students despite the fact that it has only killed one person that we know of. It is the process of distilling information through the use of simple questions. Every first-year law student feels its wrath and experiences the fear of getting called to the carpet in front of a theater of 100 other students. And for good reason: the Socratic method is the simplest form of obtaining the truth and testing knowledge. There is no hiding from a skilled questioner when its victim is compelled to answer.

Using a series of precise, focused questions, Socrates guided his fellow citizens to uncover deeper truths, reveal contradictions, and clarify their beliefs. This approach was a relentless pursuit of truth through dialogue for Socrates. Dialogue is the foundation of our current system of trials, enumerated in our constitution through the right of confrontation, and it still remains the superior way of obtaining the truth.

Socrates believed that the key to wisdom lay in recognizing one's own ignorance, and his method of questioning was designed to help others see the gaps in their knowledge. His student, Plato, preserved these dialogues, ensuring that the Socratic Method would endure through the ages. Later, Aristotle refined these ideas, emphasizing the importance of logical reasoning and empirical observation. To understand the power of the Socratic Method, imagine being in that ancient marketplace, watching Socrates engage a young Athenian in dialogue. The conversation might unfold like this:

Socrates: "Tell me, young man, what is justice?"

Young Man: "Justice is giving each person what they are due."

Socrates: "And who determines what each person is due?"

Young Man: "The laws do."

Socrates: "And are all laws just?"

Young Man: "Not always."

With this simple exchange, Socrates dismantles a simplistic definition of justice, pushing his interlocutor toward a more nuanced understanding. Each question is a stepping stone, leading to deeper reflection and greater clarity. This method of inquiry, focusing on one clear fact or concept at a time, laid the foundation for what would become a fundamental principle in education and law: the one fact per question rule.

Centuries later, the Socratic Method found a new home in the halls of Harvard Law School, where Dean Christopher Columbus Langdell transformed legal education with his rigorous application of the case method. Langdell believed that the study of law should mirror the exacting standards of scientific inquiry, and he introduced the Socratic Method as a way to challenge students' understanding of legal principles.

Langdell was a firm believer in the idea that law could be studied scientifically. He viewed legal principles as deriving from a body of cases, similar to the way scientists derive natural laws from observable phenomena. This approach defied prior teaching methods which primarily involved lectures and rote memorization of legal principles and treatises.

Instead of teaching law through abstract principles, Langdell believed that students should learn by analyzing judicial opinions. He compiled and published a collection of cases in contracts, which became the first casebook. The idea was that by studying these cases, students would learn to deduce legal principles themselves, fostering a deeper understanding of the law and developing analytical skills. But he needed a way to ensure the young minds were trained to think like lawyers, for this he adopted the time tested Socratic Method.

Langdell's teaching style involved rigorous, often relentless questioning by the professor. In a typical Socratic exchange, the professor doesn't provide answers or lecture, but instead asks a series of probing questions about a particular case or legal issue. The goal is to force students to think critically, articulate their reasoning, and engage in legal analysis in real-time.

In Langdell's classroom, the Socratic method was designed to mirror the process of legal argumentation that lawyers would face in practice. It also encouraged students to question assumptions and refine their legal reasoning, making them more effective advocates.

Langdell's innovations were initially controversial. Many contemporaries were resistant to his methods, believing that law could not be reduced to scientific principles. However, over time, his approach gained widespread acceptance and became the dominant model for legal education in the United States. Harvard Law School's prestige and success helped popularize the case method and Socratic method in other law schools as well.

While the Socratic method, adopted by Langdell was eventually accepted and became a staple of legal education in the United States, but Socrates was a bit too early for his time.

Unfortunately for Socratese, he would become a martyr to his method. He failed to understand what Plato, his student, would later teach. Questioning is important but messaging is equally as important.

The trial of Socratese in 399 BCE is one of the most famous trials in history. By the time of his trial, Socrates was an established figure in Athens, but his philosophical teachings and method of questioning had earned him many powerful enemies. The Socratic method often made influential people uncomfortable, as Socrates' relentless questioning could undermine widely held beliefs and expose ignorance, even in high-ranking individuals.

Athens had recently suffered major setbacks, including its defeat in the Peloponnesian War (431–404 BCE) against Sparta, the overthrow of its democratic government, and the brief establishment of the Thirty Tyrants, an oligarchic regime. Although Socrates himself had no direct role in these events, some of his former associates, such as Critias, were part of the Thirty Tyrants, which likely contributed to the animosity toward him.

Socrates faced two principal charges during the trial:

First, Socrates was accused of not believing in the gods of the city and introducing new deities. The specific legal charge was that Socrates failed to acknowledge the official gods of Athens and instead introduced new, spiritual entities. This accusation was tied to his philosophical inquiry into religious and moral matters, as Socrates often questioned traditional religious beliefs.

Second, Socrates was corrupting the youth of Athens by encouraging them to challenge authority and question traditional values. His teaching style often led young Athenians to adopt critical attitudes toward the political and social establishment, which may have appeared subversive to the city's leaders.

The trial took place in a public court in Athens, where a jury of about 500 Athenian citizens was chosen to hear the case. Meletus, a relatively obscure figure, was the primary accuser, though Anytus and Lycon were also key figures behind the prosecution. Anytus was a wealthy politician who may have been motivated by a personal grudge, particularly because of Socrates' critical stance toward democracy and his association with some of the city's controversial figures.

Unlike the constitutionally appointed attorney that a court provides today, Socrates was allowed to defend himself. But he was probably better off; his rhetorical abilities were unmatched. As recorded by Plato in the Apology, his defense was both defiant and philosophical. Instead of trying to win sympathy or beg for mercy, Socrates used the opportunity to explain his philosophical mission, claiming that his questioning was actually a service to the city, a form of moral examination that helped people realize their ignorance and search for truth.

Socrates famously argued that his role as a philosopher was divinely ordained. He claimed that he had a duty to question and challenge others to help them seek wisdom and virtue. He compared himself to a gadfly stirring a sluggish horse into action, saying that his constant questioning helped improve the moral fabric of the city.

Socrates did not apologize for his actions. In fact, he refused to abandon his philosophical mission- even until his death. He openly acknowledged that he would continue questioning people and challenging their beliefs if acquitted. This boldness likely alienated some of the jurors, who may have expected a more humble or remorseful tone from him.

After hearing the arguments, the jury found Socrates guilty. The vote was relatively close, with 280 jurors voting for conviction and 220 for acquittal. In Athenian trials, after a conviction, both the prosecution and the defense could propose penalties. The jury would then choose between them. Socrates' accusers proposed the death penalty. In response, Socrates provocatively suggested that, as a benefactor of the city, he should be rewarded with free meals for life. He then more seriously proposed a fine, but his earlier suggestion likely offended many jurors.

This is where Socrates could have done better, and by the end of this book you'll have a much better plan than Socrates.

Of course, the jury chose the death penalty, and Socrates was sentenced to die by drinking hemlock, a poisonous plant. After his sentencing, Socrates spent 30 days in prison while his execution was delayed for religious reasons. During this time, his friends and students visited him, offering to help him escape, but Socrates refused. He believed that escaping would violate his moral principles and show disrespect for the laws of Athens, even though those laws had condemned him unjustly. Socrates calmly accepted his fate and drank the hemlock in the presence of his friends and followers.

Plato's Phaedo provides a detailed account of Socrates' final moments, portraying him as serene and at peace with his death, continuing to discuss philosophical matters even as the poison took effect. Plato would not suffer the same fate.

Why wouldn't the Athenians understand the need for truth and justice in a developing society? Plato helps us understand in the Allegory of the Cave.

Imagine a dark, damp cave where the only light comes from the flicker of a distant fire. Inside this cave, a group of people has been imprisoned since birth, chained in such a way that they can only face forward, staring at the wall in front of them. Behind them, unknown to them, is a world they cannot see—a world of people, objects, and a fire that casts their shadows onto the wall. All the prisoners can perceive are these shadows, moving shapes that form the entirety of their reality. They've never seen the people or objects that create these shadows, nor the fire. To them, the shadows are the world, as real and tangible as anything could be.

Plato's Allegory of the Cave, found in *The Republic*, represents the human condition. The prisoners in the cave are trapped in ignorance, not by their own choice, but by the circumstances of their existence. They cannot turn around or question the nature of the shadows. This is their reality, and it's all they know. For them, to imagine a world beyond the shadows would be unthinkable, and even if someone suggested that the shadows were mere illusions, they would likely dismiss the idea.

Now, imagine one of these prisoners is suddenly freed. They stand up, turn around, and see the objects casting shadows for the first time in their lives. At first, they are blinded by the fire's light—its overwhelming brightness. Their eyes, long accustomed to the dark, struggle to adjust. The world behind them, with its objects and people, seems too vivid, too natural. It's disorienting and painful. As the prisoner makes their way out of the cave and into the sunlight, the world outside is even more dazzling, and the sunlight is nearly unbearable.

But gradually, the prisoner's eyes adjust. They begin to see the world as it is—filled with colors, shapes, and dimensions they never knew existed. For the first time, they encounter reality in its complete form. It's a revelation, but it's not easy. The journey from the cave to the sunlight is difficult and uncomfortable, and at many points along the way, it would have been easier to retreat to the familiar shadows. But once the prisoner understands the truth, there's no going back. They realize that what they had once taken as reality—the shadows—was only a distorted reflection of the real world.

The prisoners in the cave don't know that they're in the dark. They don't realize that there's a whole world outside their narrow perception. And because of this, they are content. The shadows on the wall are familiar, and familiarity breeds comfort.

Leaving the cave and challenging one's long-held beliefs or worldview is deeply unsettling. The world outside the cave—the world of knowledge, truth, and light—requires effort, discomfort, and self-examination. It means acknowledging that the world is more complicated than we once thought, and that's not an easy pill to swallow. For many, it's easier to stay in the cave, to keep staring at the shadows, and to avoid the painful process of growth and enlightenment.

This is not just an ancient problem; it's a contemporary one. With 24/7 media, social networks, and viral content, people are constantly presented with simplified, often misleading, versions of reality. Much like the shadows on the wall, these versions are easy to consume and don't require much thought. They confirm our biases, offer easy answers, and give us the illusion of understanding without the burden of critical thinking. As a result, many people remain in their own metaphorical caves, unwilling or unable to face the complexities of the real world.

The challenge for anyone trying to persuade people stuck in the cave is recognizing that logic and reason alone won't cut it. The prisoners of the cave—those who live in a world of half-truths and shadows—are not likely to be swayed by cold, hard facts. Plato's freed prisoner couldn't just return to the cave and tell the others about the real world outside. They wouldn't believe him. They would cling to their shadows because that's what they know, and anything that challenges their worldview is seen as threatening.

Here's where Daniel Kahneman's System 2 thinking, which we discuss in the next chapter, becomes essential. It's the thinking we use when critically evaluating information, weighing evidence, and challenging our assumptions. But when you're talking to people who are stuck in System 1 thinking—fast, emotional, and reliant on gut instinct—there's a disconnect. System 1 thrives on **quick** impressions and emotional responses, and for many people, this is their default mode of thinking, especially in a world filled with manipulative messaging.

You need more than logic and facts to persuade people stuck in the cave. As Plato's allegory shows, the journey out of the cave is uncomfortable and disorienting, and the person being persuaded may not even want to make that journey. That's why persuasion in this context has to be gradual and empathetic.

Acknowledge the Comfort of the Shadows: Don't dismiss the beliefs or feelings of those still in the cave. Recognize that the shadows they see feel natural to them and that their worldview provides comfort and stability. Challenging their beliefs too directly can feel like an attack, only making them retreat further into the cave.

Unlike the abrupt gut punch Socrates used to enrage his opponents, emerging from the cave requires a subtle approach. This is especially true in a hyperreal and postmodern world where the shadows on the wall are lifelike, real, and incredibly addictive.

Appeal to Their Emotions: While System 2 thinking is crucial for deep understanding, **System 1 emotions** can be the entry point. Use stories, metaphors, and examples that resonate emotionally. Much like Plato's allegory itself, a good story can bypass defensive barriers and make the listener more open to new ideas. Creating an emotional connection builds trust, which is necessary before someone is willing to engage in System 2 thinking.

Introduce Complexity Gradually: The transition from the shadows to the light doesn't happen simultaneously. People need time to adjust. Start with something small, something that challenges their assumptions without being overwhelming. Over time, as their comfort with new information grows, you can introduce more complex ideas.

Use Cognitive Biases to Your Advantage: Use it strategically rather than fighting against System 1 thinking. For example, confirmation bias is a powerful force. Find ways to frame your arguments to align with the person's beliefs, then slowly introduce new information that challenges those beliefs. This way, the information doesn't feel like a direct threat.

Be Patient: Real change takes time. People don't leave the cave in a day or suddenly abandon their worldview after a single conversation. Persuasion requires patience and persistence, especially when it involves deeply held beliefs.

Heuristics which we discuss thoroughly in the next chapter, are the subtle music that will awaken our audience.

THE TIME TESTED TOOLS OF PHILOSOPHERS: RHETORIC'S ROLE IN SHAPING HISTORY

HOW ANCIENT RHETORICAL TECHNIQUES SHAPED ICONIC MOMENTS IN HISTORY

You'd have to know it was rhetoric to watch a skilled rhetorician deftly play all of the harp's strings while maintaining balance and swooning with her unaware audience. If they do it right, absent a formal education in rhetoric - which you will get here- one may not even realize they are being swooned.

The study of rhetoric—the art of persuasion through language—was highly esteemed in ancient Greece. Philosophers and orators like Aristotle, Demosthenes, and Isocrates extensively explored rhetorical strategies to enhance speech and writing. Aristotle's work *"Rhetoric"* laid the foundation for rhetorical theory, identifying various devices and techniques that could be employed to persuade and influence audiences. Romans inherited and expanded upon Greek rhetorical traditions. Orators like Cicero and Quintilian considered rhetoric essential for public life and legal practice. Cicero's works, such as "De Oratore," discuss the importance of stylistic devices, including anaphora, for effective communication.

During the medieval period, rhetorical devices continued to be taught in the context of the trivium (grammar, rhetoric, and logic) in educational institutions. Anaphora was used in sermons, poetry, and liturgical texts to inspire and move congregations. The Renaissance sparked a renewed interest in classical rhetoric. Writers and speakers studied ancient texts to refine their craft. Figures like William Shakespeare employed anaphora and other rhetorical devices to add depth and emotion to their works. For instance, in Mark Antony's speech in *"Julius Caesar," the repeated use of "Brutus is an hono*rable man" is a rhetorical strategy to sway the public.

Anaphora, climax, antithesis, parison, and chiasmus are rhetorical devices that have endured, shaping some of the most profound speeches, writings, and dialogues in human history. Yet they are far more than stylistic flourishes—they are tools of persuasion that tap into the core of human psychology, embedding ideas deep within listeners' minds.

The principles of rhetoric represent the four humors of classical medicine; a proficient speaker, like a healer of the soul, understands each one's role in achieving harmony.

1 Logos (Reason): This involves appealing to the audience's logical faculties. If I present rational arguments and you are receptive to reason, our exchange becomes a harmonious flow of ideas, ideally leading us closer to truth.

2 Pathos (Emotion): This involves engaging the audience's emotions. It encompasses what we often call "expressiveness." By stirring feelings through tone, facial expressions, gestures, emphasis, and pauses, a speaker enhances the emotional resonance of the message, fostering empathy and connection.

3 Ethos (Credibility): Ethos is rooted in the speaker's integrity and moral character. It involves aligning with the core values of a community or ideology—be it religious, political, nationalistic, or otherwise. Establishing trust through credibility and authority and resonating with the audience's sense of right and wrong are central to ethos.

4 Kairos (Timeliness): Developed after Socratese and likely because of Socratese, Kairos, meaning "the opportune moment" in Greek, is about seizing the right time to deliver a compelling argument or insightful remark. It involves capitalizing on timing to enhance the message's

impact. Though more abstract due to its situational nature, kairos is as vital as the other rhetorical elements.

Rhetoric is not confined to grand speeches or classical literature; it permeates every facet of our daily lives. From the moment we wake up to when we retire at night, we are immersed in a sea of persuasive messages designed to influence our thoughts, feelings, and actions. Every advertisement you encounter is crafted with a keen awareness of rhetorical principles. Marketers meticulously choose words and visuals that appeal to their desires (*pathos*), present logical reasons to choose their product (*logos*), establish the credibility of their brand (*ethos*), and time their campaigns to coincide with relevant events or seasons (*kairos*). Even the layout of a webpage or a product's packaging involves rhetorical decisions intended to persuade.

The first step in becoming a persuasive communicator is to attune ourselves to the rhetoric surrounding us. By observing and analyzing the techniques used in various contexts—advertising, politics, social media, and conversations—we can learn how messages are constructed to persuade. This awareness helps us resist undue influence and equips us with the tools to craft our messages more effectively.

Soon, you can read rhetoric like the notes of emotion or even write them as such. Watch how rhetorical principles are blended into this story.

Imagine Slipping into your recliner after a long day, the bud light still secreting a fog of condensation, you flip on the television.

An infomercial appears:

"Ever stood at the cliff's edge, toes gripping the precipice, wondering if the wind would catch you or let you fall? That's how I felt every morning for ten years." [Metaphor]

I remember waking up one day, staring at the cracked ceiling of another unfamiliar room, thinking, "This isn't who I am. This isn't who I was meant to be." [Anadiplosis] But the bottle on the nightstand whispered otherwise. It told me I was trapped, that escape was a fantasy, that hope was for fools. [Personification]

"You're stronger than this," my mother used to say. "You have a light that can outshine the darkest shadows." [Antithesis] But what happens when the shadows become your only friends? When the darkness is more comforting than the light? [Rhetorical Questions]

I lost jobs, relationships, years—so many years. "Time heals all wounds," they say, but addiction is a thief who steals time and then blames you for the loss. [Hyperbole and Personification]

One night, I found myself on a bridge, the cold wind cutting through me like a knife. Below, the river raged, a mirror of the turmoil inside me. [Simile and Metaphor] I thought about letting go—of everything. But then a thought pierced the haze: If I can't save myself, maybe I can save someone else. [Chiasmus]

That's when I decided to fight back. Not just for me but for everyone who's ever felt the suffocating grip of addiction. [Climax]

I tried therapies, support groups, cold turkey—you name it. Each attempt was a step forward, followed by two steps back. It was like I was climbing a mountain with no summit. [Metaphor]

Then, I discovered Liberex—a breakthrough medication designed to help people like me regain control. Skeptical? So was I. But sometimes, the most minor key can unlock the heaviest door. [Antithesis and Metaphor]

With Liberex, the fog began to lift. Mornings weren't battles anymore but beginnings. Nights weren't escapes but restful ends to fulfilling days. I wasn't just surviving; I was living. [Parallelism]

Now, I stand before you, not as someone who was saved by a pill, but as someone who took a step—a small step that became a giant leap towards freedom. [Allusion to Neil Armstrong and Antithesis]

"Ask not what life can do for you—ask what you can do for your life," I tell myself daily. [Paraphrased Antimetabole]

If you're standing on that cliff, toes gripping the edge, know that the wind can catch you. Sometimes, all it takes is that first step back to solid ground. [Extended Metaphor]

Because the best time to reclaim your life was yesterday, the second best time is now. [Antithesis and Paraphrased Proverb]

Liberex didn't just give me a way out; it gave me a way back—to family, friends, and myself. And it can do the same for you. [Ethos and Pathos]

So, let's not let addiction write our stories. Let's take the pen and start a new chapter—together. [Metaphor and Call to Action]

Antithesis

If climax takes us on a journey upward, carefully building towards a peak, antithesis plays with opposites, illuminating the tension between two opposing ideas. This rhetorical device sets contrasts against each other in a balanced structure, sharpening the distinctions and making each idea stand out more vividly than its counterpart.

One of the most iconic antithesis uses comes from Neil Armstrong's famous statement as he first stepped onto the moon's surface: "That's one small step for man, one giant leap for mankind." This phrase marked one of the most significant moments in human history and framed it through the lens of antithesis. Armstrong juxtaposes the simplicity of his action—a single step—with the monumental achievement it represents for humanity. The contrast between "small" and "giant," between "step" and "leap," makes the moment resonate even more deeply, highlighting both the individual and collective significance of the event.

Antithesis is particularly effective in speeches and literature because it taps into how humans naturally understand the world through contrasts. By juxtaposing opposing ideas, we contrast goodness against evil, light against darkness, and success against failure. The speaker makes each concept sharper and more defined.

Consider Richard Nixon's inaugural address, in which he said, "We find ourselves rich in goods but ragged in spirit, reaching with magnificent precision for the moon but falling into raucous discord on Earth." In this statement, Nixon contrasts material wealth with spiritual poverty and technological achievement with social discord. These juxtapositions underscore the complexities of the times, showing that progress in one area often comes at the expense of another.

Antithesis not only contrasts ideas but also clarifies them. It allows the speaker or writer to frame their argument within a broader context, helping the audience see both sides of an issue and understand the importance of each. Like two sides of a coin, the contrasting ideas are inseparable yet distinct, each enhancing the significance of the other.

Some of history's greatest orators and writers have used this technique, from Shakespeare in his plays to Abraham Lincoln in his speeches. By skillfully contrasting opposing ideas, they create tension that holds the audience's attention and makes the argument all the more compelling.

In the next section, we'll examine parison and how it uses symmetrical sentence structures to create a pleasing balance that can make an argument clear and memorable. Parison, like antithesis, uses structure to enhance the audience's understanding, but it does so through harmony and rhythm rather than contrast.

Parison

Where antithesis thrives on contrasts, parison finds its power in symmetry. This rhetorical device creates harmony by repeating similar structures within sentences or clauses, making ideas feel ordered and more accessible to digest. Parison doesn't just sound good—it enhances clarity and impact by presenting ideas in parallel, ensuring that the listener or reader quickly follows along.

A perfect example of parison in action comes from John F. Kennedy's inaugural address: "Let every nation know, whether it wishes us well or ill, that we shall pay any price, bear any burden, meet any hardship, support any friend, oppose any foe..." The balanced structure of the verbs and objects creates a rhythmic cadence, reinforcing the steadfast commitment Kennedy is expressing. Each clause mirrors the next, giving his statement both weight and memorability. The symmetry ensures that each idea flows naturally into the next, building a cohesive and powerful message.

The beauty of Parison lies in its simplicity. By aligning clauses or sentences in parallel form, the speaker creates a kind of rhetorical harmony. This structure is particularly effective in speeches, where rhythm and flow can enhance the emotional resonance of the message. By presenting thoughts in a balanced, mirrored fashion, parison also lends itself to greater memorability.

Even in everyday phrases, we encounter parison without realizing it. Consider the saying, "Easy come, easy go." The symmetry of this simple phrase gives it a pleasing, almost lyrical quality, making it easy to recall and inherently relatable. The balance of words enhances the clarity of the message—that things gained with little effort are often lost just as quickly.

Advertisers often use parison for its catchy rhythm and simplicity. Take slogans like "Buy one, get one," for example. The symmetry of the structure helps create a memorable phrase that sticks in the consumer's mind. The balanced format drives home the point in a completely satisfying way.

Parison's ability to present ideas in a format makes it such a versatile tool in persuasion that feels natural and logical. When thoughts are arranged in a mirrored structure, they become more accessible and enjoyable. The symmetry creates a sense of balance, reinforcing the validity and coherence of the argument.

Next, we will explore chiasmus, where the repetition of ideas comes with a twist. Unlike Parison's straightforward symmetry, chiasmus inverts the structure of clauses or phrases, creating a mirror image that adds depth and complexity to the message. This reversal technique enhances the argument and leaves a lasting impression on the audience, making the point even more memorable.

Chiasmus

Where parison relies on symmetry and balance, chiasmus adds a twist by reversing the order of words or phrases in successive clauses, creating a mirrored structure. This technique adds depth and resonance to a message, enhancing its memorability by forcing the listener or reader to reflect on the inversion. Chiasmus reinforces an idea and encourages the audience to think more critically about the relationship between concepts.

Perhaps the most famous use of chiasmus in modern rhetoric is John F. Kennedy's iconic line: "Ask not what your country can do for you—ask what you can do for your country." By reversing the subject and object in the second half of the sentence, Kennedy flips the narrative, shifting the responsibility from the government to the individual. The structure urges citizens to move from a passive expectation to active engagement, making his message one of empowerment and service.

This use of chiasmus isn't just clever wordplay—it's a powerful tool of persuasion. By inverting the structure, Kennedy forces the audience to reconsider their relationship with their nation and aligns them with his vision of collective responsibility. The mirrored structure makes the statement not only striking but deeply memorable, embedding the call to action in the minds of his listeners.

Shakespeare was also a master of chiasmus, as demonstrated in *Macbeth* with the famous line: "Fair is foul, and foul is fair." This inversion emphasizes moral ambiguity and deceptive appearances throughout the play. By reversing the terms, Shakespeare suggests that what seems good may be harmful, and vice versa—a theme that resonates deeply with the audience and sets the tone for the unfolding tragedy.

Chiasmus balances two opposing or complementary ideas but does so through reversal, which adds an element of surprise or reflection. The audience must pause and consider how the two halves of the statement relate, often leading to a more profound understanding of the message.

In many ways, chiasmus forces the audience to think more deeply. The inversion makes the connection between ideas less obvious but more impactful. It challenges listeners to engage with the message actively, turning a simple statement into something more layered and complex. This technique is particularly effective when the goal is not just to communicate an idea but to make that idea linger in the audience's minds long after the speech or text has ended.

The following section will explore how rhetorical devices like chiasmus, parison, and antithesis can be combined to create even more powerful and nuanced messaging. By layering these techniques together, speakers and writers can craft messages that resonate on multiple levels, appealing to logic and emotion.

Combining Rhetorical Devices: Crafting Persuasive Masterpieces

Great rhetoric isn't just about using individual techniques like chiasmus or antithesis—it's about weaving these tools together to create a tapestry of meaning that resonates with an audience on multiple levels. When used effectively, these rhetorical devices can work in harmony, amplifying each other to create emotionally powerful, intellectually engaging messages that are ultimately unforgettable.

Take, for example, St. Francis of Assisi's Prayer, which seamlessly integrates anaphora and antithesis:

"Lord, make me an instrument of your peace.

Where there is hatred, let me sow love;

Where there is injury, pardon;

Where there is doubt, faith..."

In this prayer, anaphora is employed by repeating "Where there is...," creating a rhythm that draws the audience in. At the same time, antithesis sets opposing ideas—hatred versus love, injury versus pardon—against each other, emphasizing the transformative power of positive action in the face of negativity. Combining these devices doesn't just deliver a message; it creates a meditative, almost musical effect that enhances the prayer's emotional and intellectual impact.

Similarly, consider Barack Obama's 2008 election victory speech, in which he masterfully layers rhetorical techniques to build momentum and inspire his audience:

"If there is anyone out there who still doubts that America is a place where all things are possible, who still wonders if the dream of our founders is alive in our time, who still questions the power of our democracy, tonight is your answer."

Obama uses anaphora ("who still...") to create rhythm and a sense of urgency. Each successive clause adds weight to the point, culminating in the final declaration: "Tonight is your answer." The repetitive structure creates a climactic effect, allowing the audience to absorb the moment's significance fully. By combining anaphora with a climax, Obama effectively mobilizes emotion while reinforcing the logic of his message.

We also see how these rhetorical devices can be layered in literary works. Charles Dickens, in *A Tale of Two Cities*, opens with an iconic use of antithesis paired with anaphora:

"It was the best of times, it was the worst of times, it was the age of wisdom, it was the age of foolishness..."

Here, the repetition of "it was" (anaphora) provides structure, while the opposing ideas (antithesis) create a tension that perfectly captures the contradictions of the era. The combination allows Dickens to convey complex social realities with a simplicity that resonates emotionally.

When woven together, these rhetorical devices engage the mind and stir emotions, making the message intellectually compelling and deeply felt. They allow speakers and writers to create layers of meaning that resonate with their audience long after delivering the message.

In rhetoric, it's not just the ideas that matter but also how they are presented. Anaphora and alliteration are potent techniques that amplify a message's emotional resonance by creating a sense of rhythm and cohesion. When used effectively, these devices add a lyrical quality to speech or writing, making the message more memorable and persuasive.

Anaphora, the repetition of a word or phrase at the beginning of successive clauses or sentences, emphasizes key ideas and creates a rhythm that builds emotional intensity. One of the most iconic examples is Martin Luther King Jr.'s "I Have a Dream" speech, in which King repeatedly begins sentences with "I have a dream..." This repetition does more than highlight his vision—it draws listeners in, building a crescendo of hope and inspiration. Each repetition strengthens the previous point, uniting them into a cohesive, compelling narrative that resonates deeply.

In literature, Charles Dickens uses anaphora in *A Tale of Two Cities* to create a rhythmic flow that sets the tone for the entire novel: "It was the best of times, it was the worst of times, it was the age of wisdom, it was the age of foolishness..." The repetition of "it was" provides structure while emphasizing the duality of the era, making it both memorable and emotionally engaging.

Alliteration, the repetition of consonant sounds at the beginning of words, can add musicality and emphasis to critical points. It's a subtle technique that makes phrases more memorable, giving them a lyrical quality that sticks in the mind. In advertising, this is why brand names like Coca-Cola, Dunkin' Donuts, and Krispy Kreme are so influential—repeated sounds make the names catchy and easy to recall.

Alliteration is also used in poetry and literature to enhance mood and imagery. For example, Samuel Taylor Coleridgeuses alliteration in *The Rime of the Ancient Mariner*: "The fair breeze blew, the white foam flew, the furrow followed free..." The repetition of the 'f' sound mimics the rhythmic motion of the sea, pulling the reader into the scene.

These devices—anaphora and alliteration—elevate language, making it more memorable and emotionally impactful. Whether in a speech, a piece of writing, or even an advertisement, they add a layer of artistry to persuasion, engaging both the heart and the mind.

Metaphor and Allegory

While techniques like anaphora and alliteration add rhythm and structure to language, metaphor, and allegory, delve deeper, enabling communicators to express complex ideas through imagery and symbolism. These devices offer more than mere description—they allow abstract concepts to become tangible, making them relatable and more accessible. This thought transformation through imagery is compelling in rhetoric, literature, and everyday communication.

In its simplest form, a metaphor is a figure of speech that directly refers to one thing by mentioning another, creating a symbolic link between them. It's a way of describing something abstract by relating it to something more concrete. Carl Sagan, for example, famously said, "Time is a thief," suggesting that time steals moments from our lives just as a thief would steal tangible items. This vivid imagery turns an intangible concept, like time, into something everyone can understand and relate to on a visceral level.

Another brilliant use of metaphor comes from politics. In his speech about the "shining city on a hill," Ronald Reagan used this metaphor to symbolize America's role as a beacon of hope and democracy to the rest of the world.

Where metaphor is often a one-time comparison, allegory extends metaphor into a narrative form, where characters, events, and even settings represent broader concepts or ideas. George Orwell's Animal Farm is a prime example of an allegory, using farm animals to represent key figures in the Russian Revolution. The story, on the surface, is about a group of animals rebelling against their human owner, but each character and event symbolizes a deeper political reality. Napoleon the pig, for instance, represents Stalin, while Snowball is a stand-in for Trotsky.

Allegory has long been used to communicate moral, philosophical, or political lessons engagingly and memorably. It turns an argument into a story, making complex issues more relatable and easily understood. Through characters and plot, allegory provides a vehicle for ideas that might otherwise be too abstract or divisive to grasp directly.

The power of metaphor and allegory lies in their ability to transcend literal language. They connect emotionally with the audience, making intellectual and deeply felt arguments. In persuasion, these devices allow speakers and writers to communicate on multiple levels, appealing to both the mind and the heart.

Synecdoche and Metonymy

While metaphor and allegory use comparisons to build imagery, synecdoche, and metonymy work by using parts or related objects to represent a more significant idea, these rhetorical devices are subtler, often making their impact through association rather than direct comparison. Still, they are just as influential in shaping persuasive messages.

Synecdoche occurs when a part of something represents the whole or vice versa. A classic example is the phrase "All hands on deck." "hands" refers to people's hands and sailors or crew members. The part (hands) stands in for the whole (the crew). This use of synecdoche is effective because it focuses on the critical element—the hands that will help with the task—while still implying the whole person, making the phrase more concise and impactful.

Another example comes from literature. In Julius Caesar, Shakespeare uses synecdoche when Mark Antony refers to Caesar's body as "a bleeding piece of earth." Here, "piece of earth" is a synecdoche for Caesar, emphasizing his frailty after death and linking the individual with the universal theme of mortality.

Metonymy, on the other hand, involves substituting one word or phrase with another that is closely related to it. Instead of a part representing the whole, as in synecdoche, metonymy uses an associated concept to stand in for something. For instance, when people say, "The White House issued a statement," they aren't referring to the building itself but to the U.S. government or the president. The association between the White House and the executive branch of government is so strong that the building becomes a stand-in for the institution.

This device works particularly well in political and journalistic language, where concise phrasing is essential. Saying "The Kremlin" to represent the Russian government or "Hollywood" to refer to the American film industry is an example of metonymy, which uses widely recognized symbols to represent much broader ideas.

Both synecdoche and metonymy rely on shared understanding. Their effectiveness comes from the audience's ability to recognize the associations being made instantly. These rhetorical devices don't just evoke images—they evoke entire concepts or institutions with just a few words. This can be especially powerful in persuasion, where the economy of language is often necessary to make an impact.

Speakers and writers can use synecdoche and metonymy to say a lot with just a little. They add depth to language by calling on the audience's knowledge and experience, allowing the communicator to tap into a well of shared meaning.

Hyperbole and Praeteritio

While some rhetorical devices rely on precision and balance, others, like hyperbole and praeteritio, work by stretching the truth or drawing attention to what isn't said. These techniques allow speakers and writers to manipulate the focus of their audience, either through overstatement or by the sly art of omission. Both can be powerful tools in persuasion, mainly when used in conjunction with other rhetorical strategies.

Hyperbole is a deliberate exaggeration for emphasis. It isn't meant to be taken literally but emphasizes the speaker's point's importance, emotion, or extremity. When someone says, "I'm so hungry I could eat a horse," no one expects them to consume an actual horse; instead, it's a vivid way of expressing extreme hunger. Hyperbole adds a dramatic flair to language and can inspire strong emotional reactions.

In literature, hyperbole has long been a staple of descriptive writing. Homer's Odyssey, for example, describes Odysseus's journey across "wine-dark seas" and countless dangers with such exaggeration that his heroism seems larger than life. This overstatement elevates Odysseus to a near-mythic figure, making his struggles feel monumental and his victories even more awe-inspiring.

In political oratory, hyperbole is often used to heighten the stakes of a situation. A politician might declare, "This election will decide the future of our children and our children's children," knowing full well that no single election can resolve such far-reaching issues but emphasizing the significance of the moment to engage voters emotionally. It's a tool that works best when the speaker aims to inspire passion or urgency.

Praeteritio (or paralipsis) is the rhetorical technique of claiming not to mention something while drawing attention to it. When someone says, "I won't even bring up my opponent's scandals," they bring those scandals to the listener's attention. This device allows the speaker to mention something while appearing to take the high road, making it a beneficial tactic in debates, legal arguments, or political speeches.

Cicero was a master of praeteritio in his speeches. In one famous example, he stated, "I will not speak of my adversary's corruption and incompetence," thereby planting the seeds of those accusations in the minds of his audience. Cicero introduced this idea into the conversation by claiming not to say something without seeming overtly hostile or aggressive.

Praeteritio is often used in political rhetoric. It allows speakers to subtly insert information without appearing aggressive. It's clever to mention something unsavory about an opponent or situation while maintaining an air of restraint.

Both hyperbole and praeteritio work by playing with expectations. Hyperbole blows things out of proportion, while praeteritio brings things in by pretending not to. Each technique shifts the audience's focus differently, allowing speakers and writers to control how their message is received and what sticks in their listeners' minds.

Anadiplosis and Zeugma

Anadiplosis and zeugma are rhetorical devices that add depth, emphasis, and cohesion to a message. Repeating keywords or using a single word to link multiple ideas these techniques helps create fluid transitions and establish relationships between concepts, ultimately making an argument more compelling and memorable.

Anadiplosis is the repetition of the last word of a sentence or clause at the beginning of the next one. This technique builds momentum, creating a chain of thought that advances the argument or narrative. Each link reinforces the previous point while leading into the next one, giving the audience a sense of progression.

One of the most well-known examples comes from Yoda in *Star Wars*:

"Fear leads to anger. Anger leads to hate. Hate leads to suffering."

Each repetition in this statement builds on the previous one, illustrating the escalation of negative emotions. The repetition emphasizes the natural progression, guiding the listener through the logic of Yoda's warning.

In literature, anadiplosis can create tension and rhythm, as seen in the film *Gladiator*:

"The general who became enslaved. The enslaved person who became a gladiator. The gladiator who defied an emperor."

Here, the repetition emphasizes the character's transformation, intensifying the stakes with each journey step.

Zeugma, conversely, involves using a single word, typically a verb or adjective, to govern two or more words in a sentence, often in different contexts or senses. It can create a witty or impactful effect by linking ideas that might not seem connected.

For example:

"She broke his car and his heart."

In this sentence, the verb "broke" applies to the car and the heart, but in different senses—one literal and the other metaphorical. The dual meaning adds an emotional layer to the otherwise straightforward sentence.

Another example of zeugma is:

"He lost his coat and his temper."

Again, the verb "lost" links two types of loss, combining a physical and emotional experience and amplifying the statement's impact.

These devices are particularly effective because they create a sense of unity within a message, tying different ideas together economically and impactfully. Anadiplosis uses repetition to build a sequence of thought, while zeugma uses a single word to link multiple concepts, often creating a clever or surprising effect. Both can add depth and elegance to rhetoric, allowing for more sophisticated argumentation and persuasion.

Antimetabole and Tmesis

As we move deeper into rhetorical techniques, antimetabole, and tmesis offer more complex ways to play with language. These devices rely on altering the structure of words or phrases to emphasize particular ideas, often creating dramatic effects that leave a lasting impression on the audience.

Antimetabole is repeating words in successive clauses but in reverse grammatical order. This technique creates a mirror effect, reinforcing an idea by flipping its structure. The most famous example comes from John F. Kennedy's inaugural address:

"Ask not what your country can do for you—ask what you can do for your country."

The reversal of the phrases shifts the focus from passive expectation to active responsibility, making the statement memorable and inspiring. Antimetabole forces the listener to reconsider the exact words in a new light, providing a fresh perspective on the original idea.

In philosophy, Antimetabole can distill complex arguments into digestible phrases. For instance, the statement, "We do not remember days; we remember moments." This use of reversal shifts the focus from the passage of time to the significance of specific events, heightening the emotional impact and prompting the audience to reflect on the meaning behind the words.

Tmesis, conversely, involves the insertion of a word or phrase into another word or compound word. It's a more playful and dramatic device, often used to add emphasis or a conversational tone to the language. One famous example is the phrase:

"This is fan-bloody-tastic!"

Transforming "bloody" into "fantastic" emphasizes the speaker's enthusiasm. Tmesis disrupts the normal flow of speech, drawing attention to the inserted word and heightening its impact.

In casual conversation, Tmesis is often used to intensify emotions or sentiments, as in:

"Un-freaking-believable!"

The break in the word amplifies the speaker's astonishment, emphasizing the emotional weight behind the statement.

Both antimetabole and tmesis manipulate structure to enhance meaning. Antimetabole uses reversal to force the audience to engage with the statement differently, while tmesis breaks up words to add intensity or flair. These techniques offer more advanced layers of persuasion, playing with the rhythm and structure of language to keep the audience engaged.

Hyperbole and Allusion

While hyperbole and allusion seem like contrasting tools—one thrives on overstatement, while the other relies on subtlety—enhance a message's emotional and intellectual weight. These devices add layers to language, making it more vivid and memorable by heightening emotions or drawing upon shared cultural knowledge.

Hyperbole is the deliberate exaggeration to emphasize a point or convey strong feelings. It is not meant to be taken literally but to evoke a heightened emotional response from the audience. For example, saying, "I've told you a million times," doesn't mean the speaker has made the statement a million times; instead, it underscores the speaker's frustration or impatience.

Hyperbole is often used in literature and everyday speech to express the intensity of emotions or situations. Consider Shakespeare, who uses hyperbole to express the overwhelming feelings of love and desire. In *Romeo and Juliet*, Romeo proclaims, "With love's light wings did I o'erperch these walls; for stony limits cannot hold love out." Here, the exaggeration speaks to the boundless, unstoppable force of love, suggesting that physical obstacles cannot contain the power of emotion.

In rhetoric, hyperbole can be an effective way to grab attention, stir passion, or underscore the significance of an argument. Politicians might say, "This is the most important election of our lifetime," using hyperbole to motivate action and convey the urgency of a particular moment.

Allusion, on the other hand, is a more subtle technique. It involves indirectly referencing a person, place, event, or piece of literature that the speaker expects the audience to recognize. This device works because it relies on shared knowledge between the speaker and the audience, allowing the speaker to convey complex ideas or emotions with a single reference.

For example, referring to someone as "Scrooge" immediately brings to mind Charles Dickens's A Christmas Carol and the character of Ebenezer Scrooge, known for his greed and lack of generosity. This single word conveys a wealth of information and judgment without further explanation.

In his speeches, Barack Obama often used allusion to significant effect, referencing historical figures or literary works to connect with his audience on a deeper level. By alluding to figures like Abraham Lincoln or moments like the Civil Rights Movement, Obama invoked shared ideals and history, creating a sense of continuity and purpose in his message.

In persuasive writing or speech, hyperbole and allusion serve complementary purposes. Hyperbole grabs attention and amplifies emotion, while allusion connects the present to the past, tapping into shared cultural memory to give the message additional weight.

Combining Rhetorical Techniques for Maximum Impact

The true art of persuasion lies in combining rhetorical devices like hyperbole, allusion, anaphora, antithesis, and more to craft a message that resonates on multiple levels—emotionally, intellectually, and even culturally. When used together, these techniques enhance each other, creating a layered and compelling narrative that draws the audience in and keeps them engaged.

Consider how Martin Luther King Jr.'s "I Have a Dream" speech weaves anaphora, allusion, and hyperbole into one cohesive message. The repetition of "I have a dream" is the heartbeat of the speech, driving the rhythm and reinforcing the message of hope and equality. His allusions to the Emancipation Proclamation and the Declaration of Independence invoke the shared ideals of freedom and justice, while his use of hyperbole—envisioning a world transformed by love and equality—stirs the audience's emotions and inspires action.

Another excellent example is John F. Kennedy's inaugural address, which uses antimetabole, parallelism, and allusion to elevate the speech. "Ask not what your country can do for you—ask what you can do for your country" is a perfect example of antimetabole, flipping expectations and challenging the listener to reconsider their role in civic life. Throughout the speech, parallel structure reinforces his calls to action, while subtle allusions to America's historical struggles for freedom underscore his vision for the future.

When expertly combined, these rhetorical devices do more than emphasize a point; they create a narrative structure that builds toward an emotional and intellectual crescendo. Whether persuading a courtroom, rallying a nation, or writing a novel, language's power lies in its ability to unite logic with emotion, history with vision, and simplicity with complexity.

In mastering the use of these rhetorical techniques, you are equipped to not only communicate more effectively but also persuade with nuance, depth, and clarity. Each tool at your disposal—whether repetition, contrast, exaggeration, or allusion—helps to create a message that resonates far beyond the moment. Persuasion is more important than ever, crafting a message that cuts through the noise and reaches people on a deep level is invaluable.

MOBOCRACY: LESSONS FROM CICERO AND MODERN MOB MENTALITY

HOW THE ANCIENT ROMAN STATESMAN AND RECENT EVENTS WARN OF THE DANGERS OF GROUPTHINK

"Wise men speak because they have something to say; fools because they have to say something."

Plato

Cicero wasn't born with a silver spoon—or any spoon, for that matter. Born in the backwater town of Arpinum in 106 BC, he was what's known as a "novus homo," a new man in the snobbish circles of Roman politics. No noble lineage, no ancestral Senate seat—just raw talent and a determination that could move mountains.

He didn't become Rome's greatest orator overnight. Cicero spent years sharpening his skills, studying philosophy and rhetoric under the finest teachers in Greece. When he returned to Rome, he didn't just make speeches; he orchestrated verbal symphonies. His words had clarity, logic, and an emotional punch that left audiences spellbound.

Cicero believed that to sway an audience, you had to touch their hearts, convince their minds, and stand as a figure they could trust. He tailored his speeches to whoever was listening—the elite Senators, a jury in a courtroom, or the everyday Roman citizen grabbing wine at the local tavern.

His speeches were legendary. The "Philippics" against Mark Antony? Verbal daggers. The "Catilinarian Orations" denouncing Catiline? Pure rhetorical firepower. He exposed corrupt officials, defended the unjustly accused, and became the Republic's guardian. But as with any great hero, his downfall was just around the corner.

Lucius Sergius Catiline's family tree was as old as Rome, tracing back to Sergestus, a buddy of the mythical Prince Aeneas. But noble birth doesn't guarantee noble behavior. Catiline was infamous for his wild lifestyle, cruelty, and insatiable thirst for power, which made him dangerous.

By 63 BC, Catiline was drowning in debt and bitterness. He'd failed multiple times to secure the position of Consul, and watching Cicero—a nobody from nowhere—rise to power was salt in the wound. He despised Cicero, viewing him as an upstart who dared to challenge the established order. So, what's a disgruntled aristocrat to do? Plot a conspiracy, of course.

The Catiline Conspiracy was as bold as it was ruthless. To win favor among the masses, Catiline planned to assassinate critical Senators, including Cicero, seize control of the government, and wipe out debts. He gathered a rogue's gallery of co-conspirators: disgraced aristocrats like Publius Cornelius Lentulus Sura, embittered veterans under Gaius Manlius, and anyone with a grudge against the status quo.

They plotted right under Rome's nose, with Catiline's forces amassing in Etruria. The plan was to strike during the consular elections, catching everyone off guard. It might have worked, too, if not for Cicero's network of informants. Think of it as Rome's first intelligence agency, minus the gadgets.

On November 8, 63 BC, Cicero stood before the Senate and unleashed the first Catilinarian Orations. "How long, O Catiline, will you abuse our patience?" he thundered. It was a mic-drop moment. He laid bare the entire conspiracy, naming names and detailing plots. Catiline was caught off guard and tried to play it cool but soon fled to join his forces, leaving his co-conspirators to face the music.

With the Senate in a panic, Cicero was granted the senatus consultum ultimum, essentially emergency powers to protect the Republic. He ordered the arrest of the remaining conspirators. Here's where things get sticky. Roman law, specifically the Porcian Laws, protected citizens from execution without a trial. But Cicero argued that desperate times called for desperate measures.

During the heated Senate debate, Julius Caesar—yes, *that* Caesar—advocated for leniency, suggesting imprisonment. Maybe he was playing politics; perhaps he saw an opportunity down the line. But Cato the Younger, ever the stoic moralist, demanded immediate execution. Cicero, weighing the risks, sided with Cato. The conspirators were executed without trial, strangled in the dank depths of the Tullianum dungeon.

Initially, Cicero was hailed as a hero—the savior of Rome, the "Pater Patriae," or Father of the Fatherland. But glory is fleeting. He violated one of Rome's core legal principles by executing citizens without due process. Fast-forward five years, and Cicero's political enemies, led by the cunning Publius Clodius Pulcher, seized the moment. They passed a law targeting anyone who executed Roman citizens without trial. Cicero was exiled, his property ransacked, and his status shattered.

Cicero undermined the laws that held Rome together in his zeal to protect the Republic. He set a dangerous precedent that the ends justify the means in times of crisis. This is a slippery slope that future generations will struggle with repeatedly.

Drawing from Cicero's missteps, a young lawyer named Abraham Lincoln sensed a storm brewing in America's soul. In 1838, he stood before the Young Men's Lyceum of Springfield, Illinois, and delivered a speech that would echo through history: "The Perpetuation of Our Political Institutions." Lincoln warned about the dangers of mob rule—what he termed "mobocracy"—and the internal threats that could dismantle the nation.

At the time, America was barely 60 years old, still finding its footing. Economic turmoil from the Panic of 1837 had left the nation reeling. Unemployment soared, banks failed, and social tensions boiled over.

Lincoln lived modestly, sharing a room above a general store and often relying on friends for necessities.

Two incidents weighed heavily on Lincoln's mind. The first was the brutal lynching of Francis J. McIntosh, a free Black man who was burned alive by a mob in St. Louis after killing a deputy in self-defense. The second was the murder of Elijah Parish Lovejoy, an abolitionist newspaper editor, killed by a mob in Alton, Illinois. These acts of lawlessness weren't just isolated events but symptoms of a deeper malaise threatening the nation's moral fabric.

Lincoln argued that the greatest danger to America wasn't from foreign invaders but from within. "If destruction is our lot, we must be its author and finisher," he declared. He feared that unchecked mob violence would erode public trust in the government and the rule of law. His solution was a collective recommitment to legal principles: "Let reverence for the laws... become the political religion of the nation."

He cautioned that if people lost faith in the justice system, ambitious demagogues—"men of sufficient talent and ambition"—would seize power. This was a prophetic warning that underscored the fragile nature of democracy.

But history has a nasty habit of repeating itself. District Attorney Mike Nifong, facing a brutal reelection campaign, saw an opportunity in the sensational allegations against three Duke University lacrosse players accused of sexual assault.

Despite glaring inconsistencies in the accuser's story and DNA evidence exonerating the players, Nifong charged ahead. He made inflammatory public statements, withheld exculpatory evidence, and manipulated witness testimonies. This was prosecutorial misconduct at its worst.

Nifong's actions mirrored Cicero's fatal error: prioritizing ambition over the rule of law. In both cases, the mob's clamor provided cover for unethical behavior. Nifong was eventually disbarred, but not before innocent lives were nearly destroyed.

Mob mentality isn't just a relic of ancient Rome or cautionary tales from American history; it's a recurring nightmare. The Reign of Terror during the French Revolution saw thousands guillotined without fair trials. Kristallnacht in Nazi Germany unleashed orchestrated violence against Jewish communities, marking a horrifying escalation of the Holocaust.

In the United States, lynchings terrorized African Americans for decades. The Tulsa Race Massacre of 1921 saw a prosperous Black community decimated by white mobs, resulting in hundreds of deaths and leaving thousands homeless.

During the Boston Massacre, British soldiers, harassed by a jeering mob, fired into the crowd, killing five colonists. The incident inflamed anti-British sentiments but posed a critical question: Could justice prevail amid such fervor?

John Adams was a lawyer who would later become the second President of the United States. Despite overwhelming public outrage, Adams agreed to defend the British soldiers. He risked his reputation and safety because he believed everyone deserved a fair trial.

In court, Adams dismantled the prosecution's case. He highlighted inconsistencies, challenged witness credibility, and emphasized the chaos of that night. His closing argument resonated: "Facts are stubborn things, and whatever may be our wishes... they cannot alter the state of facts and evidence."

Adams appealed to the jury's sense of justice over vengeance. He warned against the perils of mob rule and the importance of upholding the law. His efforts paid off. Six of the eight soldiers were acquitted; the other two were convicted of manslaughter, not murder, and received reduced sentences.

Adams' defense wasn't just about the soldiers; it was a stand for the kind of nation America aspired to be—one governed by laws, not by the whims of the crowd.

Power is a potent force capable of upholding and undermining justice. Cicero's downfall came when he let fear and ambition override legal principles. Nifong's disgrace resulted from sacrificing ethics for personal gain. Both men crossed lines that should never have been crossed.

Lincoln and Adams, however, understood that the bedrock of a just society is the unwavering commitment to the rule of law. They recognized that when leaders succumb to the seduction of power or the frenzy of the mob, they risk unraveling the very fabric of civilization. These lessons are more relevant than ever. Prosecutors, politicians, and anyone wielding authority must exercise restraint and integrity. The siren song of public approval or personal ambition should never drown out the call of justice.

When we start justifying the erosion of legal safeguards for expedience or popularity, we set dangerous precedents. We inch closer to the point where the rule of law gives way to the rule of the mob.

Where the call of the mob rules postmodernity, fascism is sure to follow. The bent narratives of Ciceros reign and its victims are always justice, fairness, equality, and the rule of law. Maintaining this order requires two things: first, an adherence to some form of belief system that seeks to apply rational thought, and second, application of that rational thought as a matter of course. Societies naturally create this through justice systems, and religions naturally create this through commandments and religious traditions. For Carl Sagan, the creation of a guiding logical light must have common characteristics.

THE DEMON HAUNTED WORLD: LESSONS FROM CARL SAGAN ON REASON AND PASSION

USING CRITICAL THINKING TO COMBAT DECEPTION AND FIND PURPOSE

"I worry that, especially as the Millennium edges nearer, pseudo-science and superstition will seem year by year more tempting, the siren song of unreason more sonorous and attractive. Whenever our ethnic or national prejudices are aroused, in times of scarcity, during challenges to national self-esteem or nerve, when we agonize about our diminished cosmic place and purpose, or when fanaticism is bubbling up around us—then, habits of thought familiar from ages past reach for the controls. The candle flame gutters. Its little pool of light trembles. Darkness gathers. The demons begin to stir."

Carl Sagan

Carl Sagan's passion for reason and science wasn't just born out of academic curiosity—it was deeply personal. Growing up, Sagan faced significant personal tragedies, including the loss of his parents at a young age. Such emotional upheaval could have easily pushed him toward the comforting promises of mysticism and faith—the allure of afterlife reunions, unseen forces guiding us, or spiritual connections that transcend empirical understanding. But instead of seeking solace in these comforting ideas, Sagan turned to logic and science as his way of coping with life's uncertainties.

For him, science wasn't merely a method; it was a fortress against the false promises that mysticism offers. He saw firsthand how easily people could be seduced by simple answers—crystal healing, psychics, or the tantalizing promises of an afterlife. Sagan rejected these notions not because they didn't provide emotional comfort but couldn't be proven. He committed lifelong to grounding his beliefs and working in what could be demonstrated and tested—a faithful adherent to the scientific process.

In one of his most famous quotes, Sagan criticized the rise of pseudoscientific beliefs, noting how people were "clutching crystals" and placing faith in things without evidence. To him, this drift toward mysticism wasn't just a harmless exercise in wishful thinking; it was a dangerous trend. The more society placed its trust in the mystical and the unverifiable, the further it drifted from the clarity and rigor of science.

Sagan's advocacy for skepticism wasn't about being cynical or dismissive. It was about maintaining balance—being open-minded enough to entertain new ideas yet grounded enough in logic to reject those that didn't stand up to scrutiny. He understood that the human mind is prone to cognitive biases, making us vulnerable to believing things that aren't true. That's why he developed the Baloney Detection Kit—a mental toolkit designed to help us navigate the world of misinformation, false promises, and pseudoscience.

For Sagan, science and logic were the best defenses against our natural tendency to fall for comforting myths. His commitment to science was as much a personal defense against emotional pain as a public mission to protect society from ignorance.

He saw the alternative to science as dangerous. He observed that belief in mysticism and pseudoscience could lead to manipulation, false hope, and the erosion of critical thinking. The antidote was clear: reason, logic, and a firm commitment to the scientific method. These tools could safeguard humanity from the seductive pull of the unknown and the unverifiable.

Sagan warned that we are increasingly drifting toward emotionally charged rhetoric and half-truths. Logical reasoning will save us, whether we're deciding which medicine to take, how to understand the universe, or how to sift through the endless information we consume daily.

Sagan knows that mysticism's allure is strong. It offers easy answers, emotional comfort, and the promise of a reality kinder than the one dictated by science and logic. But for Carl Sagan, mysticism was more than just a harmless pursuit—it was a dangerous force that threatened to pull people away from rational thought and critical inquiry.

Sagan viewed mysticism as a retreat into false certainty. When life's biggest questions—Why are we here? What happens after death?—feel out of reach, mysticism provides a simple, prepackaged belief system. Whether it's clutching crystals, psychic readings, or claims of communicating with the dead, these forms of mysticism don't require the rigor of scientific validation. They appeal directly to our System 1 thinking—the fast, emotional, and instinctual part of our brains that seeks immediate comfort.

But the danger was apparent to Sagan: these easy answers stop people from asking hard questions. They encourage acceptance without inquiry, belief without evidence, and forgoing the arduous but rewarding process of System 2 thinking—the slow, deliberate thought that leads to fundamental understanding. Once a society begins to abandon logic and skepticism in favor of mysticism, it risks falling into ignorance and irrationality.

The comfort of mysticism comes at a high price. While it may offer emotional solace, it blinds people to the truth and leaves them vulnerable to manipulation. Mysticism, with its reliance on unverifiable claims, often acts as a gateway to pseudoscience, conspiracy theories, and even political or religious exploitation.

In his book *The Demon-Haunted World*, Sagan expressed deep concern over how mysticism could cloud public understanding of science. He referred to this as the rise of a "demon-haunted world" where supernatural explanations replace scientific reasoning. This wasn't just evident in fringe beliefs but permeated mainstream culture. He noticed how easily people turned to pseudoscientific claims about health, the universe, or human nature—because those claims were more accessible to digest than the complex, often unsatisfying realities of science.

Sagan was deeply committed to skepticism—not as a form of rejection or cynicism, but as a healthy intellectual discipline. He argued that skepticism is the counterbalance to mysticism. It's the process of questioning claims, seeking evidence, and demanding that explanations hold up to scrutiny. Skepticism, for him, was a mental shield against the comforting lies that mysticism often provides.

Sagan's philosophy was centered on the idea that while we should remain open to new ideas, we shouldn't abandon our critical faculties. He famously said we should keep our minds open but "not so open that our brains fall out." This advice is more relevant than ever, as we are increasingly saturated with misinformation, conspiracy theories, and viral falsehoods.

Sagan understood the appeal of mysticism—it offers quick, emotionally satisfying answers—but he also knew the dangers of a society that rejects evidence and logic. For him, mysticism threatened the foundations of a rational, scientifically literate society.

The battle between mysticism and rational thought isn't just an intellectual exercise. It affects our daily decisions regarding the medicine we take, the policies we support, or how we understand the world around us.

Unlike Gore, Sagan's campaign for rational thought didn't just oppose mysticism; he offered a solution. His Baloney Detection Kit was designed to give us the tools needed to evaluate the claims we encounter in our everyday lives. It was a framework for identifying falsehoods, avoiding cognitive traps, and protecting ourselves from being misled by comforting but false narratives. By empowering people with the ability to think critically, Sagan hoped to create a society that could resist the pull of mysticism and engage in a deeper, more meaningful pursuit of truth.

The kit was born from his understanding that humans are naturally prone to cognitive errors without structure. Our brains are wired to seek patterns, follow authority, and take mental shortcuts when processing complex information. While these tendencies help us navigate daily life, they also make us vulnerable to manipulation. Whether it's a false guru promising easy wealth or a conspiracy theory masquerading as truth, we're easily led astray without a structured approach to evaluating these claims.

The Baloney Detection Kit precisely provides a structured method for distinguishing fact from fiction. It's not a physical toolkit but a mental framework encouraging skepticism, critical analysis, and logical rigor. For Sagan, this toolkit wasn't just for scientists—it was for everyone because critical thinking tools are as essential in everyday life as they are in the laboratory.

At its core, the Baloney Detection Kit is built around fundamental principles:

• Independent Confirmation of Facts: Don't take anything at face value. Always seek independent verification of any claim. This principle has never been more critical in an age of viral misinformation.

• Encourage Debate on the Evidence: Scientific discourse thrives on debate. Open discussion is essential to refine ideas and test their validity. Encouraging discussion can discourage weak arguments, and only the most sound ideas prevail.

• Arguments from Authority Carry Little Weight: Just because someone is an expert doesn't mean their claims should be accepted without question. The evidence—not the authority—must stand on its own.

• Consider Multiple Hypotheses: There's often more than one way to explain a phenomenon. A claim's validity must be tested against all possible explanations, not just the most obvious or popular one. This helps avoid confirmation bias.

• Don't Get Attached to a Hypothesis: It's crucial to remain objective and willing to change your mind when new evidence emerges. Emotional investment can cloud judgment.

- Quantifiable Claims: A claim must be measurable to be scientifically valid. It's much harder to test and evaluate if it's not quantifiable. Sagan emphasized the importance of objective, data-driven approaches to truth.

- Occam's Razor: When presented with competing hypotheses, choose the one with the fewest assumptions. This helps avoid overcomplicating explanations.

- Falsifiability: A key concept in science is that a claim must be testable and capable of being proven wrong for a claim to be valid. If a claim cannot be falsified, it's not within the realm of scientific inquiry.

- Burden of Proof: The responsibility for proving a claim lies with the person making it. Extraordinary claims require extraordinary evidence.

Sagan's Baloney Detection Kit was revolutionary because it brought critical thinking down from the ivory tower and made it accessible to the general public. It wasn't just for academics or scientists—it was for anyone navigating the complexities of a world filled with dubious claims. From television ads selling questionable products to political rhetoric designed to manipulate emotions, Sagan's toolkit defended against the everyday onslaught of baloney.

His Baloney Detection Kit is relevant beyond science because it resembles the principles underlying our justice system. Just as Sagan encourages skepticism and careful evaluation of evidence, so does the legal process. In courtrooms worldwide, facts are verified through cross-examination, evidence is weighed carefully, and arguments must withstand scrutiny from all sides.

- Independent Confirmation is echoed when a jury hears evidence from multiple witnesses.

- Falsifiability aligns with the need for claims in court to be testable, with the burden of proof placed on the accuser.

- Encouraging Debate mirrors the legal process where lawyers challenge each other's claims, ensuring that only the most substantiated arguments stand.

In essence, the principles of the Baloney Detection Kit form the bedrock of critical thinking not just in science but in any field where truth, evidence, and rationality are paramount.

Sagan knew his framework could serve as a bulwark against the rise of mysticism, pseudoscience, and manipulation. However, the world he warned about has become a reality where people turn to comforting but false ideas instead of rational inquiry. His concerns about irrational thinking have manifested across the globe.

The Baloney Detection Kit provides a System 2 thinking shield against this. It forces us to pause, ask for evidence, and demand accountability from those making claims. Sagan recognized that the real danger of pseudoscience wasn't just that it was wrong—it was that it often sounded convincing. Without a system for detecting falsehoods, it's easy to fall victim to the charms of those who peddle easy answers to complicated problems. Without logic as a grounding force, we risk confusion, where nothing is verifiable, and everything is debatable. Sagan believed this was the pathway to a society built on superstition and pseudoscience, not progress and enlightenment.

Sagan's response to postmodern relativism was not to dismiss it entirely but to offer a structured alternative. His Baloney Detection Kit is, in many ways, a direct response to the postmodern condition. It provides a method for evaluating claims where truth seems increasingly elusive. It asks us to maintain an open mind but insists that we ground our beliefs in evidence—not just cultural or ideological constructs.

In rejecting the traps of postmodernism, Sagan wasn't advocating for a rigid, unyielding view of the world. His skepticism was structured but flexible—a balancing act between curiosity and doubt. For him, being skeptical didn't mean rejecting everything outright; it meant applying a formal system to evaluate claims based on the strength of their evidence. In doing so, he avoided the nihilism that postmodern thought can lead to, where everything is up for debate, but nothing can be resolved. For Sagan, skepticism was not an end but a tool for building a clearer picture of the world.

This formal system of thinking could be applied to any claim—from the mundane to the profound. Whether examining an outlandish pseudo-scientific claim or investigating a complex legal case, Sagan's principles hold up. They force us to ask hard questions, seek evidence, and apply logic in a way that guards against the emotional or cultural biases that often cloud our judgment.

In hyperreality, even the most reliable Baloney Detection Kit is prone to abuse in the era of mass media. The L.A. County Court System during the O.J. trial, or the Johnny Depp and Amber Heard case, exemplify this, as discussed in a later chapter. First, we must explore an essential victim of postmodernity that erodes the core components of our logic and communication.

THE NESTING DOLLS OF LANGUAGE: DECONSTRUCTING "TRUTH" BEYOND SEMANTICS

EXAMINING HOW LANGUAGE SHAPES REALITY AND MEANING

"Language is the source of misunderstandings."

Antoine de Saint-Exupéry

Charged with emotion and layered with complexity, our exchanges of ideas are often hijacked by the very words we use. Language has evolved beyond mere communication; it shapes realities, influences perceptions, and even commodifies our interactions. As Jean Baudrillard suggested, we live in a hyperreal world where language—once a medium to convey meaning—has become a reflection of itself, a system of symbols that create and consume our reality. Language exchanges ideas, packages them, brands them, and sells them. The language we use reflects our thoughts and influences our perception of truth.

Conversations often shift away from genuine exploration of ideas to get bogged down in debates over semantics and interpretations. We witness dialogues that drift away from substance, morphing into disputes over definitions, cultural contexts, and implied meanings. The discourse becomes convoluted, leaving less room for the clear, logical progression of thought. As language becomes increasingly performative, each word choice carries the weight of identity, allegiance, and ideological positioning. The focus skews toward winning the language game rather than uncovering the truth.

For this reason, we must return to argumentation that is precise, logical, and free from the noise of definitional differences. This is where symbolic logic holds value—offering a pathway to clarity, a means to cut through the clutter. In symbolic logic, ideas are stripped down to their core components, allowing us to examine their structure without the baggage of linguistic subjectivity. Symbolic logic forces us to confront the validity of an argument, independent of the emotional charge words might carry. By embracing this approach, we reclaim the ability to engage in meaningful debates that hinge on the integrity of ideas and not on the language that encases them.

In the intricate dance of persuasion and debate, it's not enough to present a compelling argument; one must also be skilled at recognizing and dismantling the faulty reasoning that can sway an audience if left unchecked. This is where the power of understanding logical fallacies comes into play—those subtle errors in reasoning that can seem convincing but ultimately lack the foundation of sound logic.

With his Baloney Detection Kit, Carl Sagan was an early advocate for the idea that critical thinking and logic are essential tools for avoiding the traps set by these fallacies. His principles warn against the allure of arguments made from authority, personal attacks, and emotional manipulation and encourage a return to evidence-based reasoning.

At the heart of logical reasoning lies symbolic logic, which allows us to strip an argument of its rhetoric and examine its bare structure. Consider the provocative example: "All Nazis have great teeth" and "All British have great teeth." While the content of these claims may elicit different emotional reactions, symbolic logic teaches us that both statements are equally incomplete—they are mere premises without sufficient evidence to support them. This underscores Sagan's advice to avoid taking arguments from authority or emotion at face value.

In symbolic logic, the validity of an argument doesn't depend on who is making the claim but on whether the claim is logically sound. Both the

THE NESTING DOLLS OF LANGUAGE: DECONSTRUCTING "T... | 137

Nazi and British examples fail because they lack a whole logical structure to prove the conclusion. Logic demands that we go beyond the authority or emotional weight of the speaker and focus instead on the coherence of the argument.

The syllogism, a form of deductive reasoning rooted in Aristotle's teachings, is one of the most powerful tools for constructing airtight arguments. At its core, a syllogism follows a simple structure:

- Major Premise: A broad, accepted truth.
- Minor Premise: A specific instance that relates to the central premise.
- Conclusion: A necessary outcome that follows from the two premises.
- For example:
- Major Premise: All individuals who knowingly give false testimony commit perjury.
- Minor Premise: The witness knowingly gave false testimony.
- Conclusion: Therefore, the witness committed perjury.

This form of reasoning becomes particularly potent in cross-examination, where the goal is to corner a witness with irrefutable logic. Each question leads them toward a logical trap where they cannot avoid the conclusion. In a contract dispute, for instance:

-

- Major Premise: A party knowingly breaches a contract is liable for damages.
- Minor Premise: The defendant knowingly breached the contract.
- Conclusion: Therefore, the defendant is liable for damages.

The lawyer ensures the conclusion is inescapable by guiding the witness to admit both premises. Mastering the syllogism allows you to take control of the argument and lead your opponent to a conclusion they cannot refute.

However, constructing strong syllogisms is only one side of the coin. Equally important is recognizing and dismantling faulty logic in real-time. Logical fallacies often slip into debates unnoticed, manipulating emotions or appealing to authority without offering valid reasoning. These fallacies can be particularly dangerous in legal settings, as they may mislead juries and distort the truth.

Let's explore some of the most common logical fallacies, how they appear, and how to dismantle them.

Ad Hominem Fallacy

This occurs when the focus shifts from the substance of the argument to attacking the person making it. It's one of the most frequent fallacies in legal settings and political debates.

- Example: "You can't trust this witness—he's a convicted felon!"

- Counter: "Whether or not the witness has a criminal record, what matters is the evidence he has presented."

By steering the argument back to the facts, you demonstrate that personal attacks do not invalidate an argument.

Straw Man Fallacy

This involves distorting an opponent's argument to make it easier to attack. It shifts the focus to a weaker argument, which is quickly dismissed.

- Example: "The plaintiff thinks doctors should be perfect and never make mistakes."

- Counter: "No one is arguing that doctors must be perfect. The issue is whether the doctor met the standard of care."

Clarifying the argument exposes the distortion and redirects attention to the core issue.

False Dilemma (False Dichotomy)

This presents only two choices when more possibilities exist, forcing the audience to choose between extremes and ignoring nuances.

- Example: "Either the defendant was at the crime scene, or he's lying."

- Counter: "Other possibilities exist, such as mistaken identity or faulty memory."

By pointing out other alternatives, you dismantle the fallacy and broaden the scope of the discussion.

Appeal to Emotion

This attempts to sway the audience by appealing to their emotions rather than presenting logical evidence.

- Example: "The family is heartbroken. The defendant must pay for their pain."

- Counter: "While we sympathize with the family, we must focus on whether the defendant's actions legally caused the harm."

By acknowledging the emotion while emphasizing the importance of evidence, you avoid being manipulated by emotional appeals.

Circular Reasoning

This occurs when the conclusion is restated as one of the premises, offering no new information or evidence.

- Example: "The defendant is guilty because he committed the crime."

- Counter: "Can you provide specific evidence that supports this claim rather than repeating the conclusion?"

You force the argument beyond circular reasoning by challenging the speaker to provide evidence.

Post Hoc Ergo Propter Hoc (False Cause)

This fallacy assumes that because one event followed another, the first caused the second.

- Example: "After the new manager took over, profits declined, so the manager must be at fault."

- Counter: "Other factors, such as market conditions, could explain the profit drop. Can you provide evidence linking the manager's actions to the decline?"

By pointing out other possible causes, you undermine the assumption of causality.

Slippery Slope Fallacy

This argues that small action will lead to catastrophic events without evidence of such progression.

- Example: "If we pass this law, the government will control every aspect of our lives."

- Counter: "What evidence is there that this law will lead to such extreme outcomes? Let's focus on the actual implications."

By requiring proof of the alleged chain reaction, you expose the exaggeration.

In his arguments about the definition of a woman, Ben Shapiro frequently engages in a semantic debate focused on rigid definitions based on biology. For example, during public talks and interviews, Shapiro asserts that a woman is strictly defined by biological sex, reducing the term to chromosomal and anatomical characteristics. He often juxtaposes this stance with more fluid or identity-based definitions, which he dismisses as disconnected from "truth" and "reality." By doing so, Shapiro's approach often sidesteps deeper conversations on identity and gender by insisting on a particular definition and treating it as an objective standard against which all others are measured.

This semantic argument exemplifies how debates can devolve into disputes over definitions rather than engaging with the underlying ideas. When Shapiro frames the conversation purely around biological determinism, the dialogue becomes fixated on whether words like "woman" should adhere strictly to anatomical definitions rather than exploring broader societal and philosophical perspectives on gender and identity. As a result, these exchanges can become circular and unproductive, often leading to gridlock where both sides talk past each other rather than truly engage.

This is why symbolic logic and an understanding of fallacious reasoning are so vital. By focusing on the structural validity of arguments, we can cut through these semantic tangles and analyze the core propositions at play. Symbolic logic enables us to move past subjective interpretations of terms and explore the reasoning behind claims, helping clarify arguments and identify fallacies. It allows for a more precise discourse, enabling participants to focus on whether an argument logically follows from its premises rather than getting caught up in debates over language. In doing so, we can aspire to restore communication to its original purpose: the meaningful exchange of ideas grounded in mutual understanding. This precision strengthens our discourse and helps prevent misunderstandings arising from purely definitional disputes.

PART 3

ALCHEMY, INTEGRATION AND L'ART DE LA
PERSUASION POSTMODERNE

CONFRONTING THE SHADOW

OUR INNER TRUTH IS OUR PATH TOWARDS PURPOSE

"Until you make the unconscious conscious, it will direct your life, and you will call it fate."

Carl Jung

In the early 20th Century, Carl Gustav Jung was at the forefront of this exploration. The son of a pastor, Jung was no stranger to the realms of the spiritual and the metaphysical. His upbringing had instilled in him a deep curiosity about the unseen forces that shape human existence.

One evening, Jung contemplated a recurring dream that had haunted him since childhood. In the dream, he descended into the depths of the earth, uncovering hidden chambers and ancient artifacts. Each layer he uncovered seemed to beckon him further, hinting at secrets buried within the very fabric of the human psyche. This dream, rich with symbolism, catalyzed his life's work—a journey into the collective unconscious and the archetypal patterns.

Jung's fascination with the mind's inner workings led him to study medicine and psychiatry. During his early career, he met Sigmund Freud, whose work on psychoanalysis revolutionized the understanding of mental health. The two men formed a close friendship and shared an interest in the unconscious. However, their paths would eventually diverge as Jung ventured beyond the personal unconscious that Freud had mapped into the deeper waters of the collective unconscious—a reservoir of shared human experiences and symbols.

He began to notice patterns in his patients' dreams and fantasies that could not be explained solely by their personal histories. These patterns echoed myths, legends, and religious symbols from cultures worldwide and throughout time. Jung posited that these universal symbols, or archetypes, were innate and inherited, forming the building blocks of the collective unconscious. They manifested in various forms—the wise older man, the nurturing mother, the trickster, and many others—all representing fundamental human motifs.

Among these archetypes, Jung was particularly intrigued by the concept of the shadow. The shadow represented the parts of ourselves that we reject or suppress—our fears, desires, and impulses that we deem unacceptable. He believed that acknowledging and integrating the shadow was essential for achieving wholeness. To ignore it was to risk being unconsciously controlled by these hidden forces, leading to a life that lacked authenticity.

During intense introspection, Jung engaged in "active imagination," allowing his thoughts and fantasies to surface without censorship. One such vision involved a figure named Philemon, an older man with kingfisher wings, who became a mentor within his psyche. Philemon represented wisdom and served as a guide through the labyrinth of Jung's unconscious mind. Jung believed in confronting and embracing all aspects of oneself, even those that seemed foreign or unsettling.

He recognized that the persona, the mask we wear to navigate society, often conceals our true nature. The persona is necessary to some extent —it allows us to function within social norms and expectations. However, over-identification with this mask can lead us to lose touch with our inner selves. We become performers in our lives, chasing goals and desires that are not ours but imposed upon us by external forces.

In contrast, the anima and animus archetypes represent each individual's feminine and masculine qualities, regardless of gender. Jung observed that integrating these contrasexual aspects was crucial for psychological balance. For a man, embracing the anima might involve acknowledging his capacity for empathy, intuition, and nurturing—traditionally associated with femininity. Integrating the animus could mean embracing assertiveness, logic, and strength for a woman. This integration fosters a more complete self, unburdened by rigid gender roles and societal expectations.

Jung's exploration of these concepts was not confined to theoretical musings; he delved into alchemy, mythology, religion, and art to find parallels and deeper understanding. Alchemy, in particular, fascinated him—not as a primitive attempt to turn base metals into gold but as a rich metaphor for personal transformation. The alchemists' quest mirrored the psychological journey toward individuation—becoming one's true self.

He saw alchemical symbols as representations of the inner processes of the psyche. The nigredo, or blackening, symbolized the confrontation with the shadow—the necessary descent into darkness to uncover the hidden aspects of the self. This was followed by the albedo, or whitening, representing purification and integrating these aspects. The culmination was the rubedo, or reddening, signifying the union of opposites and the emergence of the fully realized Self.

Jung's patients often benefited from this symbolic framework. One such patient, a woman struggling with recurring nightmares and feelings of emptiness, found solace in exploring her dreams through the lens of alchemy. By engaging with the symbolic language of her unconscious, she began to uncover repressed emotions and desires. Through this process, she confronted her shadow—acknowledging feelings of anger and resentment she had long denied. This confrontation was not easy; it required courage and honesty. But as she integrated these aspects, she experienced a renewed sense of vitality and authenticity.

Jung understood that the journey toward individuation was deeply personal and often challenging. It required shedding the layers of conditioning that obscure our true selves. This path can feel isolating in a society that values conformity over individuality. Yet, he believed it was the only way to achieve true fulfillment.

He warned of the dangers of neglecting this inner work. Without confronting the shadow, individuals risked projecting their unresolved issues onto others, leading to conflicts and misunderstandings. On a larger scale, this collective shadow could manifest in societal problems—prejudice, violence, and the inability to empathize with others. Jung witnessed the rise of totalitarian regimes in Europe, attributing part of this phenomenon to the collective failure to acknowledge and integrate the shadow.

In his later years, Jung reflected on the importance of reconnecting with the symbols and myths about the human condition. He lamented the modern world's disconnection from these more profound layers of meaning. The relentless pursuit of material success and external validation often led individuals away from their inner truths, resulting in emptiness and disillusionment.

He recounted an encounter with a Native American chief during his travels to New Mexico. The chief spoke of his people's belief that the white man was uneasy and restless, always seeking something but never finding it. Jung realized that this restlessness stemmed from a disconnection with the unconscious and its wisdom. By ignoring the inner voice, people became trapped in a cycle of chasing external achievements that ultimately failed to satisfy.

Jung's writings, such as *"The Archetypes and the Collective Unconscious"* and *"Psychology and Alchemy,"* delve deep into these themes. He used rich, symbolic language to convey the complexities of the psyche, encouraging readers to embark on their journeys of self-discovery. His work emphasized that understanding oneself was not a selfish endeavor but a necessary step toward contributing positively to society.=

He often used the metaphor of a tree to illustrate this idea. The deeper the roots extend into the earth (the unconscious), the higher the branches can reach the sky (conscious awareness). The tree lacks stability and cannot grow to its full potential without strong roots.

Similarly, individuals who neglect their inner worlds may find themselves ungrounded and unable to withstand life's challenges.=

In modern life, Jung's teachings resonate with those who feel adrift in a sea of superficial connections and relentless demands. The pressure to present a curated image on social media, meet societal benchmarks of success, or adhere to prescribed roles can leave one feeling fragmented. Jung invites us to look inward, face the uncomfortable truths that reside within, and embrace the entirety of our being.

By integrating the shadow, acknowledging the anima or animus, and differentiating the persona from the Self, we move closer to authenticity. But the relentless pursuit of experiences, the inundation of information, and the seductive allure of virtual realities have fostered a landscape in which individuals are both everywhere and nowhere, connected yet profoundly isolated.

Jean Baudrillard argued that contemporary society has transitioned from a world of direct experience to one dominated by simulations—representations detached from and ultimately replaced the real. Hyperreality manifests through the proliferation of media, advertising, and technology, which create an endless loop of signs without referents. The result is a culture saturated with simulacra—copies without an original. Individuals consume these simulations, internalizing them as reality, and consequently, their perceptions and identities are shaped by artificial constructs. The self becomes a collage of external influences, disconnected from genuine experiences and inner truths. They become a billboard of a fractured and unreal environment.

When we add Michel Foucault's view, we realize that the messages, symbols, and images we receive from this simulation are very powerful but capable of manipulation as a result of capitalism, oppressive government, or mob rule. His postmodernist critique dismantled the idea of universal truths and grand narratives, emphasizing instead the fluid and constructed nature of reality shaped by dominant power structures. Foucault explored how societal institutions—schools, prisons, hospitals—exert control by defining norms and deviance, thereby regulating behavior and thought.

According to Foucault, discourse propagated through media and institutions dictates what is desirable, normalizing certain behaviors while marginalizing others. This subtle coercion shapes identities, limiting the scope of self-exploration. Internalizing these norms leads to self-surveillance, as individuals police their thoughts and actions to align with societal expectations, further entrenching fragmentation.

Foucault's panopticon predicted that we would surveil each other to monitor adherence to this "truth" as a means of controlling society. This occurs on the fringes of the "woke" movement. People internalize the gaze of "woke" authority, monitoring themselves in accordance with imposed expectations. This mechanism of power operates invisibly, fragmenting the self as individuals negotiate multiple identities prescribed by various discourses. In Foucault's view, the postmodern self is decentered and fragmented, constructed through the interplay of shifting power relations.

The convergence of Jung's, Baudrillard's, and Foucault's theories paints a bleak picture of the contemporary human condition. Self-image fragmentation arises as individuals grapple with integrating their shadow selves amid a hyperreal environment that bombards them with artificial identities and desires. Fragmented societies emerge from the collective impact of these fragmented selves, where authentic connections are supplanted by superficial interactions mediated through screens and algorithms.

In this milieu, the ability to pursue everything everywhere becomes both a boon and a bane. Technological advancements have indeed expanded horizons, granting access to knowledge and experiences once unimaginable. However, this boundless potential often leads to overload and dispersion. The incessant pursuit of new experiences and identities can dilute depth and meaning, fostering a sense of rootlessness and alienation.

Baudrillard's hyperreality exacerbates this fragmentation by creating environments where the pursuit is commodified. Social media platforms, for instance, encourage the curation of idealized personas, fueling comparison and dissatisfaction. The relentless consumption and display cycle reinforces simulations' dominance over authentic self-expression. Individuals become trapped in a feedback loop of validation seeking, their self-worth tethered to external approval metrics.

By confronting and integrating the shadow, individuals can reclaim their disowned parts, fostering a sense of wholeness. This process demands introspection and courage, challenging one to peel away the layers of simulation and external influence to uncover the authentic self. Integration mitigates the projections that fuel societal divisions, promoting empathy and understanding.

Yet, the journey toward integration is fraught with obstacles in a hyperreal, postmodern world. The overwhelming influx of information and the seductive nature of simulations divert attention outward, away from inner reflection. The culture of immediacy and instant gratification undermines the patience required for deep psychological work. Moreover, power structures benefit from maintaining fragmentation, as disempowered individuals are more susceptible to control.

The dangers of a fragmented self and society are manifold. Psychologically, individuals may experience heightened anxiety, depression, and identity crises. Constantly negotiating disparate selves leads to emotional exhaustion and a diminished sense of agency. Socially, the erosion of authentic connections fosters isolation and impedes the development of cohesive communities. The prevalence of echo chambers and polarization stems, in part, from these dynamics, as individuals retreat into enclaves that reflect their constructed identities.

The pursuit of everything everywhere amplifies these issues. The illusion of limitless choice can paradoxically result in paralysis or superficial engagement. As individuals spread themselves thin across myriad experiences, they may struggle to find meaning or satisfaction. The depth is sacrificed for breadth, and the cultivation of skills, relationships, or understanding remains shallow.

A synthesis of the theorists' insights provides guidance on navigating these challenges. Jung encourages turning inward and engaging in practices that promote self-awareness and integration. Mindfulness, therapy, and creative expression are avenues through which individuals can explore their unconscious and reconcile the shadow. This inner work strengthens resilience against external pressures and fosters authentic selfhood.

The journey demands a conscious effort to peel back layers of artifice, confront the shadows within, and question the narratives imposed by external powers. It is a call to rediscover authenticity in an age of endless copies, cultivate depth in a culture of superficiality, and build connections that transcend simulations. In doing so, we reclaim the essence of what it means to be human—a being capable of self-awareness, growth, and genuine connection in a world that often conspires to fragment and distract.

MEGAPINT: SHADOW-WORK AND THE HONEST DEPICTION OF SELF

THE REFRESHING GLARE OF RADICAL ACCEPTANCE AND INDIVIDULIZATION

"It is no measure of health to be well adjusted to a profoundly sick society."

Jiddu Krishnamurti

In 2022, the defamation trial between Johnny Depp and Amber Heard captivated the world with its blend of celebrity drama, legal intrigue, and personal revelations. To fully understand the case and its impact, it is essential to explore the background that led to this high-profile lawsuit, the legal teams involved, and the public sentiment surrounding it before the trial even began.

The roots of the Depp-Heard litigation trace back to their marriage, which began in 2015 and ended in a contentious divorce finalized in 2017. Heard initially filed for a restraining order against Depp, alleging domestic abuse. The couple settled in 2016, and in their joint statement, they described their relationship as "intensely passionate and at times volatile, but always bound by love," denying any intent of physical or emotional harm for financial gain. Depp paid Heard a $7 million divorce settlement, which she publicly pledged to donate to the ACLU and the Children's Hospital of Los Angeles—a commitment that later became a focal point in the defamation trial when questions arose about fulfilling that donation.

The litigation escalated after Heard published an op-ed in *The Washington Post* in December 2018, in which she described herself as a "public figure representing domestic abuse." While she did not name Depp, he filed a defamation lawsuit in March 2019, claiming that the op-ed implied he was an abuser, damaging his career and reputation. Depp sought $50 million in damages. In response, Heard countersued for $100 million, accusing Depp of orchestrating a "smear campaign" and continuing alleged abusive behavior through litigation.

Before this lawsuit, Depp had faced a legal defeat in a separate 2020 libel case in the UK, where he sued *The Sun* newspaper for labeling him a "wife-beater." The court ruled in favor of the newspaper, finding that the majority of Heard's abuse claims had been proven to a civil standard. Despite this setback, Depp pursued his defamation case against Heard in the United States, believing he could achieve a different outcome in the Fairfax County, Virginia court.

The trial's location in Fairfax, Virginia, raised some eyebrows. Depp's legal team chose this venue because The Washington Post's online servers are in Fairfax, allowing them to file the lawsuit there under the state's more plaintiff-friendly defamation laws. This decision was strategic, as Virginia's defamation laws are considered less protective of free speech than those of other jurisdictions, such as California, where Depp and Heard reside.

Brown Rudnick represented Johnny Depp, with Camille Vasquez and Ben Chew leading his legal team. Vasquez quickly became a household name during the trial, known for her sharp, strategic questioning during cross-examinations. Her meticulous approach to highlighting inconsistencies in testimonies and her calm yet assertive style won public admiration. Ben Chew, a seasoned litigator with a strong reputation in defamation cases, helped guide Depp's legal strategy, focusing on challenging Heard's credibility through evidence and witness testimony.

Elaine Bredehoft and Ben Rottenborn represented Amber Heard, an experienced attorney handling complex civil litigation. Their defense strategy included highlighting Depp's past struggles with substance abuse in an attempt to portray him as an unreliable witness prone to erratic behavior. Rottenborn's cross-examinations aimed to cast doubt on Depp's character and suggest that the public had been misled by his charm and celebrity status.

Public sentiment before the trial was deeply divided. Depp's 2020 defeat in the UK had already impacted his reputation, removing him from key film projects, including the *Fantastic Beasts* franchise. Many saw Depp as a fallen star whose career was jeopardized by the abuse allegations. However, a substantial fanbase continued to support him, believing both Heard and the media had wronged him.

Meanwhile, Heard's op-ed and public statements positioned her as a vocal advocate for domestic abuse survivors, but she faced criticism as well. As details of the couple's volatile relationship surfaced, skepticism grew about her claims, particularly regarding inconsistencies in her narrative. Social media fueled these polarized views, with supporters of both sides engaging in a public relations battle before the trial.

This backdrop set the stage for a trial that would be a legal contest and a highly publicized battle over credibility, public perception, and the nature of truth in a media-driven world.

During the trial, Amber Heard's persona took center stage, not just through her testimony but also through her appearance and demeanor. Her courtroom fashion choices—often dark, muted tones, conservative attire, and minimalist makeup—became subjects of public scrutiny. Some observers suggested that her choices were designed to project seriousness and credibility, starkly contrasting her more glamorous public image often seen on red carpets. Commentators noted that Heard appeared to be crafting a new persona for the trial, emphasizing her role as a victim and witness to traumatic events.

However, this carefully curated image faced challenges. During cross-examination, Camille Vasquez exposed discrepancies in Heard's testimony, such as questions regarding the timeline of her charitable donations.

Even before the trial began, rumors and tabloid stories shaped the public's perception of Heard. Stories of her volatile relationships, especially with Depp and Elon Musk, were frequently discussed in the media. The public narrative often oscillated between portraying her as a victim of domestic abuse and as someone possibly manipulating the situation. These conflicting perceptions contributed to the polarized reactions to her testimony in the courtroom. The trial aired live and millions tuned in daily to watch her every move, dissecting her expressions, words, and behavior.

Amber Heard's rise to fame, her high-profile relationships, and the psychological aspects discussed during the trial were deeply intertwined with her courtroom persona. The legal proceedings exposed both the public image she had built and the underlying emotional complexities presented by forensic experts. Her attempt to control her narrative in the courtroom was met with public scrutiny, further influenced by her fashion choices and perceived inconsistencies in her testimony.

Born in Owensboro, Kentucky, in 1963, Johnny Depp was the youngest of four children. His family moved frequently, eventually settling in Florida. Depp's parents divorced when he was 15, contributing to a turbulent childhood marked by frequent relocations and family strife. He dropped out of high school at 16 to pursue a music career, joining a band called The Kids. After the band struggled in Los Angeles, Depp transitioned into acting with the encouragement of actor Nicolas Cage, landing his first significant role in *A Nightmare on Elm Street* (1984).

Depp quickly became a teen idol through the TV show *21 Jump Street* but sought to break away from mainstream fame. He gravitated toward eccentric roles in films like *Edward Scissorhands* (1990), *Benny & Joon* (1993), and *Ed Wood*(1994). By the early 2000s, Depp solidified his status as one of Hollywood's most versatile actors, earning critical acclaim in *Pirates of the Caribbean*, *Finding Neverland*, and *Sweeney Todd*.

Behind the scenes, Depp's life was complex. He has spoken openly about his struggles with substance abuse, which began in his teens. Depp described self-medicating to cope with the pressures of fame and

MEGAPINT: SHADOW-WORK AND THE HONEST DEPICTION ... | 155

unresolved personal issues. His relationships, including high-profile romances with Winona Ryder and Kate Moss, were often tumultuous.

Depp's long-term relationship with French singer Vanessa Paradis, with whom he has two children, provided some stability until they split in 2012. Shortly after, Depp began dating Amber Heard, whom he met on the set of *The Rum Diary*. Their relationship became the subject of intense media attention, marked by allegations of conflict and mutual accusations.

Johnny Depp's testimony in the defamation trial was raw, honest, and uniquely Depp. Unlike Heard, who maintained a carefully controlled demeanor, Depp presented himself with vulnerability, openly discussing his struggles with addiction, his complex relationship with Heard, and the emotional toll of the allegations.

When Depp took the stand, he candidly admitted to his issues with substance abuse, detailing how these challenges had affected his life and relationships. He spoke about his attempts to detox and the difficulties he faced during those periods: "I have not taken an opiate since, and I won't unless I plan on going through the hell of the pure horror of detoxing."

Depp did not shy away from discussing the less favorable aspects of his life—his struggles, his emotions, and the chaotic nature of his relationship with Heard. This transparency provided the jury with a multifaceted view of his character.

Drawing from Carl Jung's concept of the Shadow—the idea that individuals have a darker, unconscious side that they often suppress—Depp's testimony can be seen as an embrace of his Shadow. Acknowledging his flaws and past mistakes, he integrated these aspects into his public persona, demonstrating authenticity.

Depp recounted his childhood trauma, describing his mother's unpredictable and sometimes violent behavior: "My mother... she could become quite violent... she was very unpredictable." This acknowledgment of past pain offered context for his later struggles, allowing the jury to understand the complexities of his experiences.

His demeanor during the trial, which included moments of humor and humility, further humanized him. Depp occasionally made light-hearted remarks, and his reactions were genuine. This approach likely resonated with the jury, presenting him not as a flawless individual but as someone willing to confront and accept his imperfections.

In contrast, Heard's testimony maintained a controlled narrative. During cross-examination, inconsistencies in her statements, such as questions about specific events and timelines, were highlighted. Audio recordings played in court revealed heated exchanges between the couple.

Throughout his testimony, Depp maintained that he had never struck Heard or any woman, stating:

"Never did I reach the point of striking Ms. Heard in any way, nor have I ever struck any woman in my life."

He expressed that the allegations had deeply affected him and his family, emphasizing his desire to clear his name for the sake of his children.

Depp's willingness to expose his vulnerabilities and confront his past aligned with Jungian principles of integrating the Shadow. This authenticity may have strengthened his credibility with the jury, who could see a person acknowledging his flaws rather than hiding them.

Amber Heard's performance during the trial contrasted with Depp's approach. While Depp embraced his complexities, Heard appeared to present a carefully constructed image. Throughout her testimony, she described herself as a victim of abuse, detailing specific incidents and portraying herself as an angel.

Maintaining a false persona is nearly impossible under intense scrutiny. In psychological terms, suppressing aspects of oneself—or one's Shadow—can lead to internal conflicts and external inconsistencies. Jung suggested that failing to acknowledge one's Shadow can result in projections and misalignments between one's public image and private reality.

One of the most notable instances where Heard's constructed persona visibly cracked was during her description of an incident where her dog stepped on a bee. This moment, which quickly became a meme on social media, highlighted the dissonance between her facial expressions and the gravity of her words. While she was attempting to convey distress, her facial expressions appeared exaggerated and almost comical, leading many observers to question the sincerity of her testimony. The jury was getting to see that Amber wasn't a very good actress.

From the beginning of the trial, Amber Heard appeared intent on portraying herself as the quintessential victim of domestic abuse. In her testimony, she described herself as trapped in a toxic relationship with Depp, one where she claimed to endure emotional, verbal, and physical abuse. She referenced specific incidents, such as the infamous fight in Australia, where she described being physically assaulted by Depp to the point where she feared for her life . Heard's allegations painted a grim picture of their relationship, one where Depp was always the aggressor, and she was the innocent victim struggling to survive.

However, the construction of this victim persona seemed overly calculated. On cross-examination, Camille Vasquez, Depp's attorney, exposed various contradictions in Heard's narrative. For example, Heard claimed that she donated her entire $7 million divorce settlement to charity, a point that bolstered her image of selflessness. Yet, under questioning, it was revealed that she had not completed the donations as promised . This discrepancy, along with other contradictions, exposed the persona she had crafted as a victim as somewhat hollow, raising doubts about the authenticity of her entire testimony.

In Heard's case, admitting that she may not have been entirely truthful about certain events would have shattered the carefully crafted image of herself as a victim of Depp's abuse. For instance, when confronted with audio recordings where she admitted to starting physical fights with Depp, Heard struggled to explain her behavior. At one point, she remarked, "I'm sorry that I didn't hit you across the face in a proper slap, but I was hitting you, it was not punching you. Babe, you're not punched". The verdict? Depp was raw, honest and truthful and Heard's character on tape did not match her carefully crafted persona.

Tinkering with your image and displaying a false image while under scrutiny is tough. Amber Heard's counsel could have learned a few lessons from a well-known public figure who has conducted over 60,000 interviews with many of the most high-profile politicians, actors, and even murderers of our time.

THE ART OF THE QUESTION: HOW STORIES SHAPE OUR PERCEPTIONS

LARRY KING TEACHES US ABOUT THE POWER OF THE STORY AND THE UNASSUMING QUESTION

"Storytelling reveals meaning without committing the error of defining it."

Hannah Arendt

On May 1, 1957, a young man named Larry Zeiger prepared to go on the air for the first time at WAHR, a small Miami radio station. It was a moment he had dreamed of his entire life, but just minutes before his debut, he was thrown an unexpected challenge. The station manager told him that his name—Zeiger—was "too ethnic" and needed to be changed. With only moments to spare, he looked at an ad in *The Miami Herald* for King's Wholesale Liquors, and thus, "Larry King" was born. The name change would be the only unauthentic thing Larry King would do in his 60-year career.

Though the name change happened instantly, King's nervousness was far from gone. As the music faded and the red light flicked on, King froze. The microphone was on, but nothing came out. His boss stormed into the studio, shouting, "This is a communications business, dammit —communicate!" As King later reflected, that moment forced him to embrace the truth of the moment. Authenticity is embedded in King's System 1 thinking.

"Good morning. My name is Larry King. This is my first day on the air, and I'm scared to death. Please bear with me."

This moment of vulnerability marked the beginning of a legendary career spanning over 60,000 interviews with some of the most influential and controversial figures of the 20th and 21st centuries. King's honesty endeared him to listeners immediately, setting the stage for his career-long reputation as an authentic communicator who never tried to be anything other than himself. This early experience shaped his interviewing style, and vulnerability, openness, and authenticity became the cornerstones of his approach.

On that first day, King learned a lesson: the key to broadcasting and any form of communication was to be yourself. As he would later explain, "There is no secret. Be yourself. Answer honestly, be upfront with the audience, and you can never go wrong." This simple, powerful lesson resonates with public speakers, lawyers, and anyone who needs to engage with an audience on a personal level.

King summed up his style with an example: To a pilot: "You're taking a plane down the runway; do you know if it's going to take off?" To a doctor: "What is it like when you open someone up?" To a soldier: "What is war like?"

Larry believed that asking a question over two sentences long is "showing off." He famously does not think about or prepare questions; he listens and asks them. Throughout his career, he maintained a sense of humility and openness, never trying to present himself as someone who knew all the answers. Instead, he asked the questions that came naturally to him—often the simplest, most direct questions that resonated with audiences precisely because they were authentic. He later reflected that being vulnerable and honest was the secret to effective communication: "There's no secret, [other than] 'Be yourself.' If your self is going to work, it's going to work. You can't grab the microphone or the camera and make them like you." For King, the power of communication came not from being flawless but from being confirmed.

He followed a few simple rules:

- Never say "I."
- Don't be the star.
- Don't (over) prepare.
- Listen.
- Never state your opinion.
- Don't judge.

King shares a style similar to that of legendary defense attorney Gerry Spence. Known for his folksy style and emotional appeals, Spence often used his vulnerabilities—his frustrations, fears, and emotions—to connect with juries on a deeper level. Just as King admitted his fear during his first broadcast, Spence would admit to jurors when the evidence wasn't accessible, when the stakes were high, and when the moral weight of the case was heavy. This vulnerability allowed him to build credibility and trust, much like King built trust with his listeners.

Vulnerability is inherently linked to authenticity, and authenticity was King's defining trait. His openness about his nervousness, lack of preparation, or surprise at a guest's answers was part of what made him so beloved. He didn't try to be anything other than who he was—a curious man, asking simple questions and trying to understand the world. Authenticity builds credibility, and credibility is the cornerstone of persuasion. When a lawyer stands before a jury or a speaker addresses a crowd, the audience can sense whether they are being genuine. By staying true to themselves, speakers can create the same trust King established with his listeners.

Larry King's ability to create a comfortable, nonjudgmental environment during his interviews became his vibe. King interviewed some of the world's most powerful, controversial, and private figures throughout his career. From world leaders like Vladimir Putin and Muammar Gaddafi to reclusive celebrities such as Frank Sinatra, King's interviews were often more revealing than others could manage because his guests felt at ease. His neutral, laid-back approach allowed people to lower their defenses and speak freely, frequently uncovering personal insights that might otherwise have remained hidden.

One of Larry King's most notable interviews was with Russian President Vladimir Putin. Rather than grilling Putin or trying to force a confrontation, King allowed Putin to discuss his views on his terms, focusing on topics like his rise to power, Russia's political future, and even Putin's childhood. King asked probing but respectful questions, such as whether Putin believed in an afterlife, which prompted a candid response that humanized the otherwise stoic leader.

Another remarkable interview was with Muammar Gaddafi, the controversial Libyan leader. Once again, King approached the interview by asking questions encouraging Gaddafi to open up rather than take an adversarial stance. By maintaining neutrality and focusing on understanding Gaddafi's perspective, King allowed the Libyan leader to explain his motivations and thoughts on global affairs, providing the audience with a more nuanced view of a figure often vilified in Western media.

When King interviewed Muammar Gaddafi, Gaddafi kept him waiting for over two hours. Though he knew English perfectly well, he insisted on using an interpreter. Ten bodyguards flooded the studio for Gaddafi's grand entrance, and King sat down for what he would later label as his worst interview ever. Despite all of Gaddafi's antics, Larry approached the Libyan dictator without preconceptions. He asked questions, encouraging Gaddafi to explain his worldview and giving viewers a rare insight into the dictator's thinking.

As a result of his disarming approach toward Gaddafi, King could correctly predict that he would not run when faced with the uprising during the Arab Spring. King predicted that Gaddafi would be "done once the people revolted" but that he was too prideful to flee his country.

In both interviews, King's ability to remain neutral and create a safe space for his guests to speak their minds resulted in candid discussions that revealed the human side of these complex figures. His interviews were a reminder that even the most guarded leaders could open up when they felt comfortable and respected. King's interviews with celebrities were similarly insightful, thanks to his calming presence and curiosity. Yet, with King, Sinatra opened up about his career, struggles, and the pressures of fame. King's non-confrontational style allowed Sinatra to speak freely without feeling defensive, leading to one of the most candid interviews Sinatra ever gave.

Perhaps one of Larry King's most moving interviews involved a New York cop who was paralyzed after being shot in Central Park by a teenager. In New York, the city had a string of bike robberies. A young NYC cop investigating the robberies stopped a young Black boy, and a chase began. The 17-year-old boy on a brand new Schwinn bike stopped, pulled out a .38, and fired three shots at the cop. The officer was transported to the emergency room and survived but would not walk again. The cop, seeking closure, approached the boy after he was sentenced. He needed to understand why his life was changed. He asked the boy, "Why did you shoot me?" The boy explained, "I just got that new Schwinn bike, and you were the 15th cop who stopped me. I had a gun that my brother gave me to hold, but I'd never shot one before. But when you stopped me, I just shot." The emotional story aired for the first time on *Larry King Live* and was an incredibly emotional event. The boy asked, "Would you have stopped me if I were white?" The cop said, "No." Feeling the error of their ways, the cop and the boy became friends, and the police officer mentored the boy until he eventually graduated from the police academy.

King famously approached his interviews with minimal preparation, believing that not knowing too much about his guests in advance allowed him to ask genuine, intuitive questions. He often said that his role was to ask the kinds of questions the audience would ask if they were in the room. According to King, this approach helped him connect with his guests and viewers, creating an infectious sense of curiosity.

Following the Columbine shooting, Larry sat down with Marilyn Manson, who claimed he had been blamed for 36 school shootings, and asked him straight up: "Were you at fault for Columbine?" Marilyn didn't shy away from the confrontation because of the rapport developed by Larry. The question was not viewed as a trap but as an opportunity to tell his side of the story, and that's precisely what Marilyn Manson did. Contrast that with agenda-ridden anchors such as Don Lemon, Rachel Maddow, Tucker Carlson, and Megyn Kelly, who often ask pointed questions fueled by a known agenda before the subject even approaches the green room.

When King interviewed O.J. Simpson on the phone with Johnny Cochran, O.J. thanked Larry right out of the gate for being a fair host and cited this as his reason for being involved in the case. While O.J. didn't have much to say due to the pending civil suit, he opened up about a "shadowy figure" who ran down the hall and across O.J.'s driveway, highlighting the testimony about the "shadowy figure" from a witness in the case. King's follow-up question was, "Would you describe yourself as relieved? Angry? What?" O.J. expressed his dissatisfaction with the echo chamber in the news, reporting that essential details of the case were missed. He ended the impromptu call by saying, "Thank you for being fair."

King touched on his impartiality when his nightly show ended. Piers Morgan asked Larry King if he could voice his opinion now that he was off the air. Larry responded, "No." He reflected on his need to stay out of interviews, to not make them about himself. He refrained from using "I" and avoided voicing his opinions. Larry declined to express his opinion during that interview, stating he had other projects and implying that voicing his political beliefs would compromise his position and the trust his interview subjects placed in him.

Instead of following a rigid script, King allowed conversations to unfold naturally. He responded to the moment, reacting to what his guest said, and this flexibility allowed for unexpected turns in the discussion. One example of this was his interview with Marlon Brando. What began as a typical interview shifted when Brando kissed King at the end of their conversation, creating a memorable and unscripted television moment. King's ability to make such moments was not accidental—it resulted from his choice to listen more than he spoke. He often noted that hearing was the key to being a good interviewer. He believed that the interviewer who focused more on their next question than the guest's answer missed the opportunity for deeper engagement.

This focus on listening allowed King to pick up on subtle cues, such as tone of voice or body language, that might go unnoticed by others. His interview with Barbra Streisand is an excellent example of this. Streisand, who is notoriously private, felt comfortable enough in King's presence to open up about her struggles, and this openness stemmed from King's attentiveness and ability to create a non-threatening environment.

King trusted his instincts, let conversations flow, and allowed the unexpected to unfold. His ability to maintain curiosity while guiding discussions was at the heart of his success. This combination of flexibility and attentiveness, like in public speaking and cross-examination, created moments of real connection.

King believed that no evil person wakes up in the morning, looks in the mirror, and says, "I'm evil." King understood that it was essential to know how the interview subjects viewed themselves and ask questions to help them reveal their true self without judgment. He believed this approach created a more relaxed and honest interview subject by removing judgment and logical traps from the conversation.

THE TRIAL OF THE CENTURY

O.J. TEACHES US THAT UNIFYING IS MORE POWERFUL THAN DIVIDING

"The arc of the moral universe is long, but it bends toward justice."

Martin Luther King Jr.

In the "trial of the century," a winning narrative was manufactured mainly out of thin air due to brooding distrust and the gift of a cop with a German last name.

Steve Schwab had a ritual: every night at precisely 10:00 PM, he tuned in to watch *The Dick Van Dyke Show*. This nightly routine was so ingrained that it became almost automatic. After the show, he would leash his dog—part Corgi, part Sheltie—and take their familiar route through the quiet streets of Brentwood. He described this ritual meticulously in a sleepy LA courtroom, shifting in his witness chair and leaning into the microphone. His recollection was sharp as he tapped on the map before him, tracing his path: from his house on Bundy, down Montana, left on Gretna Green, and another series of left turns that would eventually bring him back home.

Over a year later, Schwab recalled checking his watch between 10:35 and 10:40 PM at the corner of Gretna Green and Montana. Marcia Clark, the prosecutor, punctuated his testimony with a John Madden joke, as

X's and O's were drawn on a green map to solidify Schwab's timeline for the jury.

In 1994, Brentwood was where neighbors stopped to chat and even went out of their way to help each other—at least, that's how Schwab portrayed it. His dog and cat, precise recollection of time, and strict routines made him an ideal lead-off witness for the People v. O.J. Simpson prosecution.

Kato, an Akita, was no ordinary dog. Originally bred as guard dogs by the Japanese, Akitas are known for their loyalty and strength, making them both formidable protectors and devoted companions. On the night of the murders, Kato found his way to Steve Schwab, blood on his paws, insistent and determined to lead him back to a horrific scene.

Kato followed Schwab to his apartment just after *The Mary Tyler Moore Show* began at 11:00 PM. Not wanting to upset his cat, Schwab shut Kato out, warning his wife Linda about the Akita. Steve didn't want to take Kato to animal control, fearing the dog would be alone all night with nothing to eat. Sensing Schwab's reluctance, Kato persisted, pulling at Schwab's heartstrings with the loyalty typical of his breed. Schwab tried to hand the barking dog off to a police officer, but Kato, who belonged to Nicole Brown Simpson, wasn't seeking shelter—he had a message.

Enter Sukru Boztepe, Schwab's neighbor and fellow concerned citizen. Boztepe, not a cat owner, had an easier time accepting Kato into his apartment—or so he thought. The dog pulled. The dog pulled harder. Marcia Clark mimicked the motion of holding a leash during her closing argument as she relayed Boztepe's testimony. Kato pulled with determination, leading Boztepe down Bundy toward Nicole's home. The dog stopped near a path, barked, and pulled again. Boztepe glanced up the path and saw slick black splatters and pools of blood, paw prints, and smears leading to Nicole Brown Simpson, crumpled in a heap in a tiny black dress.

Given Schwab's precise timeline of starting his walk at exactly 10:30 PM, it wasn't his first story. On June 13th, at 5:30 in the morning, when questioned by the police about the timing of his walk and discovery of the agitated Akita, he was incorrect—so incorrect that he called the police the next night to correct his statement. The June 17th police report depicting his precise timeline was the first mistake made by the Los Angeles police department. The statement claims that Schwab and Kato became friends at precisely 11:15 PM—well into *The Mary Tyler Moore Show*, a rerun Schwab recalled clearly for the jury.

The problem for the LAPD was that O.J. Simpson, the only suspect in the murder of Nicole Brown Simpson and Ronald Goldman, called his girlfriend Paula Barbieri at precisely 10:03 PM, confirmed by phone records. Prosecutors claimed that both victims were killed around 10:15 or 10:20 PM by O.J. Simpson. But Schwab contended that a "red substance" was on Kato the Akita, which means Nicole and Ron were killed before Schwab made contact with Kato. Schwab's precise timeline and his subsequent 11:15 statement to the police made at 5:30 AM on the morning of the murders prevented the prosecution from credibly starting their timeline.

The autopsy of Nicole Brown Simpson, conducted on June 14, 1994, provided a detailed account of the injuries she sustained. Dr. Irwin L. Golden, the deputy medical examiner, documented multiple sharp force injuries, including a deep incised wound of the neck that severed both the left and right common carotid arteries and the internal jugular veins, leading to fatal exsanguination. The wound, which exposed the larynx and cervical vertebral column, was so severe that it nearly decapitated her.

Nicole's body also bore multiple stab wounds to the neck and scalp, a testament to the ferocity of the attack. The autopsy detailed seven stab wounds in total, with injuries to both sides of her neck, scalp, and hands. Her hands showed defensive wounds, indicating that she had fought desperately to fend off her attacker. Among these, a 5/8-inch incised wound on the right ring finger was particularly noted as a defense wound.

In addition to the sharp force injuries, Nicole had a scalp bruise on the right parietal region, suggesting blunt force trauma. The autopsy revealed that her internal organs, including the brain, lungs, and heart, were otherwise unremarkable and showed no signs of natural disease, focusing the cause of death solely on the brutal external injuries she sustained.

The investigation quickly focused on O.J. Simpson, whose volatile relationship with Nicole was well-documented. A chilling 911 call made by Nicole on October 25, 1993, offered the Los Angeles jury a terrifying glimpse into an enraged O.J. Simpson—a persona vastly different from the beloved national icon.

"Can you send someone to my house?" Nicole asked politely, her calm voice laced with fear but somehow balanced with a delicate undercurrent.

The dispatcher's cold, pre-programmed response demanded the usual details. Nicole explained that her ex-husband, O.J. Simpson, had broken into her house and was now ranting and raving outside the front yard.

"Has he been drinking?"

"No. But he's crazy."

"Has he hit you?"

"No," she replied, her lie betrayed by the tension in her voice.

As the call progressed and O.J.'s rage grew, Nicole's fear escalated just as the call was disconnected. When she called back shortly after, her voice cracked with panic: "Could you get somebody over here now to… Gretna Green. He's back. Please? He's O.J. Simpson. I think you know his record. Could you send somebody over here?" Her escalation was evident – she had said his name.

Nicole's fear for her children became evident as O.J. continued his tirade. "The kids are up there sleeping, and I don't want anything to happen," she said, trembling. The dispatcher urged her to stay on the line and provide a continuous account of the escalating situation. Nicole's frustration and fear were palpable as she described how O.J. had broken the back door to gain entry and was now screaming incoherently.

Nicole's attempts to protect her children from the chaotic scene in their home were heartbreaking. She recounted how O.J. had pounded on her upstairs door, where the children were sleeping, and screamed until she feared they would wake up. Her attempts to soothe him, to prevent further violence, were evident as she tried to provide him with a phone number he demanded, only for him to take her phone book containing all her contacts.

Throughout the call, O.J.'s behavior oscillated between rage and incoherence. Nicole's voice, though calm at times, was underscored by a palpable fear. The dispatcher, attempting to gather more information, asked repeatedly if O.J. had hit her or was threatening her directly. Nicole's responses varied, often acknowledging the danger without explicitly stating it. "He's going to beat the shit out of me," she confessed at one point, her voice barely containing the dread she felt. Nicole's reluctance to unveil the physical violence O.J. later admitted to would have a posthumous impact.

The case against Simpson was strong, with evidence including bloodstains, a glove found at the crime scene, and Simpson's erratic behavior on the 911 tapes could have sealed his fate in most courtrooms.

To make matters worse, around 8:30 am, when Shapiro set out to turn him in, O.J. couldn't be found. Shapiro moves his turn over to the afternoon, and after he doesn't appear for a second time, the police issue a warrant. At 5:51, O.J. Simpson called 911 from A.C. Cowling's Ford Bronco. A.C. Cowlings was a close personal friend of O.J. and was taken hostage by Simpson as he drove the white Bronco. The police triangulated O.J.'s phone and sent a LAPD chopper overhead. As the chopper pilot stared at the LA rush hour traffic, he saw a white Ford Bronco near the El Toro Y interchange in Irvine. Simpson would lead the cops on a low-speed chase for another 60 miles, eventually negotiating a safe passage back to his home and the waiting 300 supporters, along with LAPD's finest, to make the arrest.

The chase earned O.J. Simpson a jail cot and three squares a day for the year-long trial. While O.J. was missing, his lawyer and father of the megastar Kim Kardashian, Robert Kardashian, delivered a bumbling press conference that ultimately damaged O.J. Simpson's defense. The letter read like a goodbye letter, leading the public to speculate that O.J. was going to commit suicide. He signed off, "Please think of the real O.J. and not this lost person."

Overcoming the Government's evidence would have been impossible for most defense teams. The bloody glove, hat, motive, 911 call, a timeline of O.J.'s departure to Chicago, as well as his decision to attempt to flee and write an apparent suicide note were robust prosecution evidence.

But this wasn't just any courtroom, defense team, or prosecutor's office. During the year-long trial, the Dream Team used heuristics and misdirection to paint a careful picture that nearly forced a jury to acquit.

The lead counsel for O.J. Simpson's first celebrity representation came early in his career. Liza Minelli called Robert Shapiro, O.J. Simpson's first "dream team" lawyer. Liza asked the young former LA County Prosecutor 6 months out of government to help out a dear friend. Shapiro rented a plane and flew to Las Vegas to help the now infamous actress who had been arrested for drug possession. Linda Loveless, the famed actress in the movie "Deepthroat," was "one the first nationally publicized cases in America," according to Robert Shapiro. She was charged with possession of cocaine, a relatively routine minor offense. But for Shapiro, who tells it as if he defended the Rosenbergs, it was the trial of the century. From then on, he became the defense attorney for the stars. This persona caused him to prefer the risk-averse plea of guilty to the "all in" high stakes of a trial.

Despite his lack of courtroom prowess, Shapiro was well respected and knew how to negotiate—an essential survival skill. His inside knowledge of the prosecutor's office would come in handy while he twisted Marcia Clark and her counterparts around the axle of the defense case.

But given O.J.'s insistence that he would not plea, Shapiro was in a pickle. As a result, F. Lee Bailey, one of the nation's most respected trial lawyers, was added to the roster. Race became a central narrative against the LAPD, so Johnny Cochrane, who had been happy on the sidelines commentating on CNN, was asked to join the team. The prosecution introduced a maze of DNA evidence, so Barry Shenck, one of the earliest DNA experts, joined the squad.

Johnnie Cochrane, known for his courtroom charisma and keen understanding of racial dynamics, slowly became the face of the defense. Cochrane's strategy was to portray Simpson as a victim of a racially biased police force.

F. Lee Bailey, with his history of high-profile cases, including the defense of Sam Sheppard and Patty Hearst, brought his expertise in cross-examination to the team. Dramatic victories and controversies marked his career. His defense of Sam Sheppard, which overturned a wrongful conviction, and his successful representation of Captain Ernest Medina in the My Lai Massacre made him one of the most sought-after trial lawyers in the United States. Bailey was known for his aggressive cross-examinations and ability to find inconsistencies. Bailey's role in the O.J. Simpson trial was to dismantle the credibility of the prosecution's key witnesses.

Nine black jurors seated amongst the four whites clarified the strategy to the defense. The prosecution, afraid to strike black jurors live on national TV and lose the "race" battle before it began, sealed their fate with this early timid mistake by permitting the race card to be dealt, and as Robert Shapiro described it to Barbara Walters, "dealt from the bottom of the deck." Christopher Darden, a black member of the prosecution team purportedly added to buffer race relations between the LAPD, the Prosecutor's Office, and the public, claimed the case was lost in jury selection. According to Darden, nine black jurors secured victory for the national treasurer, OJ Simpson.

Strictly how that "race card" would be dealt by the defense team was the primary question: The OJ Simpson defense was finely tuned to the atmospheric conditions, sensitive to the perception and beliefs of the jury, and a smokescreen of systemic injustice. The LAPD and Marcia Clark were not. Despite his apparent inexperience in such cases, an early attempt to add Christopher Darden to the prosecution team was blatantly seen as a token. Marcia Clark was roasted in the press for cultural blindness, and further efforts to shed the identity of the LAPD and its systemic racism would only put her in a deeper hole with the majority black juror.

Murder investigations are an all-hands-on-deck event, even for the LA County Sheriff's Department. A million things must be done in an instant. Cases notoriously go cold in 48 hours without a legitimate suspect. Fearing the disdain that a cold case brings and favoring the excitement of a fresh murder, legions of late model Crown Victoria patrol cars descended upon the Brentwood home when the call lit up the police scanners, lights dancing and refracting in the ink-black night. Yellow crime tape was quickly implemented to protect the scene from the inevitable press vultures driving through the night as their scanners squawked. While dozens of upstanding Sheriffs and police officers responded, one with a dark past snuck onto the scene. While not a pivotal investigation team member, happenstance put Detective Mark Fuhrman at a crucial place. Fuhrman had been dispatched to Simpson's estate to notify him of the death and take a statement. Having already left for an out-of-town trip, Simpson was out of the way, so the officers did what most would do - grabbed their oversized mag light flashlights and began looking for evidence.

Furhman then became the person who found the only connection between the grizzly murder scene and the Budny property, a single right-handed Isotoner glove soaked in blood.

The detective, a godsend to the defense, had crept behind the field house to find the bloodied glove left at Simpson's property. Fuhrman made this discovery alone and behind the field house, where the glove lay in a bed of leaves, an improbable location for Simpson to have stashed a murder weapon. The glove matched the blood-soaked glove obtained from Nicole Simpson's house at the scene of the crime.

Clouding this integral evidence was an unfortunate interview in which Fuhrman was audiotaped using the N-word repeatedly with a screenwriter working on a movie. Making matters worse for the prosecution late in the investigation, two witnesses – Kathleen Bell and Natalie Singer – claimed that Fuhrman had made racist remarks, including expressing a desire to kill black people. These allegations, coupled with

Fuhrman's attempt to obtain "stress disability leave" due to the stress of dealing with street gangs, painted a picture of a detective with significant racial animus.

F. Lee Bailey meticulously planned Mark Fuhrman's cross-examination. Bailey aimed to force Fuhrman to either admit to using racial slurs or deny it, knowing that witnesses could contradict him and the tapes could bury him. This strategy was designed to undermine Fuhrman's credibility and, by extension, the integrity of the entire investigation.

Bailey's questioning was straightforward.

F. Lee Bailey owns the silence just as many good orators do. The tone is set immediately, the silence settling on the courtroom and punctuated by the clicking of shutters or the suppressed cough of a gallery member. A conductor, before he selects his baton, Bailey prepares his space as if he's been there before a thousand times. The writhing in anticipation of a witness not accustomed to silence acts as a slow erosion of their stamina. A victim to Bailey's pace, tone, and demeanor, Fuhrman had about as little control as he had ever had at that very instant. Fuhrman had just finished a direct examination that painted him as an upstanding detective. Marcia Clark's calm and logical questions elicited a *yes ma'am, no ma'am* to the point military-esque officer style from Fuhrman. He appeared unbent by a thirst for conviction and was a diligent investigator who embodied the tired prosecutor saying, "Let the evidence be your guide." But secretly, Fuhrman was dreading this day. This is the day he would be at the end of F. Lee—Bailey's sharpest sword.

Fuhrman entered the courtroom having been blasted in the brand new 24-hour news cycle for apparent racist comments. His name could have only been worse had it been Mark *Führman*. Audiotapes, witnesses, and hours of televised hearings where this man was quickly compared to someone who would have gladly dragged Simpson from the back of a pickup from a rope.

Fuhrman made O.J. a victim. It rallied the base that O.J. needed to sway the majority black jury to forget about the blood spilling out of Nicole's apartment and the nearly decapitated head of her lover. It was a narrative that transcended the murder and spoke to the societal harms faced by Los Angeles residents. It was a theme that united the jurors under a common hatred and made the trial at least a balancing test for the jury - who do we believe? Bailey's preparatory fires pounded the battlefield of race relations and smoked out crucial pieces of evidence, including the audio tapes and several witnesses. Fuhrman was a gift that was to be respected.

This was not a bare cross to be entrusted to a garden-variety trial attorney. This was the cross of a century, and the only person in the United States who could have delivered it exactly and carefully was F. Lee Bailey.

Cochrane knew that. Cochrane was a storyteller. Bailey was a facts man. Cochrane was a soundbite machine where the tale's elements bend to the narrative; Bailey possessed the mind of a steel trap and held his credibility up high for all the jury to see. Bailey could see his target resting inside of Fuhrman. He knew that underneath the surface rested a cold, dark, racist heart likely created by overexposure to brutal gang violence. He needed to cut the surface and let the racism ooze out into the courtroom, into the city, and across the airwaves into the homes of the millions watching this race battle play out on live TV and chopped up before Seinfeld.

Bailey began by establishing Fuhrman's extensive experience as a detective, underscoring his familiarity with police procedures and evidence handling. This was a bit of Larry King's soft questioning to put Fuhrman at ease, and it was good for Bailey, too - he knew Fuhrman would play to his hero archetype and would not resist the chance to woo the jury with his wealth of experience. But we all know where this is going: experienced police officers don't make mistakes, and any errors in judgment are intentional.

Traipsing over the site of the found glove becomes an intentional act. He failed to rope off the location of the glove - a way to cover tracks and failing to interview witnesses Kato Kalin thoroughly about the events that night - an intentional act to avoid improving O.J.'s alibi. The archetype pulls one way, and the facts pull another. Bailey's questions were measured, his tone controlled, as he led Fuhrman through a series of seemingly mundane queries about his career and role in the investigation.

Fuhrman was disarmed.

Then, the abrupt switch from his gentle demeanor to the classic Bailey calculated tone. Bailey opted to say the N-word. In a volatile, predominately black community this white man used this word loudly in front of nine black jurors, two black attorneys, black members of the gallery, and the entire black community as it was broadcast live on every single TV station. He was lanced in the press for this, but he knew this would fade at verdict time.

When asked if he used this word, Fuhrman retorted, "Presently." A strange response while the public reeled from even the utterance of such a vile sound. Equivocation is evidence of a persona beginning to crack. *Presently? As if to distinguish from past uses?* Fuhrman's shadow self is revealed lightly. Snapping back, Fuhrman issued his canned, forceful denial.

In a rapid and instinctual follow-up, Bailey was off script and to engage System 1 thinking. Reflexive and instinctual. In his mind, Fuhrman was a rat searching for a way out as the water rose. Ping-ponging between his archetype and shadow, Fuhrman's battle was as much happening in the courtroom as in his head. His demeanor differed significantly from that of the poised cop on direct examination.

Bailey pounced, unleashing a waterboard of questions seeking cognitive overload. He asked Fuhrman if he had used the N-word in the past ten years. Fuhrman's response, "Not that I can recall." The equivocation was the subtle gift Fuhrman presented to Bailey. He'd seen it before. The liar always seeks a back door to escape when the odds that the truth is known are more significant than zero. A plain white denial is the minimum effective dose, and Bailey charged through the opacity of Fuhrman's response.

Based on Fuhrman's premise's error in logic - "I don't recall using the N-word"- Bailey sets up the most important single question in the year-long trial and, indeed, the most crucial question of his career.

"You mean if you called someone a N%%%, you would have forgotten it?"

Bailey used the fewest words from A to B, which are necessary for distilling complex themes to ordinary people. Fuhrman issues a reflexive denial, but it's unnecessary. The question hung in the courtroom, as those who missed the logical fallacy are now up to speed.

Bailey got what he wanted with Fuhrman's flat denials. This denial opened the door to previously suppressed evidence, which later caused Mark Fuhrman to plead the 5th in response to further questions about his use of the term.

The courtroom fell silent. Fuhrman hesitated, then replied, "No, I have not."

Bailey pressed on with perfunctory denials, "Have you used the N-word at any time while you have been employed as an LAPD officer?" Fuhrman responded again, "No, I have not." Bailey continued, "Do you have any recollection of using the N-word in conversation with any of your colleagues or any of your reports?" Sensing the danger but unable to escape, Fuhrman maintained his denial, "No, I do not." Admitting to the words would subject him to the scorn of Marcia Clark and his department. Lying could subject him to perjury. There was no way out. With objective evidence of using the term on audiotapes and with witnesses who would attest to the use, Fuhrman was now squarely in a perjury trap that would lead to his eventual prosecution and conviction.

Bailey's cross-examination set a trap and the American people watched it spring shut live on television. By forcing Fuhrman into a corner, Bailey exposed the detective's dishonesty and racism. The jurors could not ignore the discrepancy between Fuhrman's denials and Bell and Singer's compelling testimonies. This contradiction damaged Fuhrman's credibility and cast a shadow over the investigation.

If Fuhrman could lie about his use of racial slurs, what else could he lie about? Could he have planted evidence or manipulated the crime scene?

These questions lingered in the jurors' minds, planting seeds of doubt about the integrity of the prosecution's case.

As the nation awaited the verdict in the O.J. Simpson trial, those born before 1983 likely remember where they were that day. On October 3, 1995, when the jury announced Simpson's acquittal, the dissident but visceral emotions were hard to grasp by many. Either a murderer went free, and that murderer was OJ Simpson or a murderer went free, and that murderer was not OJ Simpson. But the killings were mainly rendered irrelevant at that point; LA was on trial, and race was on trial.

The defense team didn't just win on the legal front; they capitalized on psychological strategies, cognitive biases, and societal frameworks that shaped the jurors' perceptions.

Take Steve Schwab's testimony, for example. Schwab, the Brentwood neighbor who found Nicole Brown Simpson's blood-stained Akita, relied on ritual and habit in his nightly walks. He meticulously described his routine, leaning into his witness chair and tracing his familiar path on a courtroom map. Schwab's testimony fit perfectly into the prosecution's timeline—down to the minute. Yet, as it unraveled, we see how confirmation bias slipped into play. Schwab's precise recollections were later contradicted by his revised statement to the police, sowing doubt. Would the prosecution have rested its timeline on such a fuzzy witness had they understood the impact of his contradiction? Nope. Confirmation bias shielded them from the effects of his prior statement; they likely convinced themselves that it would be seen as a minor error.

But it wasn't just Schwab's shifting memory that cast shadows - it was the first error in a long string of folly. The Dream Team had the powerful impact of "recency" - scoring first blood and the first crack in the armor of a prosecution that should have been flawless. Clark presented her case as flawless during opening and framing the prosecution team, and the case as ironclad and sophisticated framed the jury for the reality that this was true. Had Clark invoked her inner Gerry Spence, she might have informed the jury that cases like this are challenging and, witnesses don't always have the best recollection, and the media coverage complicated the presentation of evidence; the jury may have accepted her mistakes as sincere or even endearing.

Detective Mark Fuhrman became the linchpin of distrust. Fuhrman's fall from grace wasn't just about the evidence he found—the bloody glove linking O.J. Simpson to the crime scene—but about the biases he harbored. When F. Lee Bailey cross-examined Fuhrman, he wasn't just probing a witness; he was dismantling the credibility of the LAPD itself, exposing deep-rooted prejudice and cognitive dissonance. However, Clark put him on that pedestal. He permitted him to adopt the LAPD's and its officers' persona, leading the jury to apply Fuhrman's characteristics to the entire department. If Clark accepted his flaws and racial hatred, she might have steered into it, minimizing his role in the case at the outset or even not calling him a foundational witness.

Clark was concerned about the prospect of dismissing black jurors live on TV. She was concerned about this because of how swiftly the race card was dealt in the case. She made this judgment call projecting a heard mentality and as a defense to her reputation and persona as the ethical race-neutral prosecutor. She made a crucial misjudgment; white jurors would not likely care about dismissing a black juror, and no one would care if she dismissed an equal number of jurors. She overestimated the impact on black jurors instead of rationally thinking that a jury would view the evidence and testimony and decide the case just as the judge instructs. She weighed the race card heavily because it sought to undermine her persona as an ethical prosecutor.

Cognitive dissonance, a psychological phenomenon where individuals experience discomfort when holding two conflicting beliefs, was evident in Fuhrman's actions. He had built his career on the perception of being a lawful protector, yet his history of racial slurs clashed with this persona. Having witnessed grotesque gang murders, crack houses, abandoned children, and call after call in the inner city - Mark Fuhrman had to protect himself from the prospect that the darkest corners of humanity he saw on those streets were not real life.

He drew distance between himself and the people he saw; he hid behind his shield and had to see himself as different and his suspects as less than human. This is the same phenomenon that was the cause of the My Lai massacre, where a platoon became out of control and bloodthirsty in the killing of Viet Nam civilians. Later, members of the platoon would recount that the platoon leadership failed to curtail offensive language and derogatory slurs toward the locals. When minor infractions such as looting or mistreatment of locals arose, they were not dealt with. Eventually, more significant infractions and, ultimately, mass murder ensued.

Fuhrman could not embrace the harm he suffered; he could not get on the stand and cry about the horrors he saw and the wall he had to build. He couldn't reveal his true self as a man who had been in danger too many times and was reacting to the impact of his public service. It would have been a heartfelt and compelling story. An L.A. juror would be moved by the damage suffered by an officer who dutifully kept the streets safe.

Fuhrman had to live behind his persona; he wore his mask proudly. Marcia Clark was happy to oblige; needing an upstanding detective on the stand, she delivered him as an Eagle Scout to the jury. Instead, as Jung teaches us, we should be raw and vulnerable. Larry King might have opened Fuhrman up and had the jury weeping for the terrors he has seen, but Marcia couldn't do that - because she hasn't read this book. Marcia Clark can't because she can't see past the courtroom and into humanity - she's too focused on her narrative and not on the truth. She forgets or perhaps fails to recognize that the only narrative is the truth.

Fuhrman denied the slurs, which led him into a trap. Everyone in the courtroom who was listening knew he had to reject the slurs. But that didn't have to happen if he was correctly presented. When evidence came forward that he used racial slurs, jurors, especially those from marginalized communities, saw this dissonance and began to question not only Fuhrman's testimony but the entire LAPD investigation. They united around their community and their social groups and made their own risk decisions about whether or not they could return home having voted for a "racist." Forced directly into the herd mentality that Marcia Clark feared, jurors could not rationalize the systemic racism when faced with a cop who disrespected them enough to lie to their faces. Without the prosecution team giving a reason for Fuhrman's lie, they had no choice - to acquit.

Fuhrman wasn't alone in his internal conflict. As a beloved sports figure, his public persona radiated charisma, charm, and success. But his violent outbursts and strained relationship with Nicole threatened to expose his shadow. The defense expertly protected this persona by shifting the narrative from Simpson's personal life to systemic racism. They framed Simpson not as a murderer but as a victim of a corrupt system—one that used Fuhrman's prejudice as its tool. The jury's anchoring bias—their initial perception of Simpson as a national hero—created a cognitive framework that was difficult to break, even in the face of damning evidence.

The defense team dealt the race card from the bottom of the deck. Fearing that O.J.'s friendships with the white community and his lack of involvement in the black community would make the race card insincere, they protected his black identity. O.J. was pictured with Donald Trump and other white business and political figures. When the jury wanted to visit O.J.'s house, the defense team filled it with pictures of O.J., his mother, and black members of his family. Later, Shapiro would say that the switch was made to make the house look more "family-friendly" and to "get the women off the walls." O.J.'s attorney, Carl Douglas, later discussed the "switch" and played it down, saying there was a statue and a few pictures changed, including a picture of O.J. blowing candles out on a provocative birthday cake.

The entire endeavor was an exercise in in-group bias. This is a cognitive bias where people tend to give preferential treatment and view members of their group in a more positive light than those outside the group. This bias stems from the human tendency to categorize people into groups based on shared characteristics, such as race, nationality, gender, political affiliation, or even something as trivial as shared hobbies or sports teams. This theory, developed by Henri Tajfel and John Turner in the 1970s, explains how individuals derive part of their self-concept from their groups. By favoring their in-group, people boost their self-esteem, reinforcing their own positive identity. In-group bias can distort decision-making processes in settings like boardrooms, jury deliberations, or political debates, where people may overvalue the contributions or perspectives of those they see as part of their group.

This strategy also played on groupthink. The predominately black jury became a collective force, subtly influenced by the racial dynamics at play. To convict Simpson was to betray their own, a decision that could reinforce negative stereotypes. Simpson's defense team, keenly aware of this, tapped into the broader societal tension between African Americans and law enforcement. With the LAPD's history of racial misconduct, the defense anchored the jurors' distrust early on, ensuring that each piece of evidence, no matter how incriminating, was viewed through the lens of racial injustice.

Prospect theory, another concept from behavioral economics, is also manifested in Fuhrman's actions. When confronted with the possibility of losing his career and credibility, Fuhrman made the high-risk decision to deny using racial slurs—despite knowing there was evidence to the contrary. This risk-seeking behavior in the face of potential loss ultimately trapped him in a perjury charge, illustrating how prospect theory often leads individuals to gamble with the truth when faced with significant personal stakes.

For the jury, prospect theory took a different form. Acquitting Simpson was a gamble, but the alternative—convicting him and reinforcing the image of a biased justice system—was an even more significant loss. The jury, particularly the African American members, weighed these risks and chose the path to deliver the least harm to their community. In their eyes, letting O.J. go free was a small price to pay for sending a message about racial injustice.

Then, there was the role of the halo effect, another cognitive bias where an individual's overall impression influences how their specific traits are perceived. Simpson's charm and celebrity status—his very persona—made it difficult for jurors to reconcile the image of the friendly football star with the brutal murderer described in court. Even when faced with blood evidence, the infamous glove, and violent 911 calls, the jurors' favorable impression of Simpson weighed heavily in his favor.

Cochran, a master of framing and psychological manipulation, effectively exploited this bias. He recontextualized the trial, framing it not as a simple case of murder but as a referendum on the LAPD's treatment of African Americans. This framing shifted the jury's focus from the crime to the broader societal issue, making the evidence against Simpson seem secondary to their message.

Moral licensing also played its part. Jurors, especially from marginalized communities, may have felt that by acquitting Simpson, they were taking a stand against decades of systemic oppression. This act of moral defiance allowed them to overlook incriminating evidence, viewing their decision as a form of justice for a community long mistreated by law enforcement. Moral licensing is also the same hook that would have caused the jurors in the Monkey Scopes trial to overlook the logical errors of Bryan's testimony and convict.

The psychological and rhetorical strategies employed throughout the trial went beyond mere theatrics; they were a calculated exercise in leveraging human biases, emotions, and cognitive shortcuts. Every aspect of the defense's strategy, from the early anchoring of the jury's perception of Simpson to Bailey's expert exploitation of Fuhrman's cognitive dissonance, was designed to manipulate the jury's decision-making process.

Jurors later spoke about the impact of Bailey's cross-examination. Carrie Bess, one of the jurors, stated, "When [Bailey] asked Fuhrman about the N-word, and he denied it, I knew he was lying. And if he was lying about that, what else was he lying about?" This sentiment was echoed by other jurors, who felt that Fuhrman's credibility was irreparably damaged.

Juror Brenda Moran noted, "Fuhrman's lies were the final straw. His words made us question the legitimacy of the evidence he presented. If he could lie so easily about using racial slurs, who's to say he wasn't lying about everything else?" Most jurors vividly remember the turbulence between 1991 and the trial as a result of the Rodney King beatings, verdict, and trial. Rodney King was brutally beaten on March 3, 1991, while being arrested for speeding and intoxication. A video was captured, and the 1991 version went viral. The offending officers were acquitted at a very public trial, sparking the LA riots. Indeed, the Rodney King beatings likely framed and anchored the Juror's impression of the LAPD.

Journalist Ellis Cose wrote in Newsweek, "The acquittal of O.J. Simpson was a stunning rebuke to a system that many African Americans felt had failed them time and again. The trial, especially the cross-examination of Mark Fuhrman, was not just about a murder case; it was about the LAPD's history of racial discrimination and abuse." Meanwhile, in an editorial for the Los Angeles Times, columnist Ron Harris remarked, "For many in the African American community, the trial's verdict was less about Simpson's guilt or innocence and more about delivering a long-overdue message to a police department with a notorious reputation for racism and brutality.

HINDUBURGER: APPROPRIATE CULTURAL APPROPRIATION

HOW THE NATION'S LARGEST RESTAURANT CONFRONTED RELIGION AND CULTURAL NORMS

"Tradition is not the worship of ashes, but the preservation of fire."

Gustav Mahler

McDonald's frontman Ray Kroc famously hailed McDonalds as a real estate company. That's a Kroc. But Ray is hiding the ball from you. McDonalds has become a master of psychology and heuristics. If Sigmund Freud, Carl Jung, and Daniel Kahneman had a baby with Ray Kroc, Ronald McDonald would be the little lovechild. A single McDonald's experience exposes the average customer to over 100 mind traps targeted directly at your dopamine and rendering your tastebuds powerless.

Forty thousand consistent locations ensure that Mcdonald's is the only constant in middle America on that long road trip, unlocking the availability heuristic - which causes us to choose Mcdonald's because it came to our mind quickly and easily. A social proof metric hangs below the "Over 1 Billion Served" sign. Get within 200 meters of a McDonalds, and chemical warfare is waged against your waistline by deploying the delicious scent of burgers and fries outside the restaurant. The smell curls into your nose, invoking a Pavlovian response that causes hunger where there is none.

The arches are masterful works of color psychology, with the colors red and yellow creating a sense of urgency. Andrew J. Elliot teaches that the color red in a logo invokes urgency and anxiety. H.E. Gerber, the author of Influence of Color on Flavor Perception, teaches that red and yellow evoke hunger and excitement.

The new double drive-through is not just for convenience; it's another hack. Pulling into the double drive-through seems shorter than other lines during a dinner rush. Without it, the prolonged wait may cause you to come to your senses. But that line does not split until it's time to order, trapping you between fellow customers as soon as you pull up.

Rolling down your window and gazing at the paradox of choice on the well-lit menu causes slight anxiety and a reflexive leap at more extensive and expensive menu items. Have you ever read the entire menu? Have you ever felt rushed? Yeah, that's intentional. The speaker is slightly too loud, and the social expectation of a swift order is anxiety-inducing. It's like waiting to get your bag from the overhead luggage on an airplane.

Notice where the dollar menu is housed on the menu next time you visit. You probably won't get there, but veteran cupon cutters tap into hyperbolic discounting, a heuristic that causes the customer to value an immediate reward. Chances are that these are merely gateway purchases, a taste that will most certainly result in a larger order when McDonalds plays its full hand.

You might be fortunate enough to be a parent of a child possessing a developing child brain that is much more susceptible to the addictive nature of even the sight of the arches. To a child, a subtle nudge, pout, or full-blown total-body tantrum might lead to a toy and a few soggy fries under the car seat. The negotiation in your mind ensues - it's just a quick stop, and a happy meal may get me through this episode of *Last Podcast on the Left* in peace.

It's okay, moms and dads; we've all been there. But did you ever wonder why the slide and ball pit is visible outside the restaurant? Or why the toy always comes in a set? Or why does the Happy Meal come in a box with arches for handles?

The uniformed employee yells at you, "Would you like to invite McDonald's into your phone, pocket, and life?" In this case, they have the digital version of your soul to use, as do you. However, the question is worded slightly differently: "Will you be using the McDonald's app today?" as if it is the only currency accepted here.

Menu arrangements gently nudge slightly more profitable decisions. Anchoring items dot the menu to make value meals seem more affordable. Limited time offers spice it up with a sense of urgency.

The McRib is back!

But the ice cream machine is still down.

I bet you will still order something.

Should you choose the restaurant instead of the drive-through, congrats, you got more exercise than 70% of McDonald's customers. But this may not be the reason you went inside. McDonald's has filtered you into a different class to apply different heuristics; the marketing tactics change just like the gambler prefers table games to slots. When you walk into the restaurant, you have the illusion of choice: a human or a menu. Those who b-line to the automated menu are likely uncomfortable with giving a human their order and historically make larger purchases even while dining alone. Men who chose the self-service menu are more likely to order meals with two burgers. Those who approach the human are often more comfortable with a longer wait, and McDonalds is their destination, not just a calorie hit on their way through middle America.

But what size to order? McDonald's perfectly uses the decoy effect here. The medium is specifically priced to make the large seem like a better value. Loss aversion is ideally deployed by adding SUPERSIZED menu items, which make customers feel like they are missing out on a better deal by not upgrading.

And now it's time to eat; their mixture of salt, sugar, and fat lights up the brain more than a heroin hit. Searching for just one more fry in the bag after pounding three thousand calories is a shocking reminder of our addiction and the appetite-suppressant qualities of McDonald's food.

The addictive quality of its food has led to the company being the most profitable restaurant in the world. A study published in the Journal Appetite in 2015 determined that this response is similar to the activation of the brain's pleasure centers seen in drug addiction. These foods can override standard satiety signals, leading to overeating and more overeating. The dopamine released after a McDonalds visit leads to compulsive eating behavior and food addiction. Food companies have a phrase for this, "bliss point," at which MRI activity has shown drastic changes to the brain.

And this is just America. The small San Bernardino restaurant in 1940 exploded to 1000 restaurants in the U.S. It went international in 1967 in Puerto Rico and Canada, and by 2024, McDonalds has over 40,000 locations in 100 countries. Burger King has a paltry 19,000 locations globally. But America was easy; for Ray Kroc, Americans are easy - he had them dialed in. But when Mcdonald's set its sights on the East and, particularly in countries where it had to take on not just consumerism but God, that's the challenge that made Ronald McDonald smile.

It was the mid-1990s, and Amit Jatia found himself sitting in a meeting room across from representatives from McDonald's. The global fast-food giant was eager to enter India, a country with a growing middle class and a burgeoning appetite for Western brands. But for Jatia, a devout vegetarian from a traditional Indian family, the idea of selling burgers—especially beef—seemed laughable. "You must be out of your mind! I'm a vegetarian. And here you are, telling me to sell beef burgers," Jatia recalled telling his friend, who first floated the idea.

However, a population of just under 1 billion people could be profitable if they ate out. But they didn't; McDonald's research showed that 2003 of the 100 meals Indian families ate per month, only three were outside the home.

To McDonald's, India represented an enticing opportunity and a market fraught with potential landmines. Roughly 80% of the population followed Hindu traditions that revered the cow, making beef not just a poor menu choice but a profoundly offensive one. Furthermore, a significant portion of the population adhered to Islam, avoiding pork due to religious dietary laws. India wasn't just another market to crack —it was a labyrinth of cultural sensitivities and dietary restrictions.

But McDonald's wasn't discouraged. It would overhaul the kitchen, reinvent its identity, and authentically adopt Indian culture to nudge the perceptions of Indian people. Thus, the McAloo Tikki was born—a burger that was not only beef-free but also a bold fusion of Indian flavors and widely accepted by a diverse but selective population.

Western ideas of fast food might not easily translate. In India, meals were a communal, family affair, and grabbing a quick bite on the go was foreign and inappropriate. So, McDonald's set out to sell food and tell a story about McDonalds. They marketed their restaurants as places where families could unite and celebrate Indian social life.

For Amit Jatia, the idea of bringing burgers to India seemed absurd. How could McDonald's possibly navigate a landscape where cows are sacred, vegetarianism is a way of life for millions, and pork is out of the question for the Muslim population?

"We were always clear we would do both veg and non-veg, but we communicated the separate kitchens and did kitchen tours to convince customers it was safe for them to eat here," Jatia recalled. This commitment to respecting dietary restrictions wasn't just a nice to have—it was essential for survival in India. In a country where trust around food purity is paramount, McDonald's went further than ever before to ensure that vegetarian food was prepared without contamination. Separate kitchens for vegetarian and non-vegetarian items became a cornerstone of their Indian operations.

But the challenges didn't stop there. McDonald's also faced the dilemma of how to offer something familiar yet acceptable. They couldn't just remove beef and pork from the menu and hope for the best. What was needed was a transformation, something uniquely tailored to Indian tastes. The answer came in the form of the McAloo Tikki—a potato-based burger spiced with cumin, coriander, and ginger, flavors that immediately resonated with the Indian palate. Far from being just a vegetarian substitute for meat, the McAloo Tikki was an entirely new creation explicitly designed for the market. It quickly became one of McDonald's most popular items in India.

"Aloo Tikki was our first local innovation," Jatia said. The decision to offer a distinctly Indian product wasn't just about avoiding beef—it was about appealing to a consumer base that appreciated familiarity with their flavors. Jatia himself, being a staunch vegetarian, understood this better than most: *"I'm so particular about vegetarianism that even if a spoon touches a non-veg gravy, I won't eat from it,"* he explained.

The burger became so popular that McDonald's expanded their local offerings, introducing other Indianized items such as the McSpicy Paneer and Maharaja Mac, which used chicken instead of beef. This approach proved to be a significant factor in McDonald's success in India. As Jatia explained, *"We didn't just adapt—we innovated. The McAloo Tikki resulted from that deeper understanding of the Indian market. It was something that people could relate to, and they loved it."* The Indian consumer wasn't just being offered an alternative—they were being given something that fit seamlessly into their food culture.

Another crucial element of McDonald's marketing strategy in India was its involvement in festivals and local celebrations whether it was Diwali or Holi, McDonald's introduced special menu items and promotions that reflected the festive spirit of the season.

Transparency was also crucial for McDonald's and Jatia so the culture would feel comfortable inviting McDonald's in. Jatia often cited this transparency as a defining feature of McDonald's success in India: *"We made it very clear from the beginning. Our kitchens were open to scrutiny because we wanted to earn that trust,"* he said.

While McDonald's made significant strides in India, not all aspects of its expansion were smooth. The brand's operations in the North and East of India, run by Vikram Bakshi through the Connaught Plaza Restaurants Private Limited (CPRL) joint venture, became mired in a lengthy and bitter legal dispute and in stark contrast to the success McDonald's was experiencing in the West and South under Amit Jatia, the relationship between McDonald's and Bakshi deteriorated rapidly after 2013, when McDonald's abruptly removed Bakshi from his role as managing director. At the heart of the dispute was a disagreement over control. While Bakshi had been instrumental in setting up operations in North India, McDonald's corporate leadership felt that the joint venture structure was no longer working. McDonald's argued that different stages of market development required different ownership models. Jatia, who ran the South and West India operations, reflected on the situation, saying, *"McDonald's believes that different ownership structures work for different stages of development. They've been tremendously supportive in our region"*.

Bakshi, who had played a key role in bringing McDonald's to North India, contested his removal, alleging that McDonald's was attempting to buy out his stake at an unfairly low price. The legal battle soon escalated into a high-profile corporate conflict that spanned years, with accusations of mismanagement and unfair business practices. For McDonald's, maintaining its brand image meant surviving the legal battle without reputational damage.

The legal wrangling between McDonald's and Bakshi dragged on for years, casting a shadow over McDonald's ability to expand in North India. While McDonald's continued to grow in the West and South, unresolved ownership issues hindered the brand's presence in the North. The prolonged dispute led to store closures and operational disruptions.

In 2019, after six years of legal conflict, McDonald's and Bakshi finally settled, with McDonald's buying out Bakshi's stake in the joint venture. The resolution allowed McDonald's to regain control of North India's operations and focus on rebuilding its regional presence. However, the damage had already been done, and McDonald's faced an uphill battle to regain consumers' trust and restore its market position in North and East India.

After McDonald's groundbreaking entry into India with the launch of the McAloo Tikki, other global fast food companies like KFC and Domino's Pizza followed suit, adapting their menus to fit local tastes. KFC introduced a range of vegetarian options and adjusted its spices to appeal to Indian palates. Domino's localized its offerings with toppings like paneer and introduced a vegetarian-only menu in certain outlets. These moves reflected a more significant trend of companies navigating cultural sensitivities and dietary habits, furthering globalization efforts.

Why is McDonald's entry into India so significant? Let's take stock. First, religious preferences predominately excluded the menu items. Second, Indian people did not eat out in a way that would have been profitable. Third, a failure could have resulted in catastrophic embarrassment to the McDonald's brand. This was a zero-sum game: either meet resounding success or alienate a rapidly expanding population. Jatia was 14 the first time he went to a McDonalds, it was in Japan. In 1994, Jaita would sit across from McDonald brass and provide a robust education on Indian culture. The decision to incorporate Jaita was its biggest gamble and most significant payoff. When Amit joined the McDonald's family in March 1995 as MD, Hardcastle Restaurants Pvt. Ltd., he was the youngest Joint Venture Partner at McDonald's. Before that, he had no restaurant experience and had a chemical manufacturing background.

Being from India but also educated at UCLA, Jatia and McDonald maneuvered the cultural integration of the concept flawlessly, utilizing each of the strategies outlined in the final section of this book. McDonald's embraced relativity and modified its all-beef patties to match norms. Transparency was essential to develop trust that its cooking practices aligned with cultural norms. Indian people were not eating out, and a strong family story and celebration were required to nudge this cultural norm. Through this, McDonalds represented similar values to this new blend of cultures, and it was accepted as authentic. It's also apparent that some challenging of traditional norms was required given the longstanding cultural norm of eating at home 97% of the time.

Even more astonishing is that Jatia and McDonald conducted this analysis in 1994. Such flexibility and adaptability in brand messaging were unheard of, and significant United States restaurant companies refrained from integration. No system or formal structure for integration was taught at primary business schools, making Jatia's first experience with cultural integration a break-out success and a model for future globalization in this post-modern world.

Jatia and another influential corporate figure have something in common. Jatia fused his heritage with his Western business culture to create a resonated message. This is common among startup successes; their grassroots origins permit an impossible-to-ignore perspective. Mark Zuckerberg, Steve Jobs, and Bill Gates ran their companies at the helm and steered them through business minefields despite modest beginnings.

THINK DIFFERENT: STEVE JOBS AND THE CREATION OF THE COMMERCIAL SUBCULTURE

CREATING YOUR OWN CULTURE AND INTEGRATING YOUR CONSUMER

"As with all matters of the heart, you'll know when you find it."

Steve Jobs

The "Think Different" commercial, which first aired in 1997, remains one of the most iconic pieces of advertising ever created, not just for its visual and emotional appeal but for what it represented to both Apple and the world. Set to black-and-white footage of some of history's most influential thinkers, rebels, and misfits, the script begins with a voiceover that has since become legendary:

"Here's to the crazy ones. The misfits. The rebels. The troublemakers. The round pegs in the square holes. The ones who see things differently."

As the narrator speaks, images of luminaries like Albert Einstein, Mahatma Gandhi, and Martin Luther King Jr. flash across the screen. The grainy and timeless footage showcases them not as distant historical figures but as visionaries who dared to defy convention. Footage of Amelia Earhart standing confidently by her plane and Muhammad Ali raising his arms in victory drives home the point: these were people who didn't just accept the world as it was—they changed it.

The ad was more than just a tribute to these icons; it reflected Apple's core philosophy. Steve Jobs, who had returned to Apple just months before the campaign aired, saw the commercial as a perfect embodiment of what Apple represented. As legend has it, Jobs was so moved when he first saw the final cut that he cried, recognizing that the campaign captured Apple's essence—unbridled passion, uncompromising self-identity, and a fearless drive to challenge the status quo.

The commercial concludes with the poignant line:

"Because the people who are crazy enough to think they can change the world are the ones who do."

"Think Different" hangs on the screen as the music plays. The commercial doesn't discuss features or products; it starts an identity. Steve knew that it would take non-conformists to reject the growing PC market, and market dominance lay not in the cheapest price but in a powerful brand identity. The Macintosh became a status symbol, but not just of wealth; it was a symbol of thought, aspiration, and creativity.

To understand how bold this strategy was, let's go back to 1997. Apple was facing an uphill battle. The company had been struggling in the years leading up to Jobs' return, and the "Think Different" campaign was more than just an advertisement—it was a statement of renewal. Apple wasn't just another tech company but a brand that stood for creativity, innovation, and the boldness to challenge conventions. At a time when competitors were focusing on specs and features, Apple was selling a vision, an idea that resonated deeply with its audience.

The deliberate use of black-and-white images of historical figures emboldened Apple's alignment with timelessness and ingenuity. By associating the Apple brand with these great thinkers and doers, Jobs created a halo effect around Apple products. The message was clear: using Apple wasn't just a technological choice but a philosophical one.

Jobs' emotional reaction to the commercial was a testament to its power. To him, Apple wasn't just a company—it was a movement. This ad captured that sentiment perfectly, giving the world a glimpse of what

Apple stood for: not just building products but pushing the boundaries of what's possible and inspiring others to do the same.

Study Jobs, and you will learn he was a master of persuasion. One key to his success was his ability to blend classical rhetorical techniques with a deep understanding of human psychology, making his presentations as emotionally engaging as they were logically compelling.

Jobs' rhetorical brilliance was rooted in ethos, pathos, and logos. Ethos, or credibility, was established through his reputation as a visionary and the founder of Apple. His return to the company after years in exile added an almost mythical dimension to his authority, reinforcing his image as the savior of Apple but also a rebel. Pathos, or emotional appeal, was another tool he mastered. For instance, Jobs often painted Apple products as revolutionary solutions to deeply personal or societal problems during product launches. Whether describing the iPhone as "magical" or the iPod as holding "a thousand songs in your pocket," Jobs connected his products to users' desires and needs in a way that made them feel indispensable.

One of Jobs' most memorable emotional appeals was in his 2005 Stanford commencement speech, where he said, "stay hungry, stay foolish." This simple, resonant message struck a chord with the audience, appealing to their aspirations for creativity and risk-taking.

His ability to weave storytelling into his speeches simplified this emotional connection, making his presentations memorable long after the products were revealed.

Logos, or logical appeal, was always present but often subtly incorporated. Jobs did not rely on overwhelming technical jargon. Instead, he used simple, clear language that anyone could understand, like when he introduced the iPhone as "three revolutionary products" combined into one,

By chunking complex ideas into digestible pieces and relating them to everyday experiences, Jobs made cutting-edge technology accessible and compelling to the masses.

By blending ethos, pathos, and logos with powerful storytelling and emotional appeal, Jobs created a style of persuasion that felt authentic and compelling. His ability to make each product launch feel like a global event made him one of the most persuasive figures of the modern era.

Jobs opened nearly every product launch up with the "labor illusion," a psychological principle highlighting the value of seeing the effort behind a product. By showing the work put into something, it increases its perceived value. Jobs would often begin his keynote presentations by emphasizing the amount of work Apple had invested. In his first keynote back at Apple in 1998, after being rehired as interim CEO, he started by saying:

"It's been 10 months since a new management team took over at Apple. People have been working hard, and because of their hard work, I'm pleased to report that Apple's back on track."

This narrative of hard work, reinforced by his comment on cars in the parking lot late at night, was more than just a remark; it was a strategic move. He was crafting an emotional appeal to show investors, employees, and customers that Apple was on the rise again because of dedication and effort.

Jobs used this labor narrative repeatedly, as seen in his introduction of the iPhone in 2007:

"This is a day I've been looking forward to for two and a half years."

By highlighting the length of time Apple had spent developing its products, Jobs made it clear that these weren't quick or thoughtless endeavors but rather the result of meticulous planning and dedication. Research shows that when consumers see the work behind the product, like a chef cooking their meal, they tend to value it more highly.

Another psychological tactic Jobs employed was the halo effect, a bias that leads people to transfer positive impressions of one thing onto another associated entity. Jobs capitalized on this with Apple's marketing, mainly through campaigns like "Think Different." The ad connected Apple with iconic figures such as Gandhi, Albert Einstein, and Picasso—people seen as revolutionary thinkers. The message was clear: just as these figures changed the world, so would Apple.

Jobs himself was often the subject of the halo effect. His status as a tech visionary gave everything he said and did more weight. Whether he was introducing a new iPod or the latest iPhone, the public's perception of Jobs as a genius transferred to their perception of Apple's products. The "Think Different" campaign, winning a 1998 Emmy for best commercial, saved Apple from bankruptcy and re-established the company as an innovative powerhouse.

Jobs also understood the power of anchoring, which is the cognitive bias where an initial reference point influences subsequent decisions. He masterfully employed this tactic during product launches, mainly when introducing the iPod in 2001. At $399, the iPod was significantly more expensive than other MP3 players, which averaged around $150. To make the price seem more reasonable, Jobs shifted the focus from the overall cost to the cost per song, stating:

"An iPod holds 1,000 songs in your pocket and costs only 30 cents a song."

This redefined how people thought about the product's value, anchoring their perception to the price per song rather than the total price.

Similarly, Jobs often used chunking to group information into easily digestible pieces. When introducing the iPhone, instead of listing hundreds of features, he boiled it down to three revolutionary aspects:

"Today, we're introducing three revolutionary products of this class. The first is a widescreen iPod with touch controls. The second is a revolutionary mobile phone. And the third is a breakthrough internet communications device."

The punchline came when Jobs revealed these weren't three separate devices—they were one, the iPhone. This strategic chunking made the presentation more digestible, memorable, and impactful.

Jobs was often said to have a "reality distortion field," a term his colleagues coined to describe his ability to convince people of seemingly impossible things. This wasn't just charisma; it was a calculated use of storytelling, optimism, and sheer confidence. Jobs could make his audience believe in his vision, no matter how outlandish it seemed. This ability to project an alternate reality was key to persuading both employees and customers to buy into his long-term plans.

He often introduced products with a story that grounded his technological achievements in a relatable, human context. For example, when launching the iPad, he framed it as a product that came not from market research or consumer demand but from an insight into how people live and work. This personalized narrative made his technology feel innovative and inevitable, as if it had always been meant to be.

Steve Jobs also understood the importance of endings. He employed the recency bias—our tendency to remember the most recent part of an experience—by ending his presentations with a surprise. His iconic "One More Thing" was a stroke of genius in closing the deal. By saving one last exciting feature for the end, Jobs left his audience in awe, making them feel like they had just witnessed something transformative. This technique made his presentations not just memorable but climactic. Eventually, everyone expected the "one more thing" ruse; during the entire launch, the audience salivated over the final stroke of prestige Jobs unleashed as if he were a stage magician.

Jobs launched a company on the brink of bankruptcy in a dynamic internet age and survived what was later called the "tech bubble," where most young technology companies were bought out or failed. He did this during one of the most dynamic aspects of the information age, and he managed to stay at the top of a cutthroat and rapidly evolving sector. He did this because he was a showman and offered a superior product. Jobs embodied the eleven principles of post-modern persuasion, and in fact, many of the principles we will discuss were used by Jobs himself.

Jobs embraced relativity by remaining neutral and focusing on his central vision, making great products for people who change the world - whatever that means to them. He embraced storytelling by creating an event around product launches instead of quarterly earnings calls. He focused on discussing the sweat his teams put into products to invest in customers. The displays were interactive and sought to anticipate customers' needs as the thought leaders of a tech revolution. Most of all, Jobs created a core of customers huddled around a central idea that he embodied: the rebel. This image of a rebel built off of the image of Gandhi, Martin Luther King Jr., Emilia Ehart, and Winston Churchill, uniting creative minds from various causes into one consumer base. Finally, he blurred the lines between creator and consumer through his products, which sought to foster creation and encourage innovation and design through seamless aesthetics, flawless packaging, and versatile features.

LET'S SEE PAUL ALLEN'S CARD

WHAT AMERICAN PSYCHO TELLS US ABOUT OUR FUTURE SELVES

If you have not seen the Movie American Psycho, stop reading and watch it now.

> "The simulacrum is never that which conceals the truth—it is the truth which conceals that there is none. The simulacrum is true."
>
> Jean Baudrillard

Nestled amongst the towering glass canyons of lower Manhattan, Patrick Bateman walks intentionally toward his individualized obscurity. Under Oliver Peoples glasses and Ferragamo shoes he exists not as an individual but as a meticulously crafted facade—a copy of a copy, endlessly replicated in the image of a society that worships at the altar of consumerism. His identity is a collage of designer labels, upscale restaurants, and exclusive clubs, exhausting routines. Bateman doesn't live life; he curates it, assembling experiences and possessions in a relentless pursuit to outdo not just others, but out replicate a false construct of himself. Yet, beneath this polished veneer lies an unsettling emptiness—a void where authenticity should reside.

Carl Jung couldn't have created a better case study for his analysis. Through the lens of Carl Jung's analytical psychology, Bateman can be seen as a personification of the conflict between the persona, the shadow, and the failure to achieve individuation.

In Jungian psychology, the **persona** represents the social mask one wears to navigate societal expectations. It is the outward face we present to the world, often hiding our true selves to fit in or gain acceptance. Patrick Bateman's persona is meticulously crafted. He is a Wall Street investment banker, embodying the pinnacle of capitalist success. His obsession with designer brands, grooming routines, and physical fitness highlights his commitment to maintaining an impeccable exterior. Bateman frequents exclusive restaurants and clubs, reinforcing his status among the elite.

Bateman's persona is exaggerated to the point of parody.

His fixation on materialism and appearances reflects a deep-seated need to conform to societal ideals of success. However, this over-identification with the persona leads to a complete disconnection from his authentic self. Jung warned that an overemphasis on the persona could result in a shallow existence, where the individual becomes merely a role they are playing, losing touch with their true nature.

The **shadow** represents the unconscious aspects of the personality that the conscious ego does not recognize or accept. It often contains repressed desires, weaknesses, and instincts. His compulsions to commit brutal acts of murder and torture out of hatred for who he has become, a hatred he cannot recognize.

Bateman's shadow is a repository for all the qualities he cannot acknowledge within himself due to societal pressures and personal denial. The more he strives to perfect his persona, the more potent his shadow becomes. Jung believed that ignoring the shadow leads to its projection onto others or its eruption into consciousness in destructive ways. Bateman's heinous acts can be seen as the uncontrolled emergence of his shadow, overwhelming his persona.

In Jungian theory, the **anima** represents the feminine inner personality in men. It is associated with emotions, intuition, and relationships. Bateman views women as objects for gratification or targets for his violence or the need to fit in at the perfect restaurant. But Bateman cannot form an emotional connection because there is nothing to connect to. He sees the Anima as a threat to his existence and a need to be fulfilled that is not fashionable - so he represses it. Bateman's rejection of his anima leads to a lack of emotional depth and empathy. Jung suggested that integrating the anima is essential for psychological wholeness. Bateman's inability to acknowledge this aspect of himself contributes to his fragmented psyche and destructive behavior.

Individuation is the process of integrating all parts of the psyche—conscious and unconscious—to achieve a complete and balanced self. Lifting his identity in turn fractures the conscious. He accepts threats to his identity by failing to correct those who mis-identify him - it no longer matters and he makes no meaningful effort to identify why this is.

Bateman's journey is the antithesis of individuation. Instead of integrating his shadow and other unconscious elements, he is consumed by them. His psyche fractures under the weight of his repressed content, leading to psychosis. Jung emphasized the importance of confronting and assimilating the shadow to avoid such outcomes Bateman's obsession with possessions replaces meaningful values. His lack of self-awareness cause his interpersonal interactions to lack depth, contributing to isolation. He lives in a society fixated on external success that neglects inner development.

In theory, if Bateman were to embark on a journey of self-discovery, acknowledging his shadow without judgment, he might begin to heal. But the glass caverns of lower Manhattan create a cave he does not know he is in. To leave this Matrix he would first have to know that he is in one. He would have to reject his worldview and risk destroying the house of cards he has created. What little identity he had would crumble. Jung felt this himself when he broke from Freud, a split that resulted in the Red Book and one of the most important works on psychology history has known.

The other problem is that Bateman has no self and this process requires the acknowledgement of an identity independent of his shadow- independent of the *Simulcrua*.

Bateman's life is the amalgamation of the tyranny of surfaces. He is a surface. He is the embodiment of what happens when a person becomes so consumed by the need to project an image that the line between the self and the facade blurs beyond recognition. He has crossed the event horizon such that he has merged fully his copy of himself and the tulpa of his capitalist religion.

Bateman's mornings are ritualistic performances:

"I shower using a water-activated gel cleanser, then a honey-almond body scrub, and on the face an exfoliating gel scrub. I apply herb-mint facial masque, which I leave on for ten minutes while I prepare the rest of my routine."

Much like a churchgoer who has merged their identity, he does this precisely so that he can tell you he has done this. This obsessive attention to detail isn't about hygiene or self-care; it's about constructing a persona that fits the hyperreal world he inhabits. Each product, each brand, is a brushstroke in the portrait of a man who has conflated consumption with existence.

Bateman has become a walking screen projecting the images of his captors as they rotate into his existence. He keeps them alive with his consumerism so that they may continue to propagate their messages. They keep him alive with their consumerism so that they may continue to propagate their messages. The darwinian urges of capitalism are to copy, copy, copy and when that is not profitable make a new copy.

How do we mass market an individualized product? The illusion of choice. Bateman's Valentino suits, the latest Rolex, reservations at Dorsia—all are tokens in a game where the rules are defined by appearances. But the products market individuality while the experiences remain mundane. When he consumes an experience, he doesn't seek experiences for their inherent value but for how they elevate his standing in the eyes of others who are equally lost in this labyrinth of materialism.

His comical but yet complex knowledge of Huey Lewis and the News shows us how serious he takes the cultural facade. At great risk of pissing my reader off, Huey Lewis and the News is about as culturally important as Aldous Snow's *African Child, from the movie Get Him to the Greek*. Given the value we place on parody, maybe even less so.

Plato's Allegory of the Cave speaks of prisoners chained in such a way that they can only see the shadows cast on a wall, mistaking those illusions for reality. The illusions become their thoughts. Bateman is one such prisoner, but the shadows he chases are cast by the iconic clop clop of a new heel on a Faragamo or Louboutin loafer or the eggshell sheen of business cards embossed with subtle off-white coloring.

"I just want to say, I'd like to have a relationship with someone special" a familiar refrain in his mind but this time delivered to a prostitute he would ultimately kill. He says this because this is what you say.

The most telling illustration of Bateman's imprisonment is the ultimate reflection of his identity:

"I flip open my card case and hand him my card. He examines it carefully. 'Nice,' he says simply. I smile appreciatively. 'But wait,' he says, pulling out his own card. 'Raised lettering, pale nimbus white...'

Bateman is trapped, the praise that accompanies hogmany is never sufficient.

In this moment, the business card transcends its practical purpose and becomes an artifact of power, a symbol laden with unspoken hierarchies. The men in the room aren't exchanging contact information; they're engaging in a silent duel where the finest details—a watermark, the thickness of the paper—can signify triumph or defeat. What subtle deviation from the pre-established rule or order nets the most profit?

Names, too, lose their anchoring to identity. Colleagues mistake Bateman for others with alarming regularity, and he does the same. In a conversation with a peer:

"Marcus, I didn't know you were into fusion cuisine," someone remarks.

Bateman doesn't correct him. Why would he? In this world, he is an individual and he is not a conformist. Rather he has chosen a group with similar tastes - a group that he ironically despises.

In Bateman's world, the business card is a perfect simulacrum—an object that has become more real than the reality it was meant to represent. Oh, the irony of agonizing over contact cards while getting names completely incorrect. The contact card superceding the true identity.

Batemen calls - all in - in this zero sum game by choking out "let's see Paul Allen's card"-- he knows he doesn't have the cards. His internal monologue spirals into envy and despair and manifests itself as sweat gathering on the Moschino collar. But game respects game, there are no haters here. Despite its undeniable damage to his existence he can't control the accolades.

"Look at that subtle coloring. The tasteful thickness of it. Oh my God, it even has a watermark."

This reaction is visceral. The card is a mirror reflecting his lack of individuality, a shadow mocking his quest for superiority. It's a reminder that in the hyperreal world, there's always another level of perfection to attain—a Sisyphean endeavor that only deepens his existential void.

Bateman's fixation on brands extends beyond mere preference; it's a doctrine he follows with religious fervor. His wardrobe isn't chosen for comfort or personal taste but for the statement it makes. A Zegna tie isn't just silk around his neck; it's a badge of honor in the unspoken competition he's embroiled in daily.

In a rare moment where the facade cracks, Bateman attempts to confess his heinous actions to his lawyer, Harold Carnes. The confession is a desperate plea for recognition—not of his crimes, but of his existence. He says:

"I just had to kill a lot of people! And I... I don't think I'm gonna get away with it this time."

But even this raw admission is swallowed by the abyss of hyperreality. Carnes dismisses it as a joke, further entrenching Bateman's isolation.

"Jesus, Davis," Carnes laughs, mistaking him for someone else. "That was hilarious. That was really good."

The interchangeability of identities strikes again. Bateman's attempt at authenticity is invalidated, his voice lost amid the echoes of a world that hears only what it wants to hear. His confession becomes another shadow—intangible, ungraspable, and ultimately, meaningless.

Bateman's descent into violence is not a break from his hyperreal existence but an extension of it. The brutality he inflicts is devoid of genuine emotion; it's another performance, an extreme attempt to feel something, anything, that might affirm his humanity.

His self wants to destroy the copies and the easiest target are the objects of his desire.

Yet, these acts fail to anchor him to reality. They go unnoticed or are misinterpreted by those around him, reinforcing the notion that in his world, the lines between reality and illusion are irreparably blurred.

"I have all the characteristics of a human being: blood, flesh, skin, hair; but my depersonalization is so intense, has gone so deep, that the normal ability to feel compassion has been eradicated."

He still doesn't get it.

His acknowledgment of this deep-seated numbness highlights the futility of his actions and is the ultimate act of his lack of self-awareness. Violence doesn't shatter the simulacrum; it reinforces it, adding layers to the facade he cannot escape. The question then arises: How does one communicate with someone like Bateman? How do we penetrate the layers of hyperreality to touch the remnants of genuine self buried within?

To approach Bateman, we must first engage with the symbols he understands. This means leveraging the very status and luxury he idolizes but reframing them to evoke introspection. Imagine presenting him with an exclusive invitation to an art exhibit featuring works that challenge consumerism—a gallery where the finest suits are made from recycled materials, where luxury is redefined not by price tags but by social impact. A ride in an electric car that is rare and expensive. Introduce anomalies into his flawless world. Ask questions that unsettle the foundations of his beliefs:

"How is the Ermenegildo Zegna tie made?"

This nudges him to reflect on the arbitrary values he assigns to objects, potentially igniting a spark of critical thought. Appeal to his logic and his pride. Point out the cracks in his hyperreal world:

"Did he mistake you for Halberstram? Perhaps you should try a different suit my guy."

This subtle challenge to his uniqueness might provoke him to question the identity he's so carefully constructed. Encourage him to consider the ephemeral nature of trends:

"Ever wonder why we switch favorite restaurants every four months?"

By highlighting the transient nature of his world, you may guide him toward contemplating what endures beyond the surface. The goal isn't to dismantle Bateman's reality in one fell swoop—that would be met with resistance and denial. Instead, it's about planting seeds of doubt, creating moments of cognitive dissonance that encourage him to seek substance over style.

Whether Bateman can ever truly escape his hyperreal cave is uncertain. His identity is so enmeshed with the shadows that stepping into the light might feel like an annihilation of self. However, the mere act of questioning—even slightly—begins to loosen the chains. For Bateman, and perhaps for society at large, the journey toward authenticity starts with recognizing the shadows for what they are: reflections without substance. It's about seeking experiences and connections that are genuine, unmediated by the distortions of consumer culture.

Bateman's story is not so extreme when we edit out the violence, yet it holds a mirror to the pervasive influence of hyperreality in our own lives.

How often do we measure our worth by the cars we drive, the clothes we wear, or the followers we have on social media?

Ignoring your children for your phone. Going into debt for a label? Unnatural adherence to name brands clearly identical to immigrations? Numbing yourself on drugs? Pretending to like popular culture that we don't like for social norms? Group-thinking our political and cultural values? These are the qualities of Bateman's existence

and yours.

In the end, perhaps the most profound act of persuasion is not to change Bateman but to learn from his descent. To recognize the shadows in our own caves and have the courage to turn toward the light, even if it means redefining who we are. By embracing authenticity, questioning the symbols that surround us, and seeking deeper meaning in our lives, we can step out of the cave. It's not an easy path, but it's a necessary one if we are to reclaim our individuality and forge genuine connections in an increasingly hyperreal world. By stepping out of the cave we can greet those who are not far behind us.

L'ART DE LA PERSUASION POSTMODERNE: MASTERING PERSUASION IN A POSTMODERN WORLD

THE TEN ESSENTIAL RULES FOR PERSUASION IN AN AGE OF AMBIGUITY

"Myth is neither a lie nor a confession: it is an inflection."

Roland Barthes, *Mythologies*

Thus far, you know that the future will be dominated by regurgitated information modified to suit the tastes of fragmented groups. This will result in more fragmented groups as consumers become more skeptical of information that does not fit their narrative or worldview. Consumers will be entrenched in their way of thought and reject that which does not conform.

We can either conform our communication to the needs of particular groups or take a much more careful approach designed to attract disparate groups. French thinker Jean-François Lyotard tells us grand narratives and universal truths are supplanted by focusing on mini-narratives and localized, context-dependent knowledge.

Lyotard posits that our experiences are no longer interpreted through the lens of overarching ideologies but through a patchwork of individual perspectives. This relativistic approach acknowledges the plurality of truths and the diverse ways individuals construct meaning, embracing the instability and fragmentation of postmodern life.

Unguided by a single dominant story, we experience truth personally and contextually, lending new value to interpretation and subjectivity.

Reject Lyotard at your peril.

Instead, embrace relativity in the message to warm the consumer or listener to a new way of thinking. Building off of Lyotard's reality, the power of persuasion lies not in declaring one "correct" way of seeing the world but in inviting the audience to consider new perspectives within their frameworks of experience.

Respecting this subjectivity is no longer optional; it's a prerequisite for connection. As you will see, the Trobriand Islanders understood this principle well in subtly reshaping cricket to align with their cultural norms. They accepted the new influence outright; instead, they creatively adapted it to resonate with their values, inviting cooperation rather than conflict. Similarly, effective modern communicators must embrace the audience's reality rather than imposing their own. French philosophers who wiped the foggy window peering into this digital renais

L'Art de la Persuasion Postmoderne *is* a set of principles that acknowledges this dynamic and seeks to bridge the gap between speaker and listener in a fluid, inclusive, and resonant way. The title pays homage to the post-war French philosophers who wiped the foggy window peering into this digital renaissance long before we would encounter it.

By respecting the audience's intelligence, communicators signal that they are not here to dictate but to engage. Transparency builds trust by revealing not just the message but the motivation behind it. Participation is welcomed, turning the audience from passive recipients to active co-creators in the narrative. In acknowledging ambiguity, communicators make room for the complexities of modern life, allowing a message to coexist with doubt and nuance. Appeals to shared values touch the very heart of human experience, tapping into a powerful collective identity. And finally, humor adds a touch of lightness, diffusing tension and easily connecting across divides.

Each element offers a way to resonate with audiences on a level that transcends mere information exchange. By meeting people where they are rather than where we expect them to be, communicators can form lasting connections grounded in respect and shared humanity. The *L'Art de la Persuasion Postmoderne* is a roadmap for this process—a guide to fostering resilient, adaptable, and deeply authentic relationships. In embracing these principles, we're not just transmitting messages; we're cultivating understanding and sparking a dialogue acknowledging the varied and multifaceted experiences of the modern world.

THE FIRST RULE

Embrace Relativity

In the early 20th century, British missionaries arrived on the Trobriand Islands, off the eastern coast of Papua New Guinea. Their mission was to spread Christianity and Western values among the indigenous population. They introduced cricket, hoping it would serve as a civilizing influence and a wholesome alternative to the Trobrianders' traditional practices, such as ritualistic warfare and elaborate social customs.

Initially, the islanders learned the game by British rules. But over time, they adapted cricket to fit their cultural context. British cricket's rigid structure and competitive nature transformed into a vibrant communal event. Matches became grand festivals with dozens of players on each side—often over 50 per team. The games were infused with traditional dances, chants, and rituals. Players adorned themselves with elaborate costumes, body paint, and decorative headdresses of feathers and shells.

One striking adaptation was the integration of tribal rivalry into the matches. Cricket became a symbolic replacement for warfare. Villages competed against each other, and the outcome reflected social status and honor. Magic and sorcery were incorporated, with teams performing spells and rituals to gain advantages. Bats and balls were sometimes treated with substances believed to possess supernatural powers.

Scoring wasn't just about runs; it also considered performance quality, including the creativity of dances and the effectiveness of chants. Matches could last several days, coinciding with harvest festivals and significant communal events. They became platforms for social interaction, courtship, and reinforcing community bonds.

Rather than accepting the game as dictated by the British, the Trobrianders reinterpreted it through their cultural lens. They received the new influence outright; they adapted it to serve their social and cultural needs. This relativistic approach allowed them to retain their identity while engaging with an external force, showcasing flexibility and creativity in the face of change.

Their adaptation was a subtle yet powerful form of cultural negotiation. By reshaping the game, they asserted their agency and resisted colonial imposition without confrontation. Their version of cricket preserved and expressed their traditions while adopting Western practices. This was persuasive because it maintained harmony with the missionaries while subtly undermining the intended cultural assimilation.

The transformed game also persuaded younger generations to engage with their cultural heritage. By incorporating traditional dances, music, and rituals into cricket, elders ensured these elements remained relevant and appealing. It reinforced community cohesion and passed down important social values engagingly.

At a time when colonial powers imposed their cultures on indigenous populations worldwide, the Trobriand Islanders' approach was both unique and inventive. They didn't passively accept cultural imports nor engage in open rebellion. Instead, they creatively appropriated an element of the colonizers' culture, transforming it into something distinctly their own. This ingenuity allowed them to navigate colonial complexities with autonomy and resilience. By reimagining cricket, they honored their past while engaging with the present—a strategic adaptation that preserved their cultural identity and resisted assimilation.

Here are other examples:

• Japan's Meiji Restoration: In the late 19th century, Japan modernized by embracing Western technology and industrial practices. However, instead of adopting these elements wholesale, Japan selectively integrated them with its cultural traditions. While modernizing its military and industry, Japan maintained its imperial system and social structures. This selective assimilation allowed Japan to become a global power while preserving its unique identity.

• African Syncretic Religions: Christianity was introduced through colonial missions in many African countries. Over time, indigenous populations blended Christian teachings with local beliefs and customs, leading to syncretic religions. Churches incorporated traditional music, dance, and languages into worship, creating a form of Christianity that resonated with local cultures. This made the religion more accessible and meaningful to indigenous communities.

• Fusion Cuisines: Blending culinary traditions has led to fusion cuisines worldwide. For instance, Peruvian Nikkei cuisine combines Japanese techniques with Peruvian ingredients, resulting in unique dishes like ceviche with soy sauce. This culinary relativity allows innovative flavors while respecting both cultures' culinary heritage.

• Multilingual Education: Educational programs incorporating multiple languages embrace relativity in linguistically diverse regions. Teaching in dominant and local languages respects cultural identities while providing broader opportunities. This fosters inclusivity and acknowledges the value of different linguistic perspectives.

• Music Genres: Genres like jazz, reggae, and hip-hop originated from blending different cultural influences. Reggae, for example, emerged in Jamaica by fusing traditional mento and calypso music with American rhythm and blues. This creative synthesis reflects embracing relativity by combining disparate elements to create something new and culturally significant.

Embracing relativity doesn't mean adopting another culture wholesale. Instead, it involves adapting messages, products, or brands to avoid rejecting cultural differences, like McDonald's and its *Hinduburger*.

Maintaining authenticity in a global market demands agility and an iterative approach. Consumer preferences, cultural dynamics, and social trends constantly evolve. Brands must adapt to these changes, stay connected to local markets, and maintain a feedback loop. This includes refining brand messaging, updating products to fit local trends, or responding to shifts in cultural attitudes.

Nike, for example, has upheld its global identity rooted in athletic performance and empowerment while localizing campaigns through collaborations with athletes and influencers who resonate with specific markets. Similarly, Airbnb balances global consistency with local relevance by encouraging hosts to share unique stories and fostering deeper connections with travelers seeking immersive experiences.

Brands like Nike and Airbnb have successfully maintained authenticity while expanding globally. Nike adapts its marketing to resonate with diverse cultures while staying true to its core identity. By collaborating with local athletes and embracing cultural diversity in ads, Nike fosters a global community that values athleticism and self-expression. Airbnb localizes its platform to cater to unique market preferences, providing localized content, supporting regional partnerships, and showcasing diverse accommodations that reflect various cultural identities.

On the flip side, failed attempts provide cautionary tales. Pepsi's controversial ad featuring Kendall Jenner attempted to align the brand with social activism but lacked cultural sensitivity, trivializing significant social movements. Similarly, Walmart's failure in Germany teaches the importance of adapting to local customs and consumer behavior. Imposing its American-centric business model without considering German cultural and shopping habits alienated customers, leading to withdrawal from the market.

Globally successful brands respect local cultures, remain open to change, and iterate their approach based on consumer feedback. Much like the transformation of cricket in the Trobriand Islands, this allows for the harmonious blending of new influences with core values, fostering mutual respect and innovation across cultural divides.

THE SECOND RULE

Use the Power of Sticky Stories

One evening in 1946, a young man named Ray Bradbury sat at his typewriter and began crafting a story about firemen—not the kind who extinguish fires. Still, those who ignite them burn books in a dystopian world ruled by censorship. The result was *Fahrenheit 451*, an enthralling tale that became an enduring metaphor for the dangers of censorship and the power of knowledge.

But here's the twist: Bradbury wasn't delivering a lecture or bombarding readers with statistics on free speech violations. He told a story. And in doing so, he planted an idea that has stuck with readers for decades. Why do stories like *Fahrenheit 451* linger long after lectures and statistics fade from memory?

Stories perform magic in our brains, making information stick in ways mere facts and figures can't. More intriguingly, stories persuade us subtly, nudging us to see the world differently without feeling coerced.

Let's delve into the science. When we hear a story, our brains light up beyond mere language comprehension. Remember the last time someone described a delicious meal? Your brain didn't just register the words "juicy burger" or "crispy fries"—it simulated the taste, texture, and smell. Your sensory cortex was activated. This phenomenon, called neural coupling, is one reason stories are so powerful: they engage multiple brain areas, allowing us to experience the story as if we're living it ourselves.

In a study by neuroscientist Uri Hasson at Princeton University, researchers found that when someone tells a story, the listener's brain activity mirrors the storyteller's. If the storyteller's brain activates in regions associated with movement, the listener's brain does the same. It's almost like the storyteller's brain is syncing up with the listener's, creating a shared experience and making the information more memorable.

But there's more. Stories are emotional experiences. As decades of research show, emotions are the glue that binds memories. Neuroscientist Elizabeth Phelps found that emotionally charged events are processed more deeply, leading to better recall. When we hear a story with an emotional arc—conflict, struggle, victory—we're far more likely to remember it.

This explains why stories like "The Boy Who Cried Wolf" or "The Emperor's New Clothes" endure across centuries. They are not just moral lessons; they are emotionally charged narratives. We feel the tension, embarrassment, and consequences, searing the message into our brains.

Stories also simplify complexity. Our brains crave efficiency—we like patterns and structures. And what's a story if not a neatly structured package of information? Beginning, middle, end.

In 2002, researchers Arthur Graesser and Melissa Olde compared how people remembered information presented as a story versus plain facts. The story format led to better recall. Why? Stories reduce cognitive load—the mental effort required to process information. Instead of remembering unrelated facts, stories offer a framework, connecting the dots and embedding facts within a narrative our brains naturally follow.

Here's where it gets even more enjoyable. Stories don't just stick with us—they change us quietly, almost stealthily. When presented with arguments, we might react with skepticism or defensiveness. No one likes being told what to think. But stories slip past our defenses.

Consider psychological reactance—people resist persuasion when they feel their freedom of choice is threatened. If someone says, "You should believe this," you might rebel. But a story invites you to step into the narrative, to experience it yourself. Often, you conclude the storyteller intended without feeling pushed.

Psychologists Melanie Green and Timothy Brock explored this in their 2000 study on narrative transportation. They found that when people are "transported" into a story, they become less critical and less likely to counter-argue. Stories persuade us without feeling like persuasion. They draw us in emotionally and let us draw our conclusions.

So, why do we remember stories more than other types of information? Stories engage us cognitively, emotionally, and neurologically. They activate our sensory experiences, tap into our emotions, and provide a framework. Most importantly, they don't make us feel told what to think—they invite us to participate.

This is why *Fahrenheit 451* remains a powerful allegory for censorship decades later. We remember courtroom stories like O.J. Simpson's "If It Doesn't Fit, You Must Acquit" long after the facts fade. And it's why brands like Nike's "Just Do It" and Apple's "Think Different" stick with us—they're stories in miniature, telling us who we can be if we step into the narrative.

We are drowning in information; facts alone are insufficient. Stories are our lifeboats—memorable, persuasive, and human. We remember them not because they tell us what to think but because they invite us to think for ourselves.

Humans are more accustomed to stories than dense factual data. For thousands of years, Australia's Aboriginal peoples navigated their vast landscape using "songlines" or "dreaming tracks." These oral narratives—stories, songs, dances, rituals—describe land features, water sources, hunting grounds, and sacred sites. Each songline recounts the land's creation by ancestral beings, connecting geography with spirituality.

As individuals travel, they sing the song associated with that route. The lyrics contain detailed environmental information, serving as a living map. Melody and rhythm encode this knowledge, making it easier to remember and pass down through generations. These songs aren't just practical guides but deeply spiritual narratives reinforcing the community's connection to the land and ancestors. One songline, the Uluru songline, is a 3,000 km journey connecting the east coast to the central deserts.

Songlines crisscross the Australian continent, linking tribes and languages through shared stories. They formed a means of communication, fostering trade and social cohesion among different Aboriginal groups. By following a songline, individuals traverse vast distances, relying on embedded knowledge to find sustenance and navigate terrain.

Songlines persuade by engaging listeners emotionally and intellectually. Captivating narratives makes information memorable, ensuring essential knowledge is retained and passed on. They also persuade individuals to respect the land, adhere to social norms, and maintain ancestral traditions.

While other societies developed written records and maps, Aboriginal Australians crafted a dynamic, living knowledge repository. Songlines could adapt over time, incorporating new information and reflecting environmental changes. This flexibility made them an enduring and effective means of knowledge transmission.

- Aesop's Fables: The ancient Greek storyteller Aesop used fables with animals and inanimate objects to convey moral lessons. Stories like "The Tortoise and the Hare" and "The Boy Who Cried Wolf" have endured for centuries, teaching valuable principles through simple, engaging narratives. These fables are used worldwide to instill ethical values in children.

- Uncle Tom's Cabin: Published in 1852, Harriet Beecher Stowe's novel depicted the harsh realities of slavery in the United States. Through vivid characters, the book galvanized anti-slavery sentiments among Northern readers without indoctrination. It's credited with sparking the abolitionist movement in the 1850s and inspiring plays across the country.

- Brand Storytelling: Companies often use storytelling in branding strategies. Teachers use storytelling to make lessons more engaging and memorable. Educators framing information within a narrative enhances students' understanding and retention. This is particularly effective in teaching history, literature, and social studies, where stories bring subjects to life.

THE THIRD RULE

Foster Authenticity and Transparency

In Norway, salaries are public information and easily accessible. The government releases tax records annually, including individual salaries, taxes paid, and wealth. This system, known as *skattelister*, promotes openness and fairness. The logic is to create a more egalitarian society where individuals can see what their peers, coworkers, and superiors earn. Some might criticize this as socialist, but it works for Norwegians and ensures public services are funded.

This transparency leads to several societal benefits. People are more likely to negotiate fair wages when they know what others in similar roles earn. By making financial information public, the Norwegian government fosters a sense of trust and accountability.

While many countries guard this information as private, Norway's radical transparency has had positive outcomes, minimizing wage discrimination and corruption. A striking example is the country's traffic fines system, which is proportional to income. Norway uses an income-based model to calculate fines for speeding and other violations, reflecting its commitment to fairness.

In a famous case, a Norwegian businessman received one of the world's most expensive speeding fines—over $100,000—for driving 27 km/h (around 17 mph) over the speed limit. The fine was based on his multi-million-dollar income, reflecting that penalties should be significant deterrents for all income levels.

This approach ensures a level playing field. A fixed fine might disproportionately affect low-income people while having little impact on the wealthy. Norway's system is perceived as more equitable because penalties are proportional to the ability to pay, preventing traffic citations from being a separate tax on the disadvantaged.

Norway's emphasis on transparency aligns with its broader social philosophy of fairness, equity, and trust. It fosters a culture where public institutions and individuals are held accountable. For a country known for high taxes and a strong welfare state, these policies ensure everyone faces the same relative consequences for their actions.

Buffer, a social media management company founded in 2010, made a bold move by implementing radical transparency. In 2013, the company publicly released employees' salaries, including the formulas used to calculate them. This information was available internally and published on Buffer's website. Buffer also shared revenue figures, user statistics, and its equity structure.

Transparency extended to other aspects: Buffer openly discussed funding rounds, including terms and valuations, and shared details about internal decision-making. Founders Joel Gascoigne and Leo Widrich believed this openness would build trust among employees, customers, and the broader community.

This was unconventional, especially in the competitive tech industry, where companies often guard such information. Critics questioned whether this would lead to talent poaching, internal dissatisfaction, or strategic disadvantages. However, Buffer persisted, continuously refining transparency practices.

The radical transparency was persuasive in several ways. Internally, it motivated employees by clarifying compensation and career progression, and knowing how salaries were determined reduced suspicions of bias or favoritism. It also encouraged accountability, as everyone understood how their contributions affected performance.

Externally, transparency built trust with customers and partners. By revealing business metrics, Buffer invited others to hold it accountable, demonstrating confidence in operations. This openness differentiated Buffer from competitors, appealing to customers who valued ethical practices.

Moreover, transparency attracted talent who resonated with the company's values. Job seekers appreciating honesty and clarity were drawn to Buffer, enhancing its ability to recruit like-minded individuals. At the time, few companies practiced such extensive transparency. Compensation, equity stakes, and financial performance were typically guarded secrets. Buffer's decision was a radical departure from the norm.

This uniqueness lies in sharing and integrating transparency into its core values. Transparency wasn't a marketing gimmick but a foundational principle guiding all aspects of the business. The inventive approach challenged traditional notions of corporate secrecy and sparked conversations about openness in business.

Authenticity and transparency reduce skepticism and resistance. Individuals who believe a communicator is genuine and forthcoming are more likely to be receptive. This applies to personal relationships, organizational settings, and public communications.

Here are some other examples of radical transparency:

• Open-source software: Projects like Linux and Apache operate with complete transparency. The source code is publicly available for viewing, modifying, and distributing. This openness fosters a collaborative community where contributors can verify code integrity and contribute improvements. Collective ownership and shared values reinforce the project's authenticity.

• Government Transparency: Some governments pursue transparency to build public trust. Estonia implemented e-governance systems allowing citizens to access public records, monitor government spending, and participate in decision-making online. This reduces corruption and enhances democratic engagement, persuading citizens of the government's legitimacy.

• Radical Candor: Kim Scott popularized this concept, encouraging leaders to provide honest, direct feedback while showing genuine employee care. This fosters authenticity in workplace relationships, improving performance and engagement. Leaders who are transparent about expectations and concerns build trust and motivate teams effectively.

• Nonprofits: Organizations like Charity: Water provide detailed reports on how donations are used, including GPS coordinates and photos of completed projects. This transparency ensures donors' contributions make a real impact, enhances trust, and encourages continued support.

THE FOURTH RULE

Create Interactive and Participatory Experiences

In 2008, researchers at the University of Washington launched Foldit, an innovative online puzzle game. The premise was simple yet revolutionary: players worldwide could manipulate virtual protein structures to achieve the most energetically stable configurations. Proteins, with their complex 3D shapes, play crucial roles in biological processes, and understanding their structures is essential for advancements in medicine and biochemistry.

Scientists have long struggled to predict protein folding due to the astronomical number of possible configurations. Traditional computational methods are time-consuming and often ineffective for challenging proteins. The Foldit team hypothesized that human intuition and pattern recognition could outperform algorithms in specific tasks.

Foldit transformed the intricate problem of protein folding into an accessible, engaging game. Players were presented with a 3D protein model and tools to twist, bend, and manipulate its structure. The game's scoring system rewarded players for achieving lower-energy, more stable configurations. No prior knowledge of biochemistry was required; tutorials and feedback guided players.

The global response was remarkable. Thousands joined the Foldit community, ranging from gamers to scientists to curious novices. In 2011, Foldit players made headlines when they deciphered the structure of a retroviral protease enzyme related to HIV/AIDS—a problem that had stumped scientists for over a decade—in just three weeks. Their solution provided critical insights for drug development efforts.

Foldit's interactive nature empowered players to contribute meaningfully to scientific research. Participants weren't passive consumers but active collaborators. The game's design fostered ownership and investment, motivating players to tackle complex problems enthusiastically.

The Foldit team persuaded thousands to dedicate time and effort by presenting the challenge in a compelling, game-like format. The persuasive power lies in making the experience enjoyable and rewarding. Gamification elements—points, leaderboards, collaborative teams—tapped into intrinsic motivations for challenge, competition, and social interaction.

By simplifying the interface and providing immediate feedback, Foldit lowered barriers to entry. The game persuaded players their contributions were valuable, regardless of background. Success stories and community recognition further motivated deep engagement.

Moreover, publicized achievements demonstrated the impact of their efforts, reinforcing the message that collective participation could lead to significant scientific breakthroughs.

At its launch, Foldit pioneered the application of citizen science and gamification to a complex, real-world problem. While citizen science projects existed, they often involved data collection or simple analysis. Foldit invited participants to engage in sophisticated problem-solving traditionally reserved for experts.

The game's inventive approach bridged entertainment and scientific research. By harnessing human intuition, Foldit opened new avenues for collaborative discovery, challenging conventional notions of who could contribute to science and how.

Creating interactive and participatory experiences involves designing opportunities for individuals to actively engage with content, contributing ideas, skills, or actions. This contrasts with passive consumption, which emphasizes collaboration and co-creation. Interactive experiences are persuasive because they involve participants directly, fostering more profound connections. Active involvement leads to internalizing messages, developing ownership, and motivating further contribution.

In a post-modern world characterized by information overload and fragmented attention, interactive experiences cut through the noise by offering meaningful engagement. They empower individuals, democratize processes, and can lead to innovative solutions through collective intelligence.

- Wikipedia: Revolutionized access to knowledge by allowing users worldwide to create and edit articles collaboratively. This participatory model harnessed the contributions of millions to build a comprehensive, ever-evolving repository. Wikipedia demonstrates how interactive platforms can democratize knowledge creation and dissemination.

- Kickstarter: This platform enables creators to fund projects by soliciting small contributions from many backers. It transforms patrons into participants, allowing them to support and shape creative endeavors. Backers often receive updates, contribute ideas, and become part of the journey, fostering a community around shared interests.

- Duolingo: Makes language learning interactive and accessible by incorporating gamification elements like points, levels, and challenges. Users actively engage with lessons, receive immediate feedback, and can compete with friends. This participatory approach keeps learners motivated and makes education enjoyable.

- OpenStreetMap: This is a free, editable map of the world created and maintained by volunteers. Users contribute by adding and updating geographic data, valuable in areas not well-covered by commercial maps. The platform relies on community participation to improve accuracy, benefiting users globally.

- Patient-Led Research: In healthcare, initiatives involve individuals with specific conditions collaborating on studies, sharing data, and influencing research priorities. Platforms like PatientsLikeMe allow participants to contribute personal health information, fostering a participatory approach that can accelerate discoveries and improve outcomes.

Interactive experiences foster deeper connections, inspire action, and can lead to breakthroughs isolated efforts might miss. Creating active participation and respect opportunities is critical to success as we navigate modern complexities. Whether in science, education, social change, or business, interactive and participatory approaches drive innovation, build communities, and achieve goals resonating with and empowering individuals globally.

THE FIFTH RULE

Acknowledge Ambiguity and Complexity

In 1628, the Swedish warship Vasa embarked on its maiden voyage from Stockholm harbor. Commissioned by King Gustavus Adolphus during the Thirty Years' War, the Vasa was intended to be the Baltic Sea's most formidable vessel, symbolizing Sweden's naval power. It was lavishly decorated and featured intricate carvings. It was equipped with 64 bronze cannons on two gun decks.

However, a gust of wind caught the sails just over a mile into its voyage, causing the Vasa to heel over. Water poured in through the open gun ports, and the ship sank rapidly, taking with it at least 30 lives.

An inquest was held, but no one was held accountable. The disaster's causes were complex: design flaws, conflicting directives, rushed construction, and lack of thorough testing. Shipbuilders and engineers had expressed concerns about stability, but the king's and court's pressures overrode caution. The Vasa was top-heavy, with insufficient ballast to counterbalance the weight of its upper structures and armaments.

The wreck remained submerged for over 300 years until salvaged in the 1960s. The well-preserved ship now resides in the Vasa Museum in Stockholm, a poignant reminder of the consequences of failing to acknowledge and manage complexity.

The Vasa disaster resulted from technical, managerial, and communication failures. Stakeholders underestimated the engineering challenges of constructing such an advanced warship.

Decision-makers pushed forward with a flawed design by ignoring or oversimplifying complexities. The ambiguity surrounding responsibility and authority compounded issues. Shipbuilders lacked clear guidance, and pressure to meet the king's demands led to compromises in safety and functionality.

King Gustavus Adolphus and court officials' urgency and authority persuaded shipbuilders to proceed despite reservations. The king's desire for a grand warship overpowered technical objections. The persuasive force of authority and the allure of prestige led to the dismissal of critical concerns. The lack of clear channels for voicing doubts meant persuasive pressure overshadowed prudent caution. This illustrates how persuasive forces can be detrimental when they suppress acknowledgment of complexity and ambiguity.

The Vasa was intended to be one of the most advanced warships of its era. Its dual gun decks and heavy armament were ambitious innovations to establish Swedish naval dominance. The ship's grandeur and artistic embellishments were meant to showcase wealth and power. However, pursuing innovation without adequately considering associated complexities proved disastrous. The design pushed the boundaries of contemporary shipbuilding knowledge, but innovation became a liability without necessary calculations and testing.

Acknowledging ambiguity and complexity involves recognizing that situations, projects, and systems often have multiple interdependent factors affecting outcomes. This principle emphasizes not oversimplifying challenges or ignoring uncertainties. In persuasion and decision-making, acknowledging complexity fosters more robust strategies. It encourages critical thinking, adaptability, and collaborative problem-solving. By accepting not all variables can be controlled or predicted, individuals and organizations can better prepare for contingencies and avoid unintended consequences.

Here are some other disasters that stem from failing to recognize ambiguity and complexity in a robust system:

- NASA's Challenger Disaster devastated the U.S. Space Program. In 1986, the Space Shuttle Challenger broke apart shortly after launch, killing all seven crew members. Investigations revealed that the disaster was partly caused by O-ring seal failures in cold temperatures. Despite engineers' concerns, the launch proceeded due to schedule pressures and managerial decisions downplaying complexity.

- Complex financial instruments, high-risk lending, and regulatory failures precipitated the Global Financial Crisis. Many didn't fully understand derivatives like mortgage-backed securities, and overconfidence and underestimation of systemic risks led to widespread fallout. Recognizing financial systems' complexity is essential to preventing similar crises.

- Climate Change presents a complex scientific, economic, and social web. Oversimplifying leads to ineffective policies or skepticism. Acknowledging ambiguity and complexity allows for comprehensive strategies considering various stakeholders, model uncertainties, and adaptive approaches.

Ambitious endeavors require careful planning, open communication, and a willingness to confront uncertainties. Acknowledging challenges' multifaceted nature, we make informed decisions, mitigate risks, and adapt to changing circumstances.

In today's interconnected world, embracing complexity is more important than ever. Recognizing and navigating ambiguity allows us to develop resilient strategies and avoid oversimplified pitfalls, whether in business, technology, policy, or personal decisions.

THE SIXTH RULE

Appeal to Values, Not Just Logic

Nestled in the bustling city of Ahmedabad, India, Seva Café offers a dining experience. Founded in 2005, the café operates on a simple yet profound principle: "Living is giving." There are no prices on the menu. Instead, guests receive a meal paid for by someone who dined before them, and they're invited to continue this chain of generosity by contributing whatever amount they wish to pay forward to the next guest.

The concept is rooted in the ancient Indian practice of "seva," meaning selfless service. Volunteers run the café, cooking and serving meals with love and care. The warm and communal atmosphere encourages conversations among strangers and fosters a sense of shared humanity. Patrons often find themselves surprised and moved by the experience. Without the transactional norms of a typical restaurant, guests reflect on the value of their meal beyond monetary terms. Many choose to contribute more than the cost of their food, inspired by the trust and goodwill extended to them.

Seva Café's model challenges conventional economic systems, emphasizing relationships and community over profit. The café has sustained itself and inspired similar initiatives worldwide, spreading the message of generosity and interconnectedness.

The café persuades individuals to contribute generously without using pressure or obligation. The persuasive power lies in the emotional resonance and moral appeal of the experience. By trusting guests and offering a gift freely, the café encourages them to reciprocate out of genuine desire rather than compulsion.

The model challenges guests to consider their values and the kind of world they wish to create. The act of paying it forward becomes a personal expression of those values. Stories and interactions within the café further reinforce the message, creating a persuasive environment that fosters generosity.

While the concept of a gift economy is ancient, implementing it as a functioning business in a modern urban setting was innovative. Relying on voluntary contributions seemed risky. Yet, the café's success demonstrated that alternative economic models could thrive. It inspired a reimagining of commerce, highlighting the potential for businesses to operate on principles of trust and community engagement.

Appealing to values involves connecting with individuals emotionally and ethically, aligning messages with their core beliefs and ideals. While logical arguments appeal to reason, values-based appeals resonate with what people care about most deeply. This approach can be more persuasive because values drive behavior more strongly than facts alone.

Communicators who tap into shared values can inspire action, foster solidarity, and motivate change.

In a post-modern context, skepticism towards grand narratives and absolute truths is prevalent; appealing to values can bridge divides. It allows for connection despite different perspectives, focusing on shared human experiences and aspirations. Here are some other examples of the power of values over grand narratives:

• TOMS Shoes: Companies like TOMS built their brand on the promise that for every product purchased, another is given to someone in need. Customers feel their purchase has a meaningful impact beyond personal use, which can be a stronger motivator than product features alone.

• Environmental Movements: Campaigns promoting conservation and sustainable practices often appeal to values of stewardship, legacy, and responsibility to future generations. For example, efforts to reduce plastic use may emphasize the moral imperative to protect marine life and preserve the planet rather than just presenting data on pollution.

• Fair Trade: Certifications assure consumers that products were made ethically, with fair wages and safe working conditions for producers. This appeals to values of justice and equality, encouraging consumers to make purchases aligning with their ethical standards.

Aligning with values creates a foundation of authenticity and connection that logic alone cannot achieve. When companies or individuals tap into what people genuinely care about—social justice, environmental stewardship, or community well-being—they foster relationships built on shared purpose and mutual respect.

This values-driven approach encourages individuals to see themselves as part of a greater whole, inspiring a sense of belonging and common purpose. Unlike surface-level appeals, which may only resonate momentarily, connections rooted in values endure because they engage the heart and soul of a person's identity. In business, advocacy, or personal relationships, aligning with values cultivates loyalty, encourages meaningful interaction, and drives action, proving that values are not merely an accessory to persuasion—they are its most essential foundation.

THE SEVENTH RULE

Leverage Fragmentation for Targeted Messaging

In the early 2010s, the retail giant Target embarked on an ambitious endeavor to refine its marketing strategies using data analytics. Andrew Pole, a statistician at Target, was tasked with a challenging question: Could the company identify customers who were likely to be pregnant even before they announced it? The motivation was clear: Pregnancy triggers significant life changes, leading to shifts in purchasing behavior. Target could build brand loyalty and capture a larger share of their shopping needs by reaching expectant mothers early.

Pole and his team delved into vast customer data collected through purchases made with credit cards, loyalty cards, and online interactions. They analyzed buying patterns, searching for indicators suggesting a customer might be expecting a child. Certain products, when purchased together or in sequence, served as signals. For example, increased purchases of unscented lotion, supplements like calcium and magnesium, or larger quantities of cotton balls could indicate early stages of pregnancy. By honing in on a combination of 25 products, Pole's algorithm could anticipate pregnancy.

Developing a "pregnancy prediction score," Target assigned each customer a likelihood. The company then used this information to send targeted advertisements and coupons for baby-related products. In one notable incident, a father in Minnesota approached a Target store manager, upset that his teenage daughter was receiving baby product coupons. Unbeknownst to him, his daughter was indeed pregnant—a fact Target's algorithms had inferred before he was aware.

The story garnered widespread media attention, raising questions about consumer privacy and the ethics of predictive analytics. While Target adjusted its approach to be less conspicuous—mixing in unrelated ads to avoid revealing their targeting—the initiative highlighted the power and potential pitfalls of leveraging fragmentation for targeted messaging.

By using data analytics to fragment their audience, Target delivered personalized content that was more relevant and timely. This approach increased the likelihood of engagement and conversion, as customers received information aligning closely with their current life circumstances and interests.

Using personal data to predict sensitive information raises concerns about privacy and consumer autonomy. Target's targeted messaging was persuasive because it reached customers with relevant offers precisely when they were most likely to need them. For expectant mothers, receiving coupons for baby products could be convenient and financially beneficial. The personalization made customers feel understood and catered to, enhancing brand loyalty.

From a marketing perspective, this approach increased efficiency by focusing resources on high-probability customers. By narrowing their focus, Target achieved better results with less wasted effort.

However, persuasiveness is a double-edged sword. When customers become aware of the extent to which their behaviors are monitored and analyzed, they experience discomfort and backlash. The perception of intrusion can undermine trust, which is crucial for long-term customer relationships.

At the time, Target's use of predictive analytics in this manner was groundbreaking. While data-driven marketing wasn't new, the sophistication and depth of Target's approach set it apart. The ability to predict life events and tailor marketing accordingly represented a significant advancement in retail strategy.

Leveraging fragmentation involves breaking down a broad audience into smaller, more specific segments to deliver tailored messages that resonate more deeply with each group. In a fragmented media landscape with diverse consumer preferences, generic messages often fail to capture attention. Targeted messaging allows communicators to address different segments' unique needs, interests, and behaviors.

This strategy enhances persuasion effectiveness by making messages more relevant and personalized. It acknowledges that audiences aren't monolithic and that customization can lead to higher engagement and conversion rates.

However, leveraging fragmentation also requires careful consideration of privacy and ethical standards. Collecting and using personal data must be transparent and respectful of individual rights. Failure to do so can erode trust and damage reputations.

• Spotify: Utilizes user listening data to create personalized playlists like "Discover Weekly" and "Release Radar." By analyzing individual music preferences, Spotify delivers curated content that aligns with each user's tastes. This targeted approach keeps users engaged and encourages continued use of the platform.

• Amazon: The recommendation engine suggests products based on a customer's browsing and purchasing history. By segmenting users according to behavior, Amazon provides personalized shopping experiences that increase the likelihood of additional purchases.

• Political Campaigns: Use voter data to segment the electorate and deliver tailored messages. By understanding the concerns and interests of different demographic groups, campaigns craft specific appeals to persuade voters more effectively.

• Netflix analyzes viewing habits to recommend shows and movies that match users' preferences. This personalization helps retain subscribers by continuously providing appealing content and leveraging fragmentation to enhance user satisfaction.

Target's use of predictive analytics to personalize marketing exemplifies the power and potential pitfalls of leveraging fragmentation for targeted messaging. By breaking down their audience into specific segments, they achieved higher relevance and effectiveness in communications. However, ethical considerations and public backlash highlight the need for responsible practices.

We are saturated with information; targeted messaging allows organizations to cut through the noise and connect more meaningfully with audiences. By understanding and addressing the unique needs of different segments, communicators can enhance persuasion and achieve better results.

Balancing personalization with respect for privacy and ethical standards is essential. Organizations must navigate these complexities thoughtfully to build trust and maintain positive relationships. Leveraging fragmentation offers significant opportunities but also demands careful stewardship.

THE EIGHTH RULE

> Challenge Traditional Authority with Subversive Humor

Banksy, the enigmatic British street artist, has emerged as one of the most influential figures in modern art—not only for his distinctive stencil-based style but for the potent social commentary embedded in his work. Banksy's art blends humor, irony, and satire to challenge traditional authority, political power, and societal norms. His rise in the art world is as much about his mystery as his message, with no one certain of his identity, though speculation runs wild.

Banksy first garnered attention in the 1990s with his witty, politically charged graffiti that often appeared overnight in various cities. His works became iconic, with pieces like "Girl with Balloon" symbolizing hope and fleeting innocence. Banksy's subversive art challenges topics ranging from capitalism and war to surveillance and environmental degradation, creating juxtapositions that force viewers to confront uncomfortable realities.

One of his most provocative pieces, "There Is Always Hope," shows a young girl letting go of a heart-shaped balloon. While simple, this artwork symbolizes Banksy's ability to evoke deep emotional responses with minimal imagery. The balloon, often interpreted as a symbol of innocence or lost dreams, paired with the title's message, strikes a chord with viewers, pulling them into reflection on societal issues like displacement or unfulfilled promises.

"Flower Thrower" is another iconic work featuring a masked protester hurling a bouquet instead of a Molotov cocktail. This piece, seen as a call for peaceful protest over violence, uses irony to juxtapose violent imagery with symbols of peace, undercutting the ferocity of revolution with humor and beauty. Its power lies in conveying that rebellion can be peaceful, subverting traditional expectations of protest.

Banksy's humor often softens the harshness of his messages, allowing his critiques to resonate more deeply. For instance, "Laugh Now," depicting a chimpanzee wearing a sandwich board with the words "Laugh now, but one day we'll be in charge," humorously critiques human arrogance and the illusion of superiority. Using animals as metaphors for societal structures, Banksy engages viewers in conversations about oppression and inequality without directly pointing fingers, using humor as a disarming force to question authority.

While celebrated for its wit and sharp social criticism, his street art hasn't been without controversy. Its unauthorized nature sparks debates about the line between vandalism and public art. Given its undeniable cultural value, city officials grapple with whether to preserve or remove his works.

For instance, Banksy's work in Palestine, like his murals on the West Bank barrier wall, stirred intense international reactions. These pieces depict themes of freedom, oppression, and conflict, gaining global attention for highlighting the Palestinian plight. One mural shows a young girl being carried away by balloons—a powerful metaphor for escapism in the face of occupation. Banksy's art on the wall was celebrated for drawing attention to the conflict but also criticized for trivializing a profoundly complex issue.

His artwork has sparked broader social movements. In 2018, during an auction at Sotheby's, his piece "Girl with Balloon" famously self-destructed moments after selling for $1.4 million. A hidden shredder within the frame partially destroyed the artwork, renaming it "Love is in the Bin." This act critiqued the commercial art world's commodification of art, generating widespread media coverage and discussions about the nature of art, ownership, and value.

Banksy has also critiqued consumerism through works like "Shop Until You Drop," where a woman plunges downward while clutching a shopping cart. This piece mocks the relentless pursuit of material goods and the idea of consumerism as a path to happiness. The humor, laced with biting truth, highlights society's obsession with consumption.

Just as Banksy used art to critique social structures, George Carlin used humor and stand-up comedy to challenge authority, push back against social norms, and encourage audiences to question the world around them. Carlin's subversive comedy addressed controversial topics like politics, religion, and life's absurdities with brutal honesty and biting humor. His routines are recognized for sharp critiques of American culture, often balancing comedy and outrage.

One of Carlin's most famous routines, "The Seven Dirty Words," questioned the absurdity of censorship in America, particularly regarding language. The bit became so influential it led to a Supreme Court case about free speech. Carlin remarked, "I don't have pet peeves; I have major psychotic fucking hatreds!"—a joke embodying his unfiltered approach to comedy and disdain for societal constraints.

In his later years, Carlin's humor grew darker yet more intelligent. In one routine, he said, "They call it the American Dream because you have to be asleep to believe it." This joke critiqued the political establishment and Americans' passive acceptance of inequality. Like Banksy's art, Carlin's comedy sought to break down societal illusions—whether blind faith in government, religion, or capitalism.

Political satire on television has followed in the footsteps of comedians like Carlin. Under Jon Stewart's leadership, "The Daily Show" became a significant source of political commentary for the younger generation, blending comedy with news to keep audiences engaged. While Banksy and Carlin used their platforms to provoke thought in visual and performance art, Stewart and his team used satire to critique political absurdities.

With Stewart at the helm, "The Daily Show" reached over 2.5 million viewers during its peak, many of whom used the show as their primary news source. Satirical segments, like the famed "Indecision 2000" coverage of the Bush-Gore election, entertained while educating viewers about the political process, media bias, and contradictions in political rhetoric.

The genius of "The Daily Show" lies in its ability to critique media coverage and political blunders without overwhelming the audience. The show creates a space through humor where viewers can laugh at political absurdities while receiving valuable insights about current events. Like Banksy and Carlin, the show uses humor to spotlight injustice, corruption, and incompetence, making complex political issues accessible to a broad audience.

For Banksy, Carlin, and Stewart, humor was the vehicle for more important messages. Satire got us to reflect on ourselves without modern dialogue's judgy and critical overtones. The Daily Show continues this tradition in political satire, blending humor with analysis to keep audiences informed and engaged. Traditional authority is often unassailable; humor becomes a way to subvert, challenge, and even change the status quo.

THE NINTH RULE

> Blur the Lines Between the Creator and the Audience

The digital revolution has fundamentally redefined the boundaries between creators and consumers. What was once a one-way relationship —creators producing content for an audience—has become a collaborative ecosystem where the lines between creator and audience are increasingly blurred. This shift is most apparent in the rise of the creator economy. Platforms like Kickstarter, Patreon, OpenAI, Minecraft, Lego, Twitch, YouTube, and TikTok now serve as global stages for individuals to create, share, and monetize their content. By 2022, this creator economy was valued at over $104.2 billion, with millions participating in a new digital marketplace built on creativity and engagement.

On platforms like Kickstarter, fans fund projects they believe in, gaining access to exclusive rewards and influencing design choices. Minecraft players modify and build expansive virtual worlds, transforming the game into an open-source community. On Twitch, audiences participate in real-time streams, influencing gameplay and contributing to the content's direction through live chat and donations. On YouTube and TikTok, creators engage directly with viewers, remixing content and fostering trends uniquely tailored to specific communities.

Modern companies are finding a wealth of success blurring lines between the creator and the audience:

• Kickstarter revolutionized crowdfunding by empowering consumers to fund creative projects they want to see come to life. Fans contribute to campaigns, providing creators financial backing while gaining unique access to exclusive content and sometimes influencing the final product's development.

• Patreon offers creators a direct funding stream, enabling artists, writers, and podcasters to rely on fan contributions for their livelihood. This decentralized funding model provides a direct connection between creator and consumer, allowing audiences to impact the creative direction of the work they support.

• Minecraft exemplifies user-generated content. Players build and create within the game, reshaping the experience through mods and custom content. The game's open-world structure allows players to become creators, establishing communities that shape their gameplay experiences.

• Twitch emphasizes real-time engagement. Streamers rely on audience interactions—through chat, donations, and subscriptions—to guide their content. This creates a dynamic where viewers feel personally involved in shaping the narrative of the stream.

• YouTube and TikTok have democratized content creation, enabling anyone with a smartphone to share their work. Creators remix content, respond to trends, and involve their audience in decision-making, fostering a collaborative experience.

The rise of Non-Fungible Tokens (NFTs) and the Metaverse allows users to buy, sell, and create digital assets directly on the blockchain, such as art or virtual real estate. This breaks traditional ownership models and puts creative power in the hands of creators and consumers, who can now influence and shape their digital worlds.

At the core of the creator economy is customization. Consumers no longer passively consume; they expect to be part of the creative process. As venture capitalist Chris Dixon once explained, "People want to be part of the creation process, not just passive consumers." Platforms that enable users to personalize their experience—whether by contributing to product design, modifying games, or engaging directly with creators—create a deeper emotional connection between the audience and the product.

Li Jin, a prominent thinker in the creator economy, elaborates on the shift: "The creator economy represents a new labor market where individuals can earn directly from their audiences without needing a middleman." This dynamic gives creators more control over their work while making consumers feel like they're actively shaping the content they enjoy.

The result?

A more loyal and engaged audience interested in the creator's success.

The IKEA Effect, a concept popularized by studies from Harvard Business Review, explains this phenomenon. People value things they helped create more—even if their contribution is minimal. In digital environments, users are more likely to engage with and support content they've had a hand in shaping, whether through financial backing, content suggestions, or real-time interaction.

Beyond Entertainment: Platforms for Social Change

Crowdfunding sites like Kickstarter and Patreon democratize access to funding, allowing underrepresented creators to bypass traditional gatekeepers. Projects focused on social justice, environmental activism, and marginalized voices have gained widespread support through these platforms, creating avenues for important messages to reach a global audience.

NFT platforms have enabled digital artists and activists to fund their work and promote their causes without relying on galleries or traditional corporate sponsors. This decentralized system allows creators to spread messages about issues they care about, furthering the impact of the creator economy beyond commerce.

Additional Examples of Blurred Lines

• Open-Source Projects: Initiatives like Linux and Mozilla Firefox rely on contributions from a community of developers and users. Participants can suggest features, report bugs, and contribute code, directly influencing the software's evolution.

• LEGO Ideas invites fans to submit designs for new LEGO sets. Community members vote on their favorites, and winning designs can become official products. Designers receive recognition and a share of the profits. This model engages fans in the product development process.

• Fan Fiction Communities: Fans of books, movies, or other media often create their own stories, art, or adaptations based on existing works. Platforms like Wattpad host vast collections of fan fiction, blurring the lines between original creators and fans who expand upon the narratives.

• Participatory Journalism: News organizations sometimes invite readers to contribute stories, photos, or insights, especially during breaking news events. This participatory approach expands coverage and incorporates diverse perspectives, involving the audience in the journalistic process.

Threadless, an online apparel company, demonstrates the power of blurring the lines between creator and audience. By fostering a participatory environment, Threadless taps into the collective creativity of its community, delivering products that resonate deeply with customers. Users submit T-shirt designs, the community votes, and winning designs are produced and sold, with designers receiving a share of the profits.

This approach aligns with modern audiences' desires for engagement, authenticity, and influence over the products and content they consume. Organizations can build stronger relationships and foster innovation by empowering individuals to contribute meaningfully. Blurring these lines challenges traditional hierarchies and encourages collaborative creation. Technology enables unprecedented connectivity, and embracing this principle can lead to richer experiences and more dynamic, responsive offerings.

Ideas will be more persuasive when customized for the receiver or when participation in creating the message is permitted. Dictating elements of the product or message is a fading concept ushered in by platforms that license creation. Platforms like Etsy, Photoshop, and Canva have developed creator communities and product customization. With the rise of 3D printing and small-batch designs, people can obtain whatever they want.

The rise of user-generated content and decentralized platforms means messages are increasingly fragmented. The official narrative of a brand or organization no longer binds users. Instead, they have the tools to create their narratives, remix content, and share alternative perspectives. This diffusion of control means persuasion is less about controlling the message and more about facilitating conversations and influencing trends through user collaboration.

The community often co-opted brand messages on Reddit and other community-driven platforms and can take on entirely new meanings. Brands that attempt to control these narratives can quickly lose credibility, whereas those that lean into user-led interpretations often succeed. Audiences are savvy and can spot insincere attempts to co-opt their engagement.

In 2006, Chevrolet launched a campaign called "Chevy Tahoe's Apprentice," an interactive initiative that encouraged users to create video ads for the Chevy Tahoe SUV using an online tool. Chevrolet hoped to engage consumers by letting them customize and promote the product, showcasing the Tahoe's features.

However, the campaign quickly backfired as users on platforms like Reddit began to hijack the tool to create sarcastic and critical ads emphasizing the negative environmental impact of SUVs, especially regarding fuel inefficiency and pollution. Users inserted messages such as:

- "Like this snowy wilderness? You better get your fill of it now. Then drive your SUV into it and wreck it forever."
- "The forests are dying, but don't worry: you've got air conditioning."

These sarcastic ads spread across the internet and social media, resulting in negative publicity. The campaign, meant to be a creative and engaging experience, turned into a viral disaster, with the critical ads receiving more attention than positive content. A later article in Wired Magazine claimed it as a win because the site received hundreds of thousands of visits, and Chevy sales did increase. The campaign drew 30,000 entries, many of them positive.

The upshot is that social media amplifies messages with viral qualities—those that appeal to System 1 thinking evoke strong emotions, encourage sharing through relatability or novelty, and leverage social connections, often with humor or surprise. The parody ads rose above the rest, and Chevy should have predicted that. However, their marketing team played along gracefully, turning a potential fiasco into a solid recovery.

Brands and creators who are upfront, honest, and genuine in their interactions build stronger connections, while those who manipulate or try to exert too much control are often rejected. The rise of influencers who share their success and struggles creates a more relatable and persuasive message.

To adapt to this new environment, the key lies in facilitating authentic user participation, providing opportunities for customization, and building genuine relationships. The future of persuasion in the creator economy is participatory, collaborative, and deeply personal.

THE TENTH RULE

> Adopt a Reflexive and Meta-Critical Stance

Tucked away on a quiet street in Culver City, Los Angeles, the Museum of Jurassic Technology (MJT) defies conventional definitions of a museum. Founded in the late 1980s by David Hildebrand Wilson and his wife, Diana Drake Wilson, the MJT presents a curious amalgamation of exhibits that blur the lines between fact and fiction, reality and illusion. Visitors entering the dimly lit spaces are greeted with displays ranging from microscopic sculptures carved from rice grains to questionable historical artifacts like the "Deprong Mori of the Tripiscum Plateau," a mythical bat that can fly through walls.

The museum's exhibits are presented with the solemnity and detail of scientific institutions, complete with descriptive plaques, audio guides, and dioramas. However, visitors may notice inconsistencies, peculiarities, or outright impossibilities in the narratives upon closer inspection. For instance, one exhibit features the "Garden of Eden on Wheels," a collection of mobile homes said to represent the pinnacle of modern living. Yet the presentation is tinged with irony and nostalgia.

The MJT does not overtly reveal which exhibits are genuine, fabricated, or exaggerated. This deliberate ambiguity prompts visitors to question the authenticity of the information and reflect on their assumptions about museums as authorities of knowledge. The experience can be both disorienting and enlightening, leading patrons to engage in meta-critical thinking about how knowledge is curated and consumed.

Over the years, the MJT has garnered a cult following and critical acclaim for its unique approach. It has inspired discussions in academic circles about museology, epistemology, and the role of institutions in shaping perceptions of reality.

The designers of the MJT museum hope that the museum acts as a mirror, reflecting not only the content of its displays but also the viewers' perceptions, biases, and societal constructs of knowledge dissemination.

This reflexivity is achieved through the museum's intentional blending of the credible and the incredible. Visitors must navigate ambiguity, prompting them to critically assess the validity of what they see rather than passively absorb it. The MJT persuades not by providing definitive answers but by inviting inquiry and self-examination. The persuasive power lies in its ability to engage visitors emotionally and intellectually, creating an immersive experience that disrupts passive consumption. The museum captures attention and fosters a sense of wonder and curiosity by subverting expectations.

The MJT's approach is subtle, allowing visitors to reach their conclusions organically. The lack of explicit declarations about the authenticity of exhibits avoids alienating the audience. Instead, it respects their intelligence and encourages them to think critically. This persuasive method empowers individuals to explore and reflect, leading to deeper, more personal insights.

When the MJT was established, the concept of a museum that intentionally blurred fact and fiction was unconventional. Traditional museums were bastions of factual knowledge, distinguishing between actual artifacts and replicas or artistic interpretations. The MJT challenged this paradigm by creating a space where the authenticity of exhibits was ambiguous, prompting a reevaluation of how knowledge is presented.

The museum's inventive approach combined elements of art installation, performance, and satire within its familiar framework. This hybridity was ahead of its time, anticipating contemporary trends in experiential and interactive exhibitions. The MJT's influence can be seen in the rise of immersive art spaces and institutions that prioritize visitor engagement and interpretation over authoritative narratives.

Adopting a reflexive and meta-critical stance involves encouraging critical reflection on thought processes and knowledge consumption. This allows individuals to recognize biases, question dominant narratives, and appreciate multiple perspectives. By being meta-critical, communicators can deconstruct arguments, identify underlying assumptions, and engage more thoughtfully with others.

Metanarratives are popping up everywhere.

- Satirical News Shows: Programs like "The Daily Show" and "Last Week Tonight" use satire to present news and critique media coverage.

Blending humor with serious topics encourages viewers to reflect on how news is reported and any potential biases.

• Meta-Fictional Literature: Authors like Jorge Luis Borges and Italo Calvino write stories that self-consciously address the nature of storytelling. Their works often include narratives within narratives or characters aware of their fictional status, prompting readers to consider the act of reading and interpretation.

• Breaking the Fourth Wall: Productions that break the "fourth wall," such as in "Deadpool" or Bertolt Brecht's epic theatre, directly address the audience or acknowledge the performance's artificiality. This technique disrupts immersion to provoke critical engagement with the content.

• Critical Pedagogy: Educational approaches encouraging students to question and challenge societal norms, such as those advocated by Paulo Freire, promote reflexivity. By examining power dynamics and assumptions in education, learners become active participants in knowledge acquisition.

• Interactive Art: Artists like Olafur Eliasson create works that require audience interaction, making the viewer's experience and perception integral to the art. This involvement prompts reflection on the nature of perception and reality.

Adopting a reflexive and meta-critical stance is essential for effective persuasion and meaningful engagement in today's fragmented and rapidly changing world. By encouraging critical thinking and self-reflection, we empower individuals to navigate complex information landscapes thoughtfully and responsibly. Through innovative museum experiences, satirical media, or participatory art, fostering reflexivity helps build a more informed, discerning, and engaged society.

THE NEW DAWN OF AUTHENTICITY

USHERING IN A NEW AGE OF ORIGINALITY AND CREATIVITY

"The intimate knowing of a single thing is worth far more than a casual knowing of many things."

Michael Polanyi Personal *Knowledge* (1958)

Rome had the Coliseum, and we have football, Instagram, Taylor Swift, and an obsession with politics. Devoid of real feelings, we cling to what we are told matters. We reinvent ourselves to be better at what we are told matters. We choose ourselves based on the menu of available options. Most people in the world of persuasion spend all their time teaching people how to manipulate this game for money, success, or beauty.

Does it matter?

Not one fucking bit. Your Instagram does not matter. Your followers don't matter. Your Lulu doesn't matter. And you probably don't like Taylor Swift. You want the sense of humanity you feel by being in the club that likes Taylor Swift. Even those with fame, money, and notoriety suffer, and they are often worse than us.

Fame has a magnetic allure, pulling people toward the spotlight with promises of admiration, success, and influence. But for many, this life in the public eye is fragile and filled with pressures that can prove impossible to bear: Kurt Cobain, the iconic frontman of Nirvana. In the early '90s, Cobain's raw talent and anti-establishment image catapulted him into global stardom. Yet, for all the success and acclaim, he felt trapped by the demands of fame. Cobain struggled with depression, addiction, and an intense discomfort with the celebrity persona that had been built around him. His tragic death at 27 became a cautionary tale, reminding us that the adoration of millions can sometimes be isolating rather than fulfilling.

Amy Winehouse, too, faced a similar fate. A singer with a once-in-a-generation voice, she became a global sensation almost overnight. Her battles with addiction and her tumultuous personal life were splashed across tabloids, feeding a media machine eager to document her every misstep. The relentless scrutiny and public spectacle only intensified her struggles, and in 2011, Winehouse joined the ranks of talented artists who died at 27, leaving a haunting reminder of fame's destructive potential. The tragedy lies in the sense that fame—rather than bringing joy or freedom—only exacerbated her battles, turning her life into a public display of vulnerability and pain.

They died of an emptiness they could not fill with drugs, alcohol, or other vices. The emptiness grew as the fame grew. In contrast, some have chosen a quieter path, deliberately sidestepping the spotlight to protect their sense of self. Keanu Reeves is a well-known example. Rather than indulging in celebrity culture, Reeves has been known for his kindness, humility, and preference for solitude. He's found contentment in preserving his privacy, focusing on his craft without letting fame consume his life. Similarly, Dave Chappelle stepped away from a wildly successful career at the height of his popularity, leaving a $50 million contract on the table to retreat to a quiet life in Ohio. Chappelle saw the toll fame took on his creativity and well-being, and he walked away to protect his sanity and rediscover his purpose.

Happiness is not found in the adoration of crowds; it's often found in moments of solitude, where one can exist freely without the pressure to perform. You are 1,000 crunches, a sterile Manhattan apartment, an epic skincare routine, and Huey Lewis and the news. But you are not a person.

You are in the cave, watching the shadows on the wall. After a few hundred pages of slowly waking up, it's time to turn around and walk toward the exit. Humanity is experiencing a five-alarm fire, a perfect storm, and the greatest threat to our existence we have ever faced. Losing this battle does not wipe us off the map but makes us slaves to the machine that pretends to feed us. We become a self-licking ice cream cone.

The grand achievement of most of society is that they kept capitalism alive. We trade our time for funny money, which we trade for necessities only made necessary because of other necessities.

We are Marcus Halberstram comparing memes and fast fashion like pale nimbus eggshell business cards. Even our unique experiences are not real. We flock to postcard destinations to copy the copy you copied and be like the false image of the person you idolize on Instagram. Your only satisfaction comes from the slow drip of social credit received along the way. You're convinced that 200 followers is less satisfying than 2,000 or 20,000. The number represents only one pure and straightforward undeniable fact - it is merely a measure of the depth of your addiction.

You are exhausted and forever onstage, acting out roles crafted not from the depths of who we are but from the algorithms and mirrors surrounding us. We're performing but not quite sure for whom, although we are convinced it's ourselves. And as we scroll, swipe, and like our way through each day, there's a sense of disconnection that hums beneath it all—a kind of liminal space where we find ourselves endlessly waiting, lingering between self and simulacrum.

Social media is an easy target. It's the abusive spouse to the rampant alcoholic—a shield for our anger and a quick change when we prefer the masturbation of self-improvement.

"I'm pausing my IG for personal time; this is just so overwhelming," Becky writes on Instagram.

In the foreword, we stepped into this concept of liminal space, a "waiting room" that has become more vivid in our digital lives. Reddit threads and social media feeds reflect our culture's restless churn, where we project, judge, and consume without anchoring in any one truth.

Liminal spaces are strange, fleeting, and evocative because they sit in between. They are airports, deserted hallways, and transitional points that stir something uncanny within us. We dwell here in our endless digital scrolling and useless lives, moving between identities, roles, and moods. It's a place of fragmentation, where we're never indeed anywhere, just perpetually passing through.

But what's at stake in all this passing through?

Our sense of self is that part of us that yearns to be authentic and grounded. We yearn to be genuine rather than participants, mannequins of an identity designed for others' eyes. But there's hope on the other side of this mirror—hope grounded in authenticity, in what Carl Jung so beautifully described as the journey to self-actualization.

For Jung, the way out of this trap is not through endless projection but an inward journey. We must be willing to face both the light and shadow within ourselves. When we accept that we're complex, even flawed, we free ourselves from constant self-curation. Compare Bateman to Johnny Depp, a figure who, love or hate him, is unapologetically himself. Depp shows us the power of letting our quirks and complexities stand unfiltered, resisting the algorithmic urge to conform to a shiny, homogeneous ideal.

Capitalism taught us that "choice" is a good thing. It's not, it's a fallacy. The more choices we're given, the fewer we seem to have. Platforms like Cambridge Analytica show how our preferences and biases are tracked, nudging us toward "choices" that are pre-engineered. This illusion of choice, both captivating and disturbing, shows how powerfully our lives are shaped by forces we rarely see. The choice becomes a narrow corridor, more a semblance of agency than the real thing.

Real choice requires awareness and perhaps even rebellion—choosing not what the algorithm offers but what we genuinely want, even if that means stepping outside the flow of easy clicks and curated feeds. It's about moving back into life, into the mess and unpredictability that no algorithm can ever fully capture.

If the illusions around us are crafted by those who control the narrative, then storytelling is our tool for resistance. Stories—real stories, messy and full of texture—break through the screens. The O.J. Simpson trial is a testament to the power of narrative. "If the glove doesn't fit, you must acquit" became more than a line; it was a rallying cry, a lens that shaped how millions viewed the case. If that's not O.J.'s glove- the LAPD is racist. If that's not O.J.'s glove, then the systemic racism you've felt can be addressed through your verdict. The facts had O.J. dead to rights. A more powerful narrative was the only path to freedom.

In the same way, the stories we tell ourselves—about who we are, what we believe, what we value—become a kind of compass, guiding us out of the hall of mirrors. Just as Aboriginal songlines map their culture and history onto the land, our stories give us roots, connecting us to something real, something beyond the glimmer of the screen.

As we reclaim the art of storytelling, we can also turn to the ancient tools of rhetoric; those classic methods are still potent in an age of hyperreality. Ethos, pathos, and logos—the trinity of persuasion—offer a structure to our communication, a way to anchor ourselves in authenticity. They remind us that communication is not about overwhelming with volume but about connecting with meaning. While ethos gives us credibility, pathos connects us emotionally, and logos grounds us in reason, these tools, used together, create a kind of armor against manipulation.

Think of these principles as a tether, grounding us in a world where messages come fast and erratic, changing as quickly as the content feeds refresh. Often overlooked in the noise, logic becomes a way of resisting, a path to clarity amid the fog of influence. If rhetoric is our compass, symbolic logic is the map, leading us out of endless scrolling and back to thoughtful, grounded interaction.

Yet, navigating these complexities also demands adaptability. Postmodernism teaches us to embrace relativity, to see the world not as a monolithic truth but as a mosaic of perspectives. Figures like Steve Jobs understood this intuitively. Jobs knew that innovation wasn't about conforming to a single idea but about allowing multiple ideas to exist together, weaving them into something new. His approach wasn't rigid; it was flexible and relative—a way of thinking that embraced contradiction and change without losing sight of core values. This resilience is essential where narratives shift and digital landscapes evolve.=

So, where does that leave us? And what does that look like? We must reclaim our humanity and creativity. This means choosing our flaws over filters and finding pride in the unique messiness that makes us human. Algorithms can imitate a lot, but they can't replicate the nuances, quirks, and rawness of unfiltered human expression. When we embrace those parts of ourselves, we step out of the simulation and into something more enduring—into the real.

Take back our narratives and resist the allure of the polished, predictable, and programmable. It's about looking in the mirror and seeing not the reflection the world expects but the face we know to be our own.

Step off the stage and reclaim the audience—the one that listens not to applause but to authenticity. And maybe, just maybe, in reclaiming our humanity, we'll find a way forward that no algorithm could ever foresee.

BIBLIOGRAPHY

Suggested Reading

Aristotle. *Rhetoric*. Translated by W. Rhys Roberts. New York: Modern Library, 1954.

Ariely, Dan. *Predictably Irrational: The Hidden Forces That Shape Our Decisions*. New York: HarperCollins, 2008.

Baudrillard, Jean. *Simulacra and Simulation*. Translated by Sheila Faria Glaser. Ann Arbor: University of Michigan Press, 1994.

Bernays, Edward. *Propaganda*. Brooklyn, NY: Ig Publishing, 2005.

Botton, Alain de. *The Art of Travel*. New York: Pantheon Books, 2002.

Cialdini, Robert B. *Influence: The Psychology of Persuasion*. New York: Harper Business, 2006.

Cicero. *On the Ideal Orator (De Oratore)*. Translated by James M. May and Jakob Wisse. New York: Oxford University Press, 2001.

Debord, Guy. *The Society of the Spectacle*. Detroit: Black & Red, 1977.

Dennett, Daniel C. *Breaking the Spell: Religion as a Natural Phenomenon*. New York: Penguin Books, 2006.

Derrida, Jacques. *Of Grammatology*. Translated by Gayatri Chakravorty Spivak. Baltimore: Johns Hopkins University Press, 1976.

Dawkins, Richard. *The Selfish Gene*. Oxford: Oxford University Press, 1976.

Festinger, Leon. *A Theory of Cognitive Dissonance*. Stanford, CA: Stanford University Press, 1957.

Foucault, Michel. *Discipline and Punish: The Birth of the Prison*. Translated by Alan Sheridan. New York: Pantheon Books, 1977.

Gladwell, Malcolm. *The Tipping Point: How Little Things Can Make a Big Difference*. New York: Little, Brown and Company, 2000.

Greene, Robert. *The 48 Laws of Power*. New York: Viking, 1998.

Harari, Yuval Noah. *Sapiens: A Brief History of Humankind.* New York: Harper, 2015.

Kahneman, Daniel. *Thinking, Fast and Slow.* New York: Farrar, Straus and Giroux, 2011.

Kant, Immanuel. *Groundwork of the Metaphysics of Morals.* Translated by Mary Gregor. Cambridge: Cambridge University Press, 1997.

Lakoff, George, and Mark Johnson. *Metaphors We Live By.* Chicago: University of Chicago Press, 1980.

Lasch, Christopher. *The Culture of Narcissism: American Life in an Age of Diminishing Expectations.* New York: W.W. Norton, 1979.

Lyotard, Jean-François. *The Postmodern Condition: A Report on Knowledge.* Translated by Geoff Bennington and Brian Massumi. Minneapolis: University of Minnesota Press, 1984.

Marcuse, Herbert. *One-Dimensional Man: Studies in the Ideology of Advanced Industrial Society.* Boston: Beacon Press, 1964.

McLuhan, Marshall. *Understanding Media: The Extensions of Man.* New York: McGraw-Hill, 1964.

Mill, John Stuart. *On Liberty.* London: Penguin Books, 1985.

Machiavelli, Niccolò. *The Prince.* Translated by Harvey C. Mansfield. Chicago: University of Chicago Press, 1985.

Polanyi, Karl. *The Great Transformation: The Political and Economic Origins of Our Time.* Boston: Beacon Press, 2001.

Said, Edward W. *Orientalism.* New York: Pantheon Books, 1978.

Sagan, Carl. *The Demon-Haunted World: Science as a Candle in the Dark.* New York: Random House, 1995.

Sen, Amartya. *Rationality and Freedom.* Cambridge, MA: Harvard University Press, 2002.

Skinner, B.F. *Science and Human Behavior.* New York: Macmillan, 1953.

Smith, Adam. *The Theory of Moral Sentiments.* London: A. Millar, 1759.

Thaler, Richard H., and Cass R. Sunstein. *Nudge: Improving Decisions About Health, Wealth, and Happiness.* New York: Penguin Books, 2008.

Toulmin, Stephen. *The Uses of Argument*. Cambridge: Cambridge University Press, 1958.

Zuboff, Shoshana. *The Age of Surveillance Capitalism: The Fight for a Human Future at the New Frontier of Power*. New York: PublicAffairs, 2019.Amit Jatia, interview by Business Today. "Westlife Development Vice Chairman Amit Jatia on Forging a Winning Partnership with McDonald's in India." Business Today, September 18, 2022. https://www.businesstoday.in.

Bibliography

Amit Jatia, interview by DNA India. "New Format Marks Next Leg of Journey for McDonald's India." DNA India. Accessed September 29, 2024. https://www.dnaindia.com.

Amit Jatia, interview by Forbes India. "Amit Jatia and McDonald's 15-Year Wait for Success." Forbes India. Accessed September 29, 2024. https://www.forbesindia.com.

American Psychological Association (APA). "The Doomsday Effect: How Fear-Based Messaging Can Backfire." APA, 2016.

Ariely, Dan. Predictably Irrational: The Hidden Forces That Shape Our Decisions. New York: HarperCollins, 2008.

Avena, Nicole M., Pedro Rada, and Bartley G. Hoebel. "Evidence for Sugar Addiction: Behavioral and Neurochemical Effects of Intermittent, Excessive Sugar Intake." Neuroscience & Biobehavioral Reviews 32, no. 1 (2008): 20–39.

Banksy. Wall and Piece. London: Century, 2006.

Baudrillard, Jean. Simulacra and Simulation. Ann Arbor: University of Michigan Press, 1994.

Becker, Amy B. "Comedy as a Gateway to Social Change: The Role of Political Comedy in Shaping Social Movements." Journal of Communication 64, no. 2 (2014): 328–336.

Boykoff, Maxwell T., and Jules M. Boykoff. "Climate Change and Journalistic Norms: A Case-Study of US Mass-Media Coverage." Geoforum 38, no. 6 (2007): 1190–1204.

Burnett, John. "Banksy's Dismaland: Satirical Masterpiece or Dark Tourism?" BBC News, August 27, 2015.

Cialdini, Robert B. Influence: The Psychology of Persuasion. New York: Harper Business, 2006.

Clarence Darrow. "The Crime of Industrial Violence: Closing Argument in the Haywood Case." 1907.

Crump, Benjamin. Open Season: Legalized Genocide of Colored People. New York: Amistad, 2019.

Dawkins, Richard. The Selfish Gene. Oxford: Oxford University Press, 1976.

Derrida, Jacques. Of Grammatology. Translated by Gayatri Chakravorty Spivak. Baltimore: Johns Hopkins University Press, 1976.

Dimmock v. Secretary of State for Education and Skills. Case No: CO/3615/2007, High Court of Justice, 2007.

Dunbar, Robin. "The Social Role of Laughter and Humor." Evolutionary Psychology 10, no. 2 (2012): 147470491201000.

Elliot, Andrew J., and Markus A. Maier. "Color and Psychological Functioning: The

Effect of Red on Performance Attainment." Psychological Science 18, no. 12 (2007): 1116–1122.
Elliot, Andrew J., Markus A. Maier, Arlen C. Moller, Ron Friedman, and Jorg Meinhardt. "Color Psychology: Effects of Perceiving Color on Psychological Functioning in Humans." Annual Review of Psychology 65 (2014): 95–120.
Festinger, Leon. A Theory of Cognitive Dissonance. Stanford, CA: Stanford University Press, 1957.
Fogg, B. J. Persuasive Technology: Using Computers to Change What We Think and Do. San Francisco: Morgan Kaufmann, 2003.
Foucault, Michel. Discipline and Punish: The Birth of the Prison. Translated by Alan Sheridan. New York: Pantheon Books, 1977.
Garber, Lawrence L., and Eva M. Hyatt. "Color and Flavor Perception." Journal of Marketing Research 40, no. 3 (2003): 72–85.
Gearhardt, Ashley N., Nicole M. Avena, and Kelly D. Brownell. "The Addiction Potential of Hyperpalatable Foods." Appetite 95 (2015): 650–658.
Gearhardt, Ashley N., William R. Corbin, and Kelly D. Brownell. "Can Food Be Addictive? Public Health and Policy Implications." Addiction 106, no. 7 (2011): 1208–1212.
Gigerenzer, Gerd. Gut Feelings: The Intelligence of the Unconscious. New York: Viking, 2007.
Gladwell, Malcolm. Blink: The Power of Thinking Without Thinking. New York: Little, Brown and Company, 2005.
Gladwell, Malcolm. The Tipping Point: How Little Things Can Make a Big Difference. New York: Little, Brown and Company, 2000.
Gore, Al. An Inconvenient Truth: The Planetary Emergency of Global Warming and What We Can Do About It. Emmaus, PA: Rodale Books, 2006.
Harari, Yuval Noah. Sapiens: A Brief History of Humankind. New York: Harper, 2015.
Harris, Ron. "Simpson Verdict and LAPD's Racial Disparities." Los Angeles Times, October 5, 1995.
Hattenstone, Simon. "Banksy—The Invisible Man of Graffiti Art." The Guardian, July 17, 2003.
Intergovernmental Panel on Climate Change (IPCC). Climate Change 2007: The Physical Science Basis. Cambridge: Cambridge University Press, 2007.
Johnson, Lyndon B. "Daisy" Television Advertisement. Lyndon B. Johnson Presidential Campaign, 1964.
Julison, Ryan. "Public Relations Strategy for Trayvon Martin Case." Julison Communications, March 2012.
Kahneman, Daniel. Thinking, Fast and Slow. New York: Farrar, Straus and Giroux, 2011.
Kahneman, Daniel, and Amos Tversky. "Prospect Theory: An Analysis of Decision Under Risk." Econometrica 47, no. 2 (1979): 263–292.
Kennedy, Randy. "Banksy Unmasked? A Gallery Show in London Revives the Debate." The New York Times, June 13, 2008.
Labrecque, Lauren I., and George R. Milne. "Exciting Red and Competent Blue: The Importance of Color in Marketing." Journal of the Academy of Marketing Science 40, no. 5 (2012): 711–727.
LaMarre, Heather L., Kristen D. Landreville, and Michael A. Beam. "The Irony of Satire:

Political Ideology and the Motivation to See What You Want to See in The Colbert Report." The International Journal of Press/Politics 14, no. 2 (2009): 212–231.

Levy, Steven. The Perfect Thing: How the iPod Shuffles Commerce, Culture, and Coolness. New York: Simon & Schuster, 2006.

Lewis, Justin, Tammy Boyce, and Kiernan McCarthy. Climate Change and the Media. New York: Peter Lang, 2010.

Lyotard, Jean-François. The Postmodern Condition: A Report on Knowledge. Translated by Geoff Bennington and Brian Massumi. Minneapolis: University of Minnesota Press, 1984.

McDonald's Franchise in India: Spiraling Toward a Deadlock." ICMR India. Accessed September 29, 2024. https://www.icmrindia.org.

Milgram, Stanley. "Behavioral Study of Obedience." Journal of Abnormal and Social Psychology 67, no. 4 (1963): 371–378.

Milgram, Stanley. Obedience to Authority: An Experimental View. New York: Harper & Row, 1974.

Moss, Michael. Salt Sugar Fat: How the Food Giants Hooked Us. New York: Random House, 2013.

Nabi, Robin L., Emily Moyer-Gusé, and Sahara Byrne. "All Joking Aside: A Serious Investigation into the Persuasive Effect of Funny Social Issue Messages." Communication Monographs 74, no. 1 (2007): 29–54.

Nabi, Robin L., and Emily Moyer-Gusé. "Toward Understanding the Humor in Persuasion: The Elaboration Likelihood Model." Communication Theory 18, no. 3 (2008): 280–303.

National Broadcasting Corporation. "911 Call Edited During Trayvon Martin Case." NBC Universal Broadcast, April 2012.

Obama, Barack. "Remarks on Trayvon Martin." White House Press Conference, March 23, 2012.

O'Connor, Cailin, and James Owen Weatherall. The Misinformation Age: How False Beliefs Spread. New Haven: Yale University Press, 2019.

Orlando Sentinel. "Details of Wrongful Death Settlement in Trayvon Martin Case." April 2012.

Pereira, Mark A., Alex I. Kartashov, Cara B. Ebbeling, Linda Van Horn, Martha L. Slattery, David R. Jacobs Jr., and David S. Ludwig. "Fast-Food Habits, Weight Gain, and Insulin Resistance (the CARDIA Study): 15-Year Prospective Analysis." The Lancet 365, no. 9453 (2005): 36–42.

Plato. The Republic. Translated by G. M. A. Grube, revised by C. D. C. Reeve. Indianapolis: Hackett Publishing Company, 1992.

Ross, Lee, David Greene, and Pamela House. "The 'False Consensus Effect': An Egocentric Bias in Social Perception and Attribution Processes." Journal of Experimental Social Psychology 13, no. 3 (1977): 279–301.

Sagan, Carl. The Demon-Haunted World: Science as a Candle in the Dark. New York: Random House, 1995.

Sagan, Carl. "Baloney Detection Kit." The Skeptical Inquirer 19, no. 1 (1995): 37–42. https://skepticalinquirer.org.

Scafidi, Susan. Who Owns Culture? Appropriation and Authenticity in American Law. New Brunswick, NJ: Rutgers University Press, 2005.

Singh, Satyendra. "Impact of Color on Marketing." Management Decision 44, no. 6 (2006): 783–789.
Springer. "Scientists Debate the Accuracy of Al Gore's Documentary 'An Inconvenient Truth'." ScienceDaily, April 15, 2008. www.sciencedaily.com/releases/2008/04/080414115107.htm.
Stice, Eric, Kyle Burger, Jonathan Yokum, Sonja Veling, Cendri Hutchins, and Diane E. Shaw. "Relation of Obesity to Neural Activation in Response to Food Stimuli: A Meta-Analysis of Functional MRI Studies." Science 322, no. 5900 (2008): 449–452.
Strick, Madelijn, Rob W. Holland, Rick B. van Baaren, and Ad van Knippenberg. "Humor in Advertising: Revealing the Effects of Humor on Brand Evaluation." Journal of Advertising 38, no. 1 (2009): 49–64.
Sutherland, Rory. Alchemy: The Dark Art and Curious Science of Creating Magic in Brands, Business, and Life. New York: William Morrow, 2019.
Thaler, Richard H., and Cass R. Sunstein. Nudge: Improving Decisions About Health, Wealth, and Happiness. New York: Penguin Books, 2008.
The American Psychological Association (APA). "The Doomsday Effect: How Fear-Based Messaging Can Backfire." APA, 2016.
Tversky, Amos, and Daniel Kahneman. "Judgment Under Uncertainty: Heuristics and Biases." Science 185, no. 4157 (1974): 1124–1131.
Wade, Nicholas. "Origin of COVID — Following the Clues: Did People or Nature Open Pandora's Box at Wuhan?" Bulletin of the Atomic Scientists, May 5, 2021.
Wason, Peter C. "On the Failure to Eliminate Hypotheses in a Conceptual Task." Quarterly Journal of Experimental Psychology 12, no. 3 (1960): 129–140.
Watts, Duncan J. The Daisy Ad: Fear, Loathing, and the Most Controversial Political Advertisement in American History. Princeton, NJ: Princeton University Press, 2011.
Yu, Lionel. "Dubstep Moonlight Sonata" [Performance at the Kennedy Center]. YouTube video, 6:07. Posted November 10, 2016. https://www.youtube.com/watch?v=EtIwhvSa7kw.
Zhang, Yong. "The Effects of Humor in Advertising: An Individual-Difference Perspective." Journal of Advertising Research 36, no. 1 (1996): 16–26.

www.ingramcontent.com/pod-product-compliance
Lightning Source LLC
Chambersburg PA
CBHW031611210526
45464CB00004B/1530